D0403703

Developments in Mathematical Education

Developments in Mathematical Education

Proceedings of the Second International Congress on Mathematical Education

EDITED BY

A. G. HOWSON

Senior Lecturer in Mathematics
University of Southampton

CAMBRIDGE
at the University Press
1973

Published by the Syndics of the Cambridge University Press
Bentley House, 200 Euston Road, London NW1 2DB
American Branch: 32 East 57th Street, New York, N.Y.10022

Library of Congress Catalogue Card Number: 72–97880

ISBNS:
0 521 20190 X hard covers
0 521 09803 3 paper back

Printed in Great Britain
at the University Printing House, Cambridge
(Brooke Crutchley, University Printer)

Those fortunate beings who find mathematics a joy and a fascination will probably get on, whatever the standard of teaching. It requires real genius to light a flicker of understanding in the minds of those to whom mathematics is a clouded mystery. The subject is so vitally important for everyone in this technological age that any advance in the techniques of teaching is to be welcomed.

I hope all the delegates to the 2nd International Congress on Mathematical Education will find the business interesting and full of fruitful ideas. I also hope that they will have a thoroughly enjoyable time between sessions, meeting old friends and making new ones.

Philip

CONTENTS

EDITOR'S ACKNOWLEDGEMENTS

The prompt and rapid preparation of this book was only made possible through the cooperation and help of many people. In particular, I am indebted to Dr T. J. Fletcher, Professor G. Matthews, Mrs E. M. Williams and the rapporteurs of the various working groups for their assistance in the compilation of the congress survey, to Professor R. B. Davis, Dr T. J. Fletcher, Professor H. Freudenthal, M. Maurice Glaymann and Professor T. Varga for their help in selecting from contributed papers those to be reproduced in this volume, and to the authors of the papers for the swiftness with which they produced final versions. I received speedy and willing secretarial assistance from Miss Janet Watson of Exeter University and have also benefited greatly from the resources of the Department of Mathematics at Southampton and wish especially to note the help given to me there by Miss Sibyl Young and her able team of typists.

The papers originally written in languages other than English were translated by Joan Bliss (Piaget and Fischbein), Jennifer and Geoffrey Howson (Thom) and Owen Storer (Sobolev).

I

A CONGRESS SURVEY

An international congress which took two years to plan, embraced a vast range of activities and was attended by some 1400 educators from all parts of the world, could scarcely be satisfactorily described and evaluated within the covers of a single book. Certainly, the provision in printed form of some of the many papers presented at the congress, whilst valuable enough in itself, would convey little impression of the context in which the papers were presented – of the thoughts which prompted them, and of the feelings and reactions they aroused. It was for this reason that the Programme Committee, the committee responsible for planning the professional work of the congress, decided that the official proceedings of congress should attempt to do more than merely present a selection of papers. It should also contain some account of the lengthy preliminary discussions which determined the shape and thus, effectively, the scope of the congress, as well as an attempt to describe the general spirit of the meeting and to identify those themes which arose in the working groups and which could profitably repay further study by individuals and groups before the Third International Congress on Mathematical Education is convened in the summer of 1976.

In this way it was hoped that the congress proceedings would succeed in conveying to those who could not be present at Exeter not only what twenty or so distinguished authors judged to be worthy of study and concern, but, even more importantly, the problems which over one thousand committed and enthusiastic mathematical educators had identified as those which they most desired to consider and discuss. Such a report, it was thought, would have a more widespread appeal and be of correspondingly greater value.

Similar considerations led the Programme Committee to break with tradition and to recommend that the proceedings should be published entirely in English. Translations have therefore been prepared of those papers originally presented in languages other than English. Copies of these papers in their original form have, however, been made available to congress members, and it is hoped that part, at least, of these proceedings will appear elsewhere in languages other than English.

I-2

1 PRELIMINARIES AND PLANNING

A major difficulty in planning a Second International Congress is that one suffers from a shortage of precedents. In this respect, of course, the members of the Programme Committee were more fortunate than their colleagues who had planned the First International Congress on Mathematical Education, held at Lyons in August 1969, for we at least had the experience of that meeting on which to build.

The format of the Lyons meeting was based upon that of the International Congress of Mathematicians – indeed the sections of the ICM devoted to education can be viewed as embryonic congresses on mathematical education. Thus, the meeting was built around a series of one-hour invited lectures supplemented by a number of short (15-minute) contributions by congress members. The limitations of this procedure were soon apparent. Mathematical education is a topic totally different in nature from mathematics. Although there is no shortage of *theories* in the former, there is a noticeable lack of *theorems* – for, indeed, there is no accepted axiom system which even crudely models, and is modelled by, the educational process. Contributors to a congress on mathematical education cannot, therefore, be expected to emulate their mathematical colleagues (or even their mathematical selves) by presenting new proofs or new theorems, by producing generalisations or new characterisations. Primarily, they bring their experience, their personal judgement, and accounts of their work in the classroom – not that these are in any way the less valuable! Again, although mathematics possesses a basic vernacular which has international validity, the words used in mathematical education have to be interpreted afresh by each congress member in the light of his educational environment. Professor Thom has pointed out (see p. 204) how, once one strays from the 'common stem', the difference of semantic universes amongst mathematicians can lead to problems of interpretation and understanding. How true this is of mathematical education which, as yet, lacks even this 'common stem'. Traditionally, mathematicians have sought to ease their problems by discussion, and the need for encouraging this type of interaction was soon recognised at Lyons and manifested itself in the hasty provision of discussion groups arranged on site. In the event, the success of the congress in attracting some 600 members – a most encouraging response to this novel venture – militated against the organisers' attempts to provide these facilities at short notice.

The need to provide for effective discussion was, therefore, one lesson of the Lyons Congress. One hint as to how this might be encouraged other than through groups constituted to examine specific issues was provided by the *Mathematics Workshop* mounted at Lyons by the Association of Teachers of Mathematics. This presentation, which included a class of children at work, provoked considerable discussion and comment. It transmitted an image and a philosophy in a way that could not have been achieved by any number of plenary lectures and, as we shall see, influenced the design of the Exeter Congress.

Even before the Lyons Congress had closed, the thoughts of many began to turn to its successor, for which, at that time, no venue had been decided. The British National Committee for Mathematics had extensively discussed the possibility of inviting the International Commission on Mathematical Instruction (ICMI) to hold the Second Congress in Britain. In February 1970 it determined upon Exeter as a suitable site and by the summer of 1970 its invitation to ICMI to hold the congress there had been accepted. The detailed planning of the congress could now begin.

The arrangements for the congress were to be made by various committees working under the auspices of the Royal Society. The Organising Committee, chaired by Professor M. J. Lighthill (shortly afterwards to be honoured for his contributions to mathematics by the award of a Knighthood), was the body responsible for formulating fundamental principles and for liaison with international institutions. The Programme Committee appointed by the Organising Committee was to be responsible for the preparation of a detailed programme – the selection of invited speakers, the establishment of working groups, etc. This committee consisted of a number of British educators later augmented as the need arose, together with a number of distinguished, international 'corresponding' members, and was chaired by Mrs Elizabeth Williams. A third committee, chaired by Mr G. Duller (and, after his unfortunate withdrawal because of ill-health, by Dr D. Hammond Smith), was in charge of local arrangements, excursions, social events, etc.

The Programme Committee held the first of its many meetings in October 1970. Some matters which fell into its domain, such as arrangements for translation facilities and publicity, although essential to the success of the congress, do not merit detailed discussion in these pages. More relevant was the early attempt to identify a 'theme' for the congress.

The committee began its work with the conviction that the response to the Lyons Congress justified it in planning a much fuller programme and in anticipating one thousand active participants, and with the belief that a congress of this nature could have a world-wide influence on the development of mathematical education.

Would that influence be greater if the congress concentrated upon a particular theme? Could a theme help give direction and focus to our work during the short period we had together – shorter, in fact, than was the case at Lyons? After lengthy discussion, and the rejection of several proposals, the idea of a central theme was abandoned. Mathematical education, a discipline still in its formative years, appeared to embrace too many interests for any such circumscription to be profitable, or even possible. The congress, it was felt, should attempt to cater for all interests and, as far as one could describe its purpose, it should 'Study recent work in the field of mathematical education and stimulate further developments'.

The discussions devoted to finding a 'theme' were not without value, however, for they helped the committee better to comprehend and identify those issues which should be raised at Exeter. Many different aspects of mathematical education were distinguished.

The international nature of the congress served to emphasise the great range of conditions in which mathematical education takes place. Environmental factors, such as the extent to which the student's background and surroundings stimulate or militate against an interest in mathematics, are of vital importance. Cultural influences, including scientific attitudes, can play a crucial role. These problems, which can occur within a single country, loom particularly large when one considers mathematical education on a world-wide basis and contrasts the situation in a village in Malawi or India with that in, say, a residential suburb of Boston (Mass.). Not only would members be drawn from all parts of the world, but their interests would range over all sectors of education. Problems on the formation of ideas on number by the pre-school infant would be matched by those concerning what an old man in retirement studying for an Open University degree should know about the calculus. (The fact that the Lyons Congress – along with most of the ICM section meetings which preceded it – had chosen to interpret 'mathematical education' as something which affected only schoolchildren, had been noted, and it was agreed that university and other higher and further education should also be considered at Exeter.)

Mathematics, then, is being taught to, and learned by, a multitude of students in a bewildering variety of conditions. But what mathematics? Here was another leading question for discussion and comment. During the past two or three decades, the influence of mathematics in contemporary society – scientific, technical and socio-political – has grown tremendously. What are the consequences of this for mathematical education? What is the place of mathematics in the total education of the individual? Mathematics itself has expanded rapidly and whole new fields for study have been uncovered. What is the relevance of these advances in mathematics at a research level to mathematics teaching at lower levels? Attempts to answer these questions have been made during the last decade and are still being made. To what extent have the solutions proposed been justified? To what extent do they appear to be practicable?

The teacher has, of course, received a great deal of advice on how he should tackle the problems which confront him. Indeed, the proliferation of educational aids and research reports has become positively bewildering. But what problems can educational technology and educational research solve? What assistance can they provide for the mathematical educator? Again, these were aspects of mathematical education which merited consideration at the congress. Some idea of what technical developments have made possible has been given by the multi-media courses provided in Britain by the Open University and the BBC. What are the lessons to be learned from these and similar experiments? Equally important questions can be asked about the computer, which clearly has a crucial role to play in mathematical education both as a technical aid to student and teacher and as an integral part of mathematics itself – for its power is such that it has been able to influence mathematical thought and even the nature of mathematics. Such considerations of mathematical thought lead naturally to questions concerning the growing insights one possesses into the nature of mathematics as an activity of the human mind. How does this develop in a child? Why has it become the fundamental instrument in shaping the structures of the physical and social sciences? How has it affected philosophy and man's view of the universe?

These questions concern the philosophical and psychological bases of mathematical education – foundations which will demand even greater study if we are to have any confidence in the durability of the structures of mathematical education which we are now creating.

These then were some of the facets of mathematical education that were discussed by the Programme Committee as it sought to decide upon a 'theme' for the congress. When the idea of a single theme was rejected, it was then necessary for the committee to provide congress with a framework within which all these different facets could be examined.

2 THE PROGRAMME

When deciding upon the range of activities to be included in the congress programme, the Programme Committee was, as indicated above, very much influenced by the Lyons Congress. Obviously, there was still a place in the programme for the invited lecture. Certain broad issues should be aired before the congress as a whole and, equally, the opportunity to hear distinguished speakers – previously only names attached to articles or books – is one which most congress attenders value. What was not so evident was the amount of time that could profitably be allocated to such talks. Eventually, after the views of colleagues abroad had been sought, it was decided that, in addition to the Presidential Address, there should be six plenary lectures (compared with twenty at Lyons). The 15-minute contributions by congress members were abandoned entirely, since it was thought that, as a means of pooling the experience of teachers, such individual accounts were not enough and that they consumed valuable time in a prodigal manner. The active participation of the members themselves was considered essential and it was thought that the most acceptable means of communication would be papers submitted before the congress for limited distribution there, and discussion by small groups constituted according to specialist interests. The administrative problems consequent upon these proposals were daunting, particularly since it was hoped to arrange for a preparatory exchange of views prior to the congress, but the committee agreed that the ends appeared to justify the risks which attended such an ambitious undertaking. The third major contribution to the congress programmes would be in the hands of various national committees. The ATM contribution at Lyons had indicated the value of workshops in which one could discuss particular developments and even see mathematical learning and teaching taking place. This idea was now extended to that of a National Presentation at which educators could talk about developments and projects in their own country and in which they might arrange demonstrations both of materials and of actual classroom practice.

The bricks with which the formal congress programme was to be built were, therefore, plenary sessions, working groups and national presentations – the necessary mortar would be the intervals provided in the programme for informal exchanges of views.

The selection of the speakers to give the six key lectures was a most difficult task. When the committee surveyed the international field many possibilities emerged. Two names, however, were in a slightly different category from all the others, for they appeared to be present in everyone's mind: those of Pólya and Piaget. It is difficult adequately to describe the influence of this pair on mathematical education. Professor Pólya's distinguished contribution to many branches of mathematics has been matched by his outstanding work in the field of mathematical education. Through his books *How to Solve It*, *Mathematics and Plausible Reasoning*, and *Mathematical Discovery* he has helped to explain the process central to mathematics – that of solving problems. The term 'heuristic' – the study of the methods and rules of discovery and invention – is for many inseparably linked with his name. In a similar manner, the phrase 'concept formation' automatically evokes the name of Piaget. The work of Professor Piaget, and that of the Geneva school which he created, has had enormous influence on primary education during the past two decades and has generated research work in universities throughout the world. Such books as *The Psychology of Intelligence*, *The Child's Conception of Number*, *The Early Growth of Logic in the Child* and *The Child's Conception of Geometry* have been read and studied by mathematical educators everywhere. His theories are not universally accepted, but it is indeed a measure of his greatness that they should generate controversy – and even on occasion provide the headlines of the British daily press!

The committee after noting this unanimity, proposed that, rather than being asked to address congress, these two great educators should be invited to attend as 'Distinguished Guests' and to contribute papers which, by being made available to all members, would help to direct congress thought. It was to the delight of all that both Professor Pólya and Professor Piaget accepted the invitation offered to them by ICMI, a delight only tempered by the fact that Professor

Piaget had later, reluctantly, to decide on medical advice that he could not make the journey.

In the event, the choice of speakers was circumscribed to some extent by the themes which the Programme Committee wished to emphasise. There was the need to see mathematics not only as a world in itself, but as part of a greater universe. How did mathematics evolve? What were its social and cultural roots? What is its place in general education, indeed in 'civilisation'? To help draw attention to these questions and in the hope of encouraging study of the relevance of the findings of anthropologists, sociologists and others to mathematical education, the committee invited the distinguished anthropologist Dr Edmund Leach to address the congress. It is significant that other plenary speakers, notably Professor Philp, also chose to emphasise such considerations.

Such anthropological study provides us with opportunities to identify primitive examples of mathematical creativity and of those processes of thought which we can describe as 'mathematical'. The study of such processes and their cultivation – problems of learning, knowing, thinking and teaching – are central to the development of a discipline of mathematical education. As an acknowledgement of this, two speakers, Professor Hawkins and Professor Philp, were specifically invited to lecture on aspects of educational philosophy and psychology.

Having indicated the importance which it attached to these facets of mathematical education, the Programme Committee turned to problems of content and selection. What mathematics should be taught and for what reasons? Here the committee was able to fall back on precedents, for it has long been the case that certain (even if, almost of necessity, a small minority of) professional mathematicians have sought not only to advance the study of mathematics itself, but also to improve the way in which it is taught at all levels. The committee was fortunate, therefore, that it could turn for guidance and advice to such eminent mathematicians as Freudenthal, Sobolev, Thom and the congress President, Sir James Lighthill.

The French professional mathematicians have been very much involved in the discussions on mathematical education that have taken place during the past fifteen years. In particular, Professors Lichnerowicz, Choquet and Dieudonné have contributed greatly to the debate through OECD and other seminars, and through their textbooks. More recently, Professor René Thom's voice has been heard and his contribution has been along very different lines from those of his compatriots. The committee was most grateful, therefore, when Professor Thom accepted its invitation to speak at Exeter about 'modern' mathematics as he saw it. Professor Thom's contribution is, of course, doubly valuable, for it emphasises – if further evidence is still required – that although the mathematical educator should seek advice and guidance from professional mathematicians, he should not expect the professionals to reply in a unanimous and unequivocal manner. The educator will still have the responsibility for making decisions.

The interest which Russian mathematicians have taken in fostering mathematical talent in schools is well known. The committee naturally turned, therefore, to the USSR for suggestions regarding principles that might govern mathematical education. Originally it was hoped that Academician Kolmogorov would be able to attend the Exeter meeting. Unfortunately, circumstances prevented his attending and we were fortunate that Academician Sobolev, one of the international corresponding members of the Programme Committee, agreed to lecture in Kolmogorov's place and to tell us how mathematical educators in the USSR are attempting to solve some of the problems which face them.

One professional mathematician who will always be remembered for his contribution to mathematical education is Felix Klein. His books on *Elementary Mathematics from an Advanced Standpoint* are still read throughout the world – indeed, some of his suggestions, such as the use of calculating machines for teaching arithmetic to children, still have a modern ring about them! In recent years, many new approaches to the teaching of geometry in schools have been based on his *Erlanger Programm*. By a happy coincidence, our meeting in Exeter marked the centenary of Klein's inaugural address at Erlangen, and the committee's thoughts turned to how this anniversary might best be celebrated. It was decided to invite a geometer, who, like Klein, had contributed greatly not only to mathematics but also to mathematical education, to talk on some subject closely allied with Klein's work. We were fortunate that the Programme Committee contained just such a person, Hans Freudenthal, and that he was willing to accept the invitation offered to him by its other members.

Finally, the committee wished to stress the importance it attached to teaching mathematics for, and through, its applications. We in

Britain have a tradition of teaching 'Applied Mathematics' in schools, where it is often found on the timetable alongside 'Pure Mathematics'. It can, of course, be argued that such a dichotomy is pedagogically undesirable or even meaningless, yet, despite these and other objections, this tradition is one which the British tend to value greatly and which makes them apprehensive about the 'purer' programmes that they see advocated elsewhere. The committee wished, therefore, to draw the attention of all congress members to this aspect of mathematics and was extremely grateful when Sir James Lighthill, who is renowned for the manner in which he has applied mathematics in a variety of fields, suggested that he should devote part of his Presidential Address to this topic.

All the time allotted to plenary sessions had now been filled. The committee realised that it had not accorded a mention at plenary level to many aspects of mathematical education – to computers, educational technology, the history of mathematics, etc. – but hoped that these deficiencies would be remedied through the work of the various discussion groups, in the showing of films, and in the display of equipment and materials. A more significant omission, perhaps, and one which the working groups could not remedy, was an account of developments within mathematics itself. Many of those who, in the past, attended ICM congresses primarily for the work of the Education Section also greatly enjoyed the opportunity to make contact with leading research mathematicians and to learn of the most recent developments. It must be admitted, however, that the rapid expansion of mathematics has tended to diminish the value of such contacts, for now a vast amount of specialist knowledge is frequently required before one can comprehend the significance of developments – particularly when they are presented in a manner which assumes specialist competence in the listener. The idea of attempting to bridge this gap by means of a series of expository lectures intended for a more general audience was discussed by the committee. In the event, it was unable to mount such a programme – but it remains the hope of the committee that this idea will be re-examined and followed-up at future ICMI congresses.

3 THE CONGRESS IN ACTION

The congress was officially opened at 8 p.m. on Tuesday 29 August at a ceremony in the Great Hall of Exeter University. The President of Congress, Sir James Lighthill, read to the meeting a message received from H.R.H. The Prince Philip, Duke of Edinburgh. (This message is reprinted on p. v.) An opening speech of welcome was given by Mr Kenneth Rowe, M.B.E., Pro-Chancellor of the University of Exeter, and this was followed by the Presidential Address (p. 88). The closing session of the congress was held at 8 p.m. on Saturday 2 September, when the President announced the decisions of the Executive Committee of ICMI on future meetings and the congress resolutions (p. 305) were read out.

The congress was attended by 1384 full members and 300 associate members. In all, 73 countries were represented.

The scientific programme of the congress consisted of six invited lectures, meetings of thirty-eight working groups (see p. 300), and presentations mounted by seventeen different countries (see p. 71). Mathematical films were shown throughout the working hours of the congress. In addition there were independent exhibitions and displays arranged by the Educational Equipment Association and the Educational Publishers Council, the Open University, the School Mathematics Project, the Schools Council Mathematics for the Majority Continuation Project, and the Nuffield Project.

The official representatives of the International Commission on Mathematical Instruction met on Friday 1 September and the Executive Committee of that body met on Saturday 2 September.

The social programme included a reception given by the City of Exeter and the University of Exeter, held on Thursday 31 August, the Congress Dinner, held on Friday 1 September, and late-night film and theatre shows. On the afternoon of Friday 1 September a wide variety of excursions was available to members. Special excursions were provided for associate members on three other days.

4 THE WORK OF CONGRESS

It is the aim of this book to transmit to its readers something of the general spirit of congress. This it does, in part, by reprinting papers presented to congress by the invited speakers, and by reproducing some of the papers submitted to the working groups. The difficulties of conveying 'spirit' are manifest. Perhaps the inclusion of '(Laughter)' or even '(Gallic whistles)' at suitable points in the texts of the plenary lectures might help to transmit more of that sense of occasion, but it would be impossible adequately to describe, say, the warmth of the congress greeting to its distinguished visitor Professor George Pólya.

If the printed texts fail to do justice to the plenary lectures, how much more do the papers reprinted in Part III fail to indicate the breadth and depth of the discussions which took place within the working groups. The committee which met to select those papers to be reprinted in the proceedings had a well-nigh impossible task. First, it must be emphasised that many of the papers submitted to working groups were clearly intended to provoke discussion and, because of their format, were not suitable for reprinting in this volume. This is by no means a criticism of their authors, for, indeed, such papers were exactly what were required by the various groups. Again, there were outstanding papers which were too specialised for this publication and which one hopes to see reprinted in one or other of the technical journals that now exist – for it must be emphasised that the selection committee attempted to choose papers of general interest which could be read by any mathematics teacher. Those papers reprinted, therefore, represent only a small part of those considered by the selection committee and, for the reasons given above, are not wholly typical of the many papers submitted by authors from so many different countries.

It would be wrong, however, to suggest that the committee suffered from an embarrassment of riches. Obviously, all the papers considered did not reach the same standard of readability, excitement or depth of research. As we have said before, mathematical education is in its formative years and criteria and objectives are not yet sharply defined.

The constraints of space and the time available to a prospective reader, rule out any attempt to present a meeting-by-meeting account of the activities of the working groups, and we have, therefore, chosen instead to survey the major themes which arose in the group discussions and to attempt to indicate problems to which mathematical educators will be paying especial attention in the coming years.

In general, the names of contributors to working groups have been omitted. However, where research results or reports are available the names of the persons concerned and brief details of the institution to which they belong have been added. The names and addresses of the chairmen and secretaries of the working groups can be found on pp. 300–4.

Where appropriate, the activities of two or more groups have been described under the same subheading. This is but one way in which an attempt has been made to impose some structure on this particular section of the proceedings. However, it is important to realise that any such structure is bogus in the sense that the groups formed themselves in an unstructured way; they represent neighbourhoods of interest which, not unexpectedly, reveal some complicated patterns of connectivity.

Some working groups concentrated their attention on specific age levels or even on particular sections of the curriculum within a given age-range, others ranged across all levels of education. The accounts of the former type of group are collected together and separate the descriptions of the work of the wider-ranging groups.

The psychology of mathematics learning

It is perhaps fitting that the survey of the activities of the working groups should begin with consideration of that on the psychology of learning mathematics, for not only does this study underpin the whole of mathematical education, but also this was the most popular group in terms of numbers attending. The papers of this working group were divided into four categories: the first dealt with theoretical problems concerning the psychology of learning mathematics; the second was concerned with the results of learning experiments which had been based on theoretical-psychological sources; there were practical demonstrations and films related to children learning; and problems of research related to the psychology of mathematics learning were raised.

The chairman of the group, Professor E. Fischbein (see p. 222), introduced three themes, the relation between intuition and reasoning processes, the concept of structure in mathematics and psychology, and heuristics and the solving of mathematical problems. Research was needed on the child's primitive intuitive knowledge, on which the school must later try to help the child to build his conceptual structures. It was suggested, reciprocally, that the various mathematical operations readily available in elementary mathematics might indicate the presence of certain developmental stages in the child.

Other speakers covered various aspects of studies arising from Piaget's work which it was claimed allowed the child's cognitive growth to be described with some precision. Miss Joan Bliss talked about the relation between concept and image, emphasising that the concept derives from the 'interiorised' actions of the child. It is the coordination of the results of the child's actions on objects, not the objects themselves, that forms the basis of his first interiorised logical thinking.

Joint sessions were held with the working group on research in the teaching of mathematics. A number of speakers described experiments in teaching logical and mathematical structures to young children. Miss Colette Hug (France) stated that she could teach such structures with success when she used situations which were 'pure', that is, which were stripped of any significance in the real world. Dr Seymour Papert (USA) described his teaching method, which was essentially enabling children to abstract a formal scheme from its concrete materialisation.

It was suggested that there is a real communications gap between teachers and researchers, not merely a difficulty of communication. This stems from the differences in the tasks facing them: the first having complex problems to solve in 'real time', the latter having to locate definable problems capable of solution in some rigorous sense. There are problems of transferring ideas from research to teaching, among them a danger that results will be inflated, and applied in circumstances well beyond those in which they have research validation. There is also a danger of the confusion of research terms with the looser language necessarily used in teaching. The language developed in curriculum projects might be one way of bridging the gap as it is at the same time precise enough to convey distinct meanings but also rich enough to be effective in the confusing, value-judgement-laden classroom situation.

A number of theoretical problems were discussed in the working group sessions. The relation between images and concepts influenced greatly the learning of mathematics. The discussion made it clear that consideration of the different types of image and their role needs to be studied in greater depth. There are images which reproduce more or less directly the objects and world around them, there are other images which have varying degrees of schematisation, there are post-conceptual images which are, in fact, figural abstractions. All these different types of image and their relation to the concept concerned need to be known, as part of mathematical learning depends upon imagery. Another area in which research is needed is in the study of intuition, both primary (primitive forms of knowledge) and secondary (constructed by the teaching process in the different branches of mathematics).

It was felt that practical demonstrations and discussion have shown that the learning of mathematical structures through different 'embodiments' at the elementary level is a promising direction. However, it was stressed that longitudinal research is necessary in order to determine the value of such teaching procedures for the development of mathematical thought.

The group's discussions led to the following conclusions:

It is vital that psychologists and mathematics teachers should attempt to communicate with each other so that they can better understand each other's work and problems. It is necessary for both groups to know in greater depth each other's language and working style. Research in psychology and the learning of mathematics is practically all concerned with the child's first learning experience in elementary mathematics in the primary school. It would seem desirable that research should be started in children's spontaneous learning processes of more complicated mathematical structures, for example, the notion of continuity, limits, derivatives, integrals and problems concerning axiomatisation.

Periodical meetings (in the form of symposia, seminars, etc.) should be organised between psychologists, mathematicians and teachers. Such meetings would not only help in bridging the gap between these various groups of people but would possibly also be the source of team work in research at the international level. It is requested and hoped that ICMI would support such meetings. The group generally hoped that at the next congress more mathematics teachers and children could be present.

Investigation and structure

In the introductory paper written by Professor Piaget for circulation to members of congress (pp. 79–87) he discusses the relationship of 'activity with objects' to 'the comprehension of arithmetical as well as geometrical relations'. 'Real comprehension of a notion or theory' he says 'implies the re-invention of this theory by the subject.' Here we have a clear statement that the manipulation of things leads to an understanding of relations through the inventive mind of the learner.

This question of the connection between practical exploration of situations and the growth of generalisations was the major theme of the group considering *Creativity, Investigation and Problem-solving*. In the opening session Miss E. E. Biggs (UK) stressed the importance of free investigation if spontaneity and creativity are to be preserved in mathematics learning. Starting points need not be obviously mathematical but the teacher can so structure situations for children that they can rapidly make a discovery or frame a generalisation. A workshop, well equipped with materials, apparatus and books, is a useful setting in which the teacher has a role different from that of an instructor. As Piaget says in his paper, the teacher becomes 'someone who organises situations'.

Some interesting points were made in subsequent meetings. For instance it was emphasised that spatial factors are involved in the treatment of number systems, a fact which becomes evident when children use some forms of number apparatus. It also draws attention to the varied ways in which children learn and the consequent need for a wide variety of techniques in teaching. It was reported that an investigation of the effects of learning through individual discovery had shown that pupils learn more quickly and show greater interest when the initiative lies with them.

Problem-solving can be carried beyond the practical and become a dialectic in which the young investigator conducts an argument with himself as proponent and opponent. He may assure himself about the solution of some simple instances and can then move on to more complex examples.

After valuable discussions of the thinking that develops through discovery methods the group welcomed Professor Pólya to their final session at which he spoke on the role of heuristics in mathematical education, using an investigation by Euler to illustrate the success of unsophisticated lines of enquiry. He urged that young people should not have problem-solving techniques thrust upon them but should be encouraged to establish a pattern of relations from which they could make their own generalisations.

Finally this group recorded two conclusions: that many ways of presenting problems are required if the curiosity of all pupils is to be aroused; and that problem-solving abilities develop only in an atmosphere of free investigation.

Structure and activity was the chosen topic of another group. The question whether structure or activity should introduce a new mathematical idea was one of the most controversial raised during congress. This group set out to study different learning programmes. Discussion was based on two contrasting schemes: one was from the Experimental School in Mathematics of Francheville-le-Haut, near Lyons; the other was contained in the Essex County Council (UK) pamphlet *The Impact of Modern Mathematics on Primary Schools.* In the Francheville programme structure was presented first and applications followed. In the Essex plan practical experiences of many kinds were used as starting points from which generalisations could be derived and structures could be identified and used. Video tapes and verbal descriptions were used to present schemes from Holland and West Germany also.

The analyses of these schemes revealed substantial differences and stimulated vigorous discussion. One positive comment on the practical approach stressed the importance of progressing from experimentation by the children to an organised review of their experimental findings. This links up with the observation that the Essex scheme, which has an experimental basis, asks the children to record their discoveries in some form, whereas the other plans postponed recording until later. Another difference was in the earlier introduction of number in the Essex programme than in the other schemes. It was reported that the later start with numbers had had no ill effects and had benefited children who, although socially disadvantaged, appeared to take well to logic, sets and relations during the early years. It was considered that schools where a definite programme is not laid down give more scope for the creative and imaginative powers of a child.

This group limited its investigations to the primary stage. The topic is equally relevant at later stages and discussion will doubtless be extended to the middle and secondary years. Meanwhile this group was so keenly interested in the well-defined themes discussed that they hoped to maintain individual contacts made at Exeter and perhaps to make some contribution to the Symposium on Primary Mathematics to be held in Hungary in June 1973 (see p. 305).

Mathematics and language

'Lekgolo le masome a mabedi le metso e mebedi' is the Northern Sotho way of saying 'one hundred and twenty two' when one is counting people. When counting cattle, the expression one uses, literally translated as 'one hundred and tens which are two and ones which are two', differs grammatically. This was but one of the many indications given at Exeter of the way in which language patterns can affect the learning and teaching of mathematics. Several other examples can be found in this book and the reader's attention is especially drawn to Professor Philp's paper (p. 154), to the account of the work of the Developing Countries Group (p. 62) and to the decision of ICMI (p. 305) to sponsor a regional symposium on *Mathematics and Language*. Yet although the problems of language may be more apparent in the developing countries, they exist everywhere; indeed there are universal problems not only related to mathematics *and* language, but also to *mathematics as a language*. It was this latter phrase which was taken as a title by one of the groups that met at Exeter.

The group chairman, Professor Schweiger, suggested that mathematical reasoning can be seen as a highly specialised language and referred to the increasing use of mathematical methods in linguistics. For example, the concept of a relation can be applied to natural languages and to formal languages; in particular to mathematics itself. The general feeling of the meeting was that this sort of analysis was in its infancy as yet, and that it became difficult beyond certain limited applications. But it was also felt that this was no reason not to try to continue applying to mathematics what was potentially a useful theory.

Dr H. Davies (UK) first pointed out the obvious: one learns a first language. The beliefs and values of folk linguistics which result from this learning can be characterised by the facts that most people have a large operational knowledge, yet only a small descriptive knowledge of their first language, and popularly consider that the written word is automatically better than the spoken word. Tape recorded readings and experiments within the group showed how the context changed the information supplied by the same sentence, and how the position of the prominent pitch within the sentence affected the meaning. In particular it became evident that the speaker gave prominence to what he considered to be the new information imparted by the sentence. With this in mind the group listened to tape recorded readings from a mathematical text on sets by a mathematician and by a ten-year-old. The school boy obviously found a lot more that was new to him than did the mathematician. More important, what he thought to be the important new information was not what the writer intended him to learn.

This was disturbing, and various ideas for improving textual layout were discussed: should we underline key words or leave more spaces for example. It was agreed that authors and printers of textbooks should bear in mind the need to make explicit, and more obvious than most seem to, just what is new and what is assumed.

The importance of intonation while teaching was also underlined by Professor Papy who gave a demonstration lesson with no words; just drawing while 'groaning' the intonation. We could, he claimed, sometimes use too many words and so confuse, not enlighten. The group agreed.

The subject of notation was also tackled. Children had to be taught to read a textbook, and to be shown how the order of action was not necessarily the order in which the signs were written, nor as read. The linear form of our notation makes certain things very difficult. Dr Turnau (Poland) advocated the use of a 'reasoning graph'; that is the steps of a proof laid out in a tree alongside the linear text. This principle gained support and it was shown how, for example, diagrams served to make proofs of commutability unnecessary for children. Just as music is something more than the score, mathematics is something more than our codes for it. Our texts must allow children to appreciate the mathematics, they can learn to read the 'score' afterwards.

It was suggested that many difficulties arose from the fact that, although children learned their own language in a natural way from native speakers, they are taught mathematics by people who were taught by people who were taught by people...who were taught by mathematicians. Some mathematical concepts seem to develop out of a repeated need in a given situation, become a body of knowledge and then undergo a third stage where the knowledge is organised. This theme was illustrated with examples from matrix and set theories, and by descriptions of experiments with children who were finding the need for mathematical methods to help them discover the outcome of some action without having to do it. At first the children invented their own notation, until sufficient examples had been built up for a unifying system to be employed. This system took on a generality which gives it a life of its own. The system can now be studied in its own right, and applications chosen at will. The group thought that this provided a natural way for children to begin learning mathematics.

Throughout the group meetings the feeling was expressed that viewing mathematics as a language could contribute to our insight into what mathematics is, allow for more ready discussion of rigour when it is needed, and, in particular, could make available to us an understanding of how we might improve communication in our teaching methods. All possible encouragement should be given to these studies as well as to promoting a better awareness of the relationship between the language of mathematics and the mother tongue.

The first eight years

We now turn to questions of objectives, organisation and content during the early stages of mathematical education: a period taken to cover both those years which Piaget describes in his paper (p. 82) as 'the age where material actions and logico-mathematical experience are necessary' (before 7/8 years old) and also the years on towards 11/12 years, up to 'the age where abstract thought begins to be possible', with a year or so more, perhaps, of development in deductive thinking. We are therefore concerned here with both the 'pre-operational stage', with its dependence on actions, and the 'concrete operations stage' (in Piaget's terms) when a child 'in order to arrive at a coherent deduction, needs to apply his reasoning to manipulable objects (in the real world or in his imagination)'.

The crucial importance of a child's surroundings and opportunities before he begins formal schooling is now being fully recognised. It is not surprising that a group set up to study primary mathematics chose for its title *Pre-school and primary mathematics*. When children start school they normally come after several years of family life in which many of the things in use and the round of daily activities will have given them experiences of a mathematical kind. But family situations vary widely and some children will have done little exploring and will have had only very restricted contact with other children. Teachers must therefore take into account the great variations in ideas, power of expression in words or drawings, skill of hands, and responses to new experiences. Mathematical education in school must begin for some children with the free play and experiments with materials which other children have enjoyed for two or three years. So important did the group think this problem that their introductory paper described the plight of many disadvantaged children and urged the need for compensatory experience.

A teacher must take each child as he is at entry, find out his individual needs and ensure that he is given as rich a programme as possible so that he may have a chance to catch up with others in his age-group. Points of potential mathematical growth must be identified and curiosity aroused by materials, conversation, and a variety of surprising happenings. Films and descriptions, from Japan and elsewhere, of such programmes confirmed the view of the group that they were the foundation of the first mathematical steps. Other interesting films showed experiments to test the readiness of a child to begin mathematics. One of these, using Piagetian tests, led some members to express the opinion that it was preferable to assess young children in the learning situation rather than under test conditions.

A discussion of the significance of Piaget's work was introduced by Miss Mary Sime, whose paper appears on pp. 272–82. She said that a study of his findings made many intending teachers aware that they did not themselves have some of the fundamental concepts, such as conservation, on which the understanding of number depends. Such awareness made a teacher a more competent guide to children's learning.

Under the title *Are we off the track in teaching mathematical concepts?* Professor Hassler Whitney (see p. 283) carried further the examination of the place of concepts (using the word in its broadest sense) in the primary school. It was pointed out that concepts cannot be directly taught; they must be acquired by the learner through his own experience. The student must *do* the right things before he can see meanings. There was a lively exchange of views and it was evident that there were various interpretations of the word 'concept'. This is one aspect of the argument about the role of abstraction in mathematical education and is of great importance. It deserves further consideration at another conference.

A main difficulty in establishing new mathematics schedules in primary schools is the fear and dislike that the subject rouses in very many teachers. They seek a false security in a retreat into teaching as they were taught. Plans for in-service courses to remedy this condition are discussed on pp. 49–50.

Several new programmes were described and the group found great satisfaction in the 10-point plan put forward, with practical examples, by Professor Tamas Varga (Hungary). He cited combinatorics as a great source of problems and listed these activities: (1) acquaintance with materials, (2) games, (3) searching, (4) classifying and arranging, (5) calculating, (6) the beginning of proof, (7) tabulating, (8) finding and extending patterns, (9) formulating rules, (10) varying the situation.

A plea for non-numerical activities, such as manipulating logical or attribute blocks, or work on probabilities with matches, led to the conclusion that numerical and non-numerical ideas should develop side by side.

Reviewing the week's discussions it was agreed that the development of children's thinking is so complex and as yet so little is known about it that generalisations about material and methods could be dangerous. The teacher's greatest need is flexibility in meeting the needs of every child.

A separate group considered the later part of the 8-year period under the title *Middle school mathematics* (*ages 9–13*). There would naturally be some overlap with both primary and secondary programmes but the group looked upon the Middle School as a new type of unit which is being developed in some countries, notably in Britain which had supplied the background papers. A brief account of the British development was given but ten countries in all were represented in the group and major contributions also came from Holland, Japan, and the USA.

It was agreed that mathematics teachers should play their part in the broad educational aims of this stage: social integration, active learning, readiness to investigate, the exercise of imagination, the acquisition of necessary skills and techniques, and the fulfilment of promise and latent ability. But it was thought that short-term objectives should be stated in specifically mathematical terms. This seems to differ from the views of the primary group but in fact the middle school group agreed on the general inclusion of computational, manipulational, and problem-solving abilities, which could cover a wide range of related topics.

Further discussion concerned the place of mental arithmetic, number, probability and statistics, and algebra, but standards and the point at which topics are introduced varied from country to country. Geometry programmes from different countries were compared. In the end the major problem was defined as whether geometry in the 9–13 age range should be about the properties of geometrical figures or about transformations. This certainly could be further debated.

It was suggested that middle schools should have flexible timetables so that meaningful links between subjects could be arranged to form 'areas of knowledge'. Nevertheless the mathematical activities should, in the opinion of the group, be timetabled separately and be under the supervision of a competent mathematics teacher.

A wide range of materials and technical aids were listed as desirable at this age and a variety of types of class organisation were proposed. Believing that the mathematical curriculum for the middle years requires careful study, the members of the group hoped to continue their discussions through correspondence. They recommended that there should be joint studies between ICMI committees and those of organisations concerned with the teaching of other subject disciplines.

Subject matter at secondary level

Separate working groups considered specifically the teaching at secondary level of algebra, geometry, calculus, logic, and probability and statistics. The fact that mathematical education is still at its formative stage was reflected by the uncertainties expressed and the local differences highlighted. Indeed, these differences, due to variations in conditions and traditions, and to the dissimilar goals of those responsible for designing curricula (see p. 59), make the task of identifying 'themes' extremely difficult. The value of these groups' work cannot, therefore, be adequately assessed from what is written below. Some idea of the approaches they employed can be gained from reading the papers of Professors Meserve and Shibata (pp. 241 and 262). It is also to be hoped that some of the more technical papers contributed to these groups will appear in those journals devoted to mathematics and mathematical education, for they contained much that was of more than passing interest.

There were, however, certain problems which seemed to be encountered by all the groups. In particular, there is clearly much work still to be done on the question of the amount of rigour which might reasonably be expected and the stages at which it might be required.

'Much more needs to be known about the way in which children learn algebra. . . there is clearly scope for a great deal of research in this area.' The relative merits of groups and vector spaces remained unresolved; but there was agreement that even simple informal abstractions from concrete situations demand a great deal of children in general, not just the less able. It is important, too, not to introduce the rigorous axiomatic definition of structures before it is possible to make useful deductions which have relevant applications for the pupils.

There was more of a consensus of opinion among the geometers.

Three arguments put forward in favour of transformation geometry were (*a*) the children find it easy, (*b*) children like it, (*c*) teachers, even those previously antagonistic to mathematics, readily adapt to it. Problems take pride of place over axioms, which 'will only be taken off the shelf (which may hold a strictly superfluous supply) if and when demanded by the pupil'. The trend is towards the introduction of a variety of geometries (coordinate, vector, transformation, even informal Euclid). In this way the children have a battery at their disposal, and the very selection of the best approach for a particular problem gives opportunities for genuine mathematical thinking.

In addition to the main geometry group there was also a smaller group which devoted all its discussions to lattice geometry. This group was distinguished by the limited area it sought to study and it was significant that there was general agreement within the group about the value of looking at a restricted topic and considering its relevance at all stages of education. The group ably demonstrated, therefore, how an ICME can provide a meeting place for, and stimulate discussion between, enthusiasts for a particularly specialised branch of mathematical education. It is hoped that one outcome of this group's work, both at and after the congress, will be a booklet on this approach to teaching geometry in schools and colleges.

'Too much rigour too early can easily spoil the pupils' confidence' was a slogan of the calculus group. Nevertheless, difficulties should be pointed out: when the teacher is skating over something he should warn the pupils that he is doing so. Counterexamples are very helpful in de-bunking the plausible.

Numerical and graphical methods will undoubtedly receive impetus from the advent of computers, and in particular the whole treatment of differential equations is likely to undergo a thorough change.

The logicians on balance came out in favour of integration within the mathematics curriculum rather than isolated, straight 'logic courses'. In any case, concepts should be formed before symbols are introduced. First logical ideas can be introduced at about the age of 8 or 9, with a variety of teaching materials. The principle of making the mathematics encountered at school intelligible and relevant, and the need for further research into how this may be done, are exemplified by the resolution put forward by the logic group.

In order to improve and to develop the efficiency of logical thinking and practice in pupils it is not enough to give formal elementary notions about propositional and predicate calculi. Moreover it is necessary to integrate those notions of symbolic logic to help to understand mathematical reasoning and to make use of them to clear up some logical difficulties.

In this field more research is urgently needed.

The probability and statistics group, in addition to a programme of technical papers and discussions on the teaching of these topics from the primary school to higher education, devoted one of their sessions to consideration of future work. It was stressed by many members that there was need for greater communication between those who had tried different teaching programmes for statistics – it being recognised that such courses were not so readily produced as those in probability. Also, it appeared that the special equipment created in some countries for teaching these topics was not so widely known as it should be. In an attempt to improve matters the group agreed to inaugurate a news bulletin. It was hoped that this bulletin would also carry contributions on those areas of needs and interests which the group saw as being particularly worthy of study prior to the 1976 ICME, namely:

(*a*) the development of new aids and technologies for teaching statistics,

(*b*) ways of using government and other official statistics in teaching,

(*c*) the search for points in the curriculum at which statistical concepts can be introduced and/or used,

(*d*) suggestions for statistical field trips and data collection activities suitable for students of various ages,

(*e*) proposals for interdisciplinary work (with computing, biology, physics, geography, social science, etc.),

(*f*) outlines for suitable courses for teachers (it was felt that at present many such courses are unsuitable, being but pale imitations of those given to intending research workers),

(*g*) outlines for statistics courses for pupils for whom secondary education is terminal,

(*h*) ways in which statistics can be applied to research in mathematical education.

Papy–Cemrel workshop

A separate group was devoted to the joint work of Papy's Centre Belge de Pédagogie de la Mathématique (CBPM) and the Comprehensive School Mathematics Program (CSMP) of CEMREL.[1] The

[1] Cemrel Inc., A National Educational Laboratory, 10646 St Charles Rock Road, St Ann, Missouri 63074.

main objective is to introduce the basic notions of *number*, *set*, *relation*, and *function* by means of simple languages; 'strings', 'arrows' and the minicomputer.[1] The 'strings' language employs Venn diagrams with certain conventions, the 'arrows' show relation-

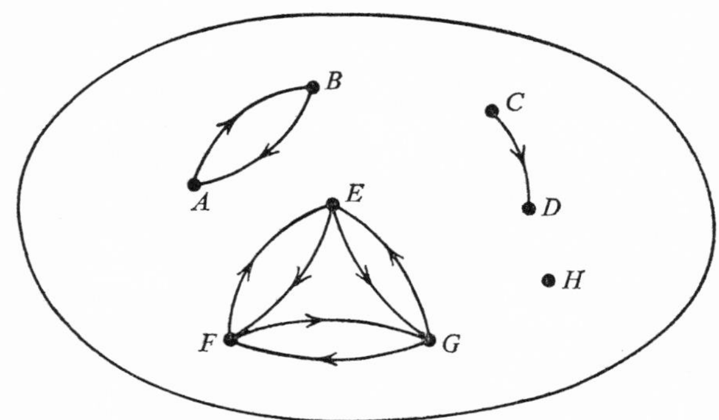

ships; both are combined in the example in which children are pointing at their sisters. The children can deduce from the diagram, for example, that

(*a*) *A* and *B* are sisters,
(*b*) *D* is a girl,
(*c*) *H* has no sisters (in the playground),
(*d*) *C* is a boy.

The innovations and experiments are well documented elsewhere, e.g. 'Affine geometry at 7',[2] the introduction of vectors as equivalence classes,[3] 'Real Numbers at 9',[4] 'A Purchase Vector Space'.[5] Of special interest is the application of the simple languages to the education of mentally handicapped children.[6, 7, 8]

[1] Cf. *Proc. 1st Int. Congress on Math. Ed.*, Reidel Pub. Co., 1969, pp. 201–13.

[2] Martin, E., Quelques remarques au sujet de la rencontre entre la géométrie et des enfants de la deuxième année, *NICO* 12. (*NICO* is a publication of the CBPM, Avenue Albert 224, 1180 Bruxelles.)

[3] Frédérique, Initiation à la Géométrie Affine Plane, *NICO* 10.

[4] Frédérique, Nombres réels, *NICO* 10.

[5] Frédérique, Introduction vectorielle de l'équation de la droite à 10 ans, *NICO* 13. See also Frédérique, *Les Enfants et la Mathématique*, vols. 1 to 5.

[6] Dieschbourg, R., Un enseignement moderne de la mathématique à des enfants mentalement handicapés, *NICO* 10.

[7] Dieschbourg, R., Un enseignement moderne de la mathématique à des enfants mentalement handicapés – 2e année, *NICO* 13.

[8] Vandeputte, C., Un enseignement moderne de la mathématique à des enfants paralyses cérebraux, *NICO* 13.

Links with other subjects at secondary level

This is a major growth-point in mathematical education and a resolution by the working group concerned, calling for further action, was received with sympathy at the final plenary session of the congress (see p. 306). There is, however, much spade work still to be done. Considerable quantities of relevant source materials exist in a diversity of areas, and the urgent task is to sift, collate, edit and test in schools.

Science is a major 'user' of mathematics. Despite the common complaints of science teachers, studies of particular recently developed courses in the USA and in the UK have shown that the difference between what is required and what is provided is *apparently* slight (see, for example, the paper by A. J. Malpas, pp. 233–40). The difficulties might be less in the subject matter covered than in the poor communication between teachers of mathematics and of science and in the different phraseology and approach used by each. One expression of this was that scientists 'feel' the phenomena, but mathematicians 'feel' the logical implications in any particular area.

The key to breaking down the barriers between subjects lies in mathematical modelling.[1] The approach is to start from experience, and from this to make the appropriate abstractions (models) rather than to develop the abstract structure first.

A biological example of mathematical modelling was described in some detail in which the consequences of enlargement applied to animals were explored. This involved construction of mathematical models of *concrete* models of the animals, and dealt with the relations (for animals with bodies of similar proportions) between linear dimensions and length or thickness of leg needed to support the body. An important stage was to go back from the model to experience to check whether its predictions corresponded to what is actually found, both at the concrete model level, and with real animals. It would not be correct to describe this example merely as science using mathematics, nor as the science being a starting point for the mathematics: both subjects develop together.

The ideal is for teachers of mathematics and other subjects to work together in preparing such work, but for the diffusion of ideas it is

[1] Cf. Bell, M. S., Mathematical Models and Uses in our everyday world, SMSG Studies in Mathematics, 1972.

necessary eventually to publish possible strings of inter-disciplinary work.[1]

Important questions arise about the closeness or otherwise of the mathematical abstraction to the student's experience (for example in an experiment on the expansion of a gas there are several levels of abstraction from the varying volume of the gas: the length of the scale on which volume is indicated; a graph of measured volume against temperature; and an equation to represent the relation).

Apart from science, links with philosophy, art, music, geography and economics are all ripe for exploration.

Impediments to learning mathematics

Three main topics usually arise in discussions on mathematical education: the value of mathematics as an ingredient in education; the appropriate mathematics for particular individuals having regard to their circumstances; the ways in which mathematical ideas and processes can be presented to a pupil. But it is an uncomfortable fact of experience that some children do not learn mathematics with interest or ease. Their environment has not stimulated their curiosity or their urge to construct; they seem to have no capacity for understanding mathematics or using its language. This twin problem of lack of willingness or ability to learn was studied by two groups, one interested in the apparent sterility of some children's environment, the other in the poor progress of some pupils.

The main aim of the first group (*Mathematics and the socially disadvantaged child*) was to look at, compare and try to evaluate projects being worked out for the mathematical education of disadvantaged children in many parts of the world. The first point made was that children from poor homes often lacked the language to describe, for instance, such comparisons as big/small, bigger/smaller; this deficiency could hinder the growth of the concept of comparison. Other factors were insufficient possessions to learn how to share with others, lack of toys to manipulate, absence of books and tools in the home.

There then followed the observation of a lesson given by the chairman of the group, Professor William F. Johntz, to a group of children from Brixton, a rather poor part of London with a large

[1] The project SUM (Science Uses Mathematics), based on the Centre for Science Education, Chelsea College, University of London is preparing some 15 interdisciplinary 'modules of work' aimed at pupils from 11 to 16 years old.

number of immigrants. The lesson was planned to illustrate the methods of Project SEED (Special Elementary Education for the Disadvantaged) in which graduates in mathematics teach high school and college-level mathematics to full-sized classes in which nearly all the children come from poverty backgrounds. Professor Johntz, Director of SEED, presented a topic from abstract algebra in a Socratic group-discovery format. This topic had the advantage of being relatively culture-free and not associated with previous failures. The lesson sparked off animated discussion in which many members expressed doubts as to the relevance of the topic and the long-term understanding achieved, while an equal number was impressed with the learning which had taken place.

An account of the Michigan State University Inner City Mathematics Project turned discussion to the need for meaningful in-service training for teachers in the atypical and often restricted environment of inner-city schools. The desirability of selecting able children in such schools for 'enriched' educational experience to enable them to proceed to higher education in mathematics provoked controversy. Other experiments in Australia, Italy and Norway were described. This led to a further consideration of teacher-training. It was emphasised that a deep transformation in training was required so that teachers could develop an approach based on inter-pupil communication.

One session was held jointly with the other group (*Mathematics for slow/reluctant learners*) in which the focus was a showing of films, including one produced by the Mathematics for the Majority Continuation Project (see p. 309). This formed an interesting contrast with the SEED lesson, because it used the environment as the source of mathematics. Group opinion remained evenly divided between the view that abstract mathematics was suitable material for these children and the belief that the mathematics relevant to the life around them was more appropriate. Consequently the group made no definite recommendation. Yet it can be expected that future discussions will resolve the conflict since children enjoy both the exercise of their minds on arguments within their grasp and also the investigation of practical problems within their experience.

The second group, concerned with slow/reluctant learners, decided that it was their task to discuss how to teach children who had already failed in most of their mathematical work and were reluctant to undertake any sort of further work connected with mathematics.

The group therefore agreed on the fundamental requirements before any progress could be made. Their first principle was that the mathematics programme must consider each child in the totality of his situation: personal, educational, social and economic. This may demand different individual programmes and a correspondingly small class. Administrators should encourage the maximum freedom of choice for teachers planning the work and in their turn teachers must provide choices for their pupils who need to build up confidence through success. Rigid adherence to a prescribed course is bound to aggravate the problem. Inexperienced teachers need help in planning the various alternative starting points and rates of development. The responsibility for the success of these pupils must rest with the teacher even within an externally imposed scheme of work.

Teaching reluctant and slow learners demands ample resources. They are generally quite inadequate; authorities should look for ways to ensure a generous share of staff, materials and equipment for slower classes. Their development is as important as that of abler children and working with them may demand greater teaching skills than work with more academic children. It should have equal status and financial rewards.

Highly qualified staff should take part in this work and care should be taken to avoid separating reluctant learners from those who are more successful. The group thought it undesirable that specialists should be trained to work only within this problem area.

The following recommendations were put forward:

(*a*) There should be a systematic rather than a piecemeal approach to this problem and national projects will be necessary to develop materials and train teachers.

(*b*) The group did not think it necessary to hold a separate meeting before 1976 but a section of the 1976 congress should be devoted to this problem. Meanwhile a coordinator should be found to gather information from various countries and prepare a report for 1976. Such a scheme would, however, probably depend upon financial assistance from ICMI.

University and college level

As was remarked earlier (p. 6) the Lyons Congress had not specifically considered mathematical education beyond the secondary level, apart from teacher-training, and it was, therefore, particularly encouraging that a number of groups should have been set up at

Exeter to look at various aspects of mathematical education at a higher level.

One group chose to consider the mathematics taught to specialists, that is to students for whom mathematics constitutes the greater part of their studies. Besides looking at more general questions, the group considered two areas, geometry and applied mathematics, in depth. The congress heard many pleas for the restoration of geometry as a major discipline in the curriculum at all levels – one such is reprinted on p. 241 and, of course, this is one of Professor Thom's main theses (p. 194). Strong pleas were made in the group discussions for the return at a university level of analytic geometry and, in particular, the treatment of conics, both analytic and projective. The importance of geometry as a medium for conveying fundamental concepts of mathematical thought, such as proof, was mentioned. Another topic which arose in the plenary sessions was that of applied mathematics (see p. 37) and this was taken up again in group discussion. It was argued that the teacher of applied mathematics should have considerable familiarity with the discipline to which the mathematics was being applied and that this familiarity should be transferred to the students. To aid this transfer it was suggested that perhaps a quarter of course time should be spent on a descriptive treatment of the area of application. There was also a need to ensure that students were given the theory of practical applications rather than that of idealised models. It was agreed that the area of application was of less importance than the manner in which the process of application was taught (although the opportunity was taken to reaffirm the usefulness of mechanics as a medium for teaching applied mathematics *provided* the work was closely related to that of the practising engineer). The time spent on the descriptive part of such courses would inevitably mean that the mathematics available for use would be more elementary than would otherwise be the case but it was pointed out that there are many powerful examples in which relatively elementary mathematics is applied.

Amongst the other more general points considered was that of the students who cannot cope with courses as they are given at present. Discussion of this point was complicated by the fact that the members present came from widely differing educational systems, but some pertinent questions were raised which would seem to have universal relevance, for example:

(*a*) Is the purpose of an undergraduate education to enable the student to ‘know’ some mathematics, or to ‘do’ some mathematics?

(*b*) Are the standard specialist courses designed to produce productive mathematicians?

(*c*) Are lectures intended to ‘straighten out’ the students’ minds or that of the teacher?

(*d*) Is there a place for survey courses as well as specialist ones?

(*e*) To what extent should mathematics students be exposed to other disciplines?

Similar questions were raised by the groups considering the problems of those students who study mathematics as an ancillary subject, for example, engineers, biologists and social scientists. Here the difference in the mathematical aptitudes of the students is more marked – some are able mathematicians capable of reading, say, biomathematics or econometrics whilst others fight shy of mathematics. One’s aim for this latter type of student is that he should arrive at some understanding of mathematics and its use in his own subject so that he might make, or recognise, informed decisions. The big problem is finding sufficient teachers who are knowledgeable in both mathematics and the discipline in which it is to be applied (here the group’s thinking resembled that of the group discussing mathematics for specialists (see p. 33). This is necessary in order to provide an abundance of elementary examples (especially in model-making) which can be used with many of the weaker students. The work of the Committee of the Undergraduate Program in Mathematics (USA) in collecting suitable examples was welcomed and the forthcoming publication of a collection is eagerly awaited.

The shortage of those qualified both in mathematics and another discipline can only be solved by the provision of joint courses, i.e. ‘integrated’ rather than ‘two-subject’, for those students referred to above as ‘able mathematicians’. Again there are difficulties of staffing such courses and also often difficulties of recognition both within and without universities. Courses of this nature will only be produced after considerable discussion and developmental work and clearly this is a major priority, for once a few courses have been successfully developed then others will assuredly follow.

Although mathematics has been taught to engineers and physicists for many years and its importance for these students has long been recognised, there remain two opposed schools of thought on how it should be taught. It was apparent in group discussion that participants from a number of European and Asian countries believed that mathematics was such an important subject that it should be taught in the same way to the mathematics specialist and to his engineering or scientist counterpart – indeed mathematics should be taught to all these in a common group. The respective science and engineering teachers would then be responsible for teaching applications of this mathematics. Such a system was certainly possible in some countries since the students admitted to these courses were highly 'motivated' and, furthermore, selection procedures ensured that the students had a good mathematical training and background.

The other school of thought, however, believed strongly that mathematics should be taught separately to engineering/science students and that the material should be strongly 'motivated' all through their course. An essential part of this course was the inclusion of applications and a demonstration of the relevance of the mathematics taught. Additionally, the discussion of real problems, mathematical modelling and the solution of physical problems arising from their courses and from their experience was regarded as an important feature of such a course in mathematics.

The discussion quite clearly revealed that there was a need for a continuing discourse on these and other topics and it was unanimously agreed that a conference, devoted entirely to the mathematical education of engineers, should take place in the near future.

It will be seen that many of the problems raised above hinge on finding ways of encouraging students to participate in mathematics, and to apply mathematics, in an active, meaningful way. These latter problems were given particular attention by the group which met to discuss teaching methods at university and college level. The group was concerned at the way in which undergraduate teaching is largely regarded as the transmission of information by means of expository lecture-type courses and associated tutorial classes.

The need to describe the goals of one's teaching adequately and the qualities and modes of thought and action one seeks to generate in one's students was seen as the initial problem to be solved. There is a danger that vague descriptions such as 'encouraging creativity', 'developing thinking' and 'learning to function as a mathematician' will mislead us into believing that these aims can be achieved through the act of learning mathematical subject matter. The group felt that one area which appeared to need, and would repay, investigation was that of explicitly formulating the ways in which we should like students to think and act. This might possibly be done by considering how these ways would differ from those that are to be observed in our students at present.

Another problematic area was that of using one's professional mathematical expertise when teaching students having different levels of understanding to one's own. This is a problem of translation – translation of a piece of mathematics from the teacher's conceptual framework to that of the student, which is generally less complex and less mathematically sophisticated. This issue was raised particularly in connection with the training of school and college teachers who are constantly faced with these problems and who get little if any chance to discuss such matters in traditional courses. Some work in progress was described and again it was apparent how one was involved as much with *attitudes towards mathematics* as with *knowledge of mathematics*.

This concerns motivation, a matter which also entered the group's discussions through a consideration of the relationships between mathematics and the physical world. It was told how simple laboratory situations were being used as a means for encouraging students to grapple with problems of constructing their own mathematical models.

Particular teaching methods discussed included types of project and investigational work intended to encourage students to employ and develop a variety of skills. For, in addition to those manipulative and conceptual skills traditionally required, it was thought important to develop skills in the formulation of problems, asking questions in particular mathematical situations, relating work from different sources, the making of value-judgements and decisions about their work, and skills in communication. Research into the ways of bringing out these skills in the course of one's teaching – within the constraints of the system in which one must work – should be encouraged.

Since much undergraduate teaching will still be done by means of lecturing, this must be made as productive as possible. Joint lectures were discussed as a possible means whereby, through having another teacher share the teaching, teaching technique might be improved and the *ex cathedra* nature of lectures lessened. Students also require guidance as to how they can make most effective use of lectures.

The need to consider ways of relating a student's mathematical activity to his future needs was discussed, particularly in relation to those intending to be teachers and further investigation of this problem seems urgently to be required.

Finally, it was remarked that teachers cannot be certain of obtaining optimal solutions to their problems: conditions are constantly changing and, most importantly, they have to establish relationships through their teaching with *individuals*.

Vocational mathematics

One working group studied 'vocational mathematics for technicians and business personnel'. The students concerned have left school but are not pursuing a university course. A number of factors contribute to the difficulty in making proper provision for them:

(*a*) the age-range of the students, say 16 to 60;

(*b*) the wide range of their separate interests and requirements;

(*c*) the variety of school courses (after a decade of curriculum reform);

(*d*) the variety of needs of industry.

The mathematics required ranges from arithmetical calculations (for crafts such as building, plumbing), through traditional topics for engineering or technical qualifications, to the direct use of mathematics in statistics and computing.

This wide variation in age, ability and requirements poses so many problems that the working group considered the possibility of setting up a Centre for Further Education in Mathematics, where research could be conducted into syllabus content, teaching methods, assessment techniques and equipment needs, in the fields of mathematics, statistics and computing. An impetus for the massive re-shaping of courses, which was generally agreed to be necessary, has been given in the UK by the implementation of the 'Haslegrave Report'.[1]

Applications of mathematics

The reader will already be aware of the emphasis given at Exeter to the application of mathematics. Examples of how mathematics is applied engender motivation, and the need to bring modern applications to students has been recognised in industry (for example) and has attracted financial help from funding agencies. This need was also acknowledged by the formation of a working group specifically to consider the problems of teaching how mathematics is applied and – what is not the same – how to apply mathematics.

The essential requirement of course is to find problems which arise from situations of genuine interest which recognisably really exist.

[1] *Report of the Committee on Technician Courses and Examinations*, HMSO, 1969.

The situations will certainly vary from one age group to another and one community to another; they can be drawn from sport, social sciences, music, physical science and many other sources. The problem itself need not necessarily be new to the teacher but it is essential that a very thorough investigation of the background to it should be undertaken by the student before and during any attempt to formulate a model. The students themselves should participate in the formulation of this mathematical model and, ultimately, also in the assessment and evaluation of any conclusions which are drawn from the consideration of the model. The search for a 'right solution' (which may be known to exist because it is in an answer book or may, in fact, not exist at all in any precise sense) and emphasis on the most elegant solution (which may be classical and known to the teacher) should be made less important than the acquisition of insight into the nebulous situation which gave rise to the problem. The students may derive some numerical results, recognise some structure but, even if they never achieve a complete solution, they will have gained valuable experience in formulating the model itself. The final interpretation and criticism of any results may well lead to discussions of a non-mathematical and very general nature.

It is believed that human science in particular is a rich source of problems and even new mathematics, and that there is a very great need for mathematicians and human scientists to work together on them.

A number of informal accounts were given of work in this field, but a source book of ideas and possible projects would be invaluable. The field ranges from young students in danger of becoming 'mathematical drop-outs' to the highest university level. An account was given of study groups held at Oxford University[1] for industrial mathematicians, faculty members and graduate students at which attempts were made to formulate and solve industrial problems which had been triggered off and found intractable in the firms concerned.

History of mathematics

One feature of mathematical education in recent years has been an attempt to find a place for history in the mathematics curriculum. Its current neglect and its fall into disrepute have been the cause for much concern,[2] and it was encouraging, therefore, that some seventy

[1] By Dr J. Ockendon.

[2] See, for example, Wilder, R. L., History in the Mathematics Curriculum: Its Status, Quality and Function, *Amer. Math. Monthly*, **79**, 5, 1972, 479–95.

congress members elected to attend the group established to discuss the relations between the history and the pedagogy of mathematics.

Contributors illustrated and stressed the way in which a study of the history of mathematics could, amongst other things, reveal mathematics as a human activity – with a future – rather than as a ready-made structure, provide an increased awareness of the relationships between mathematics and the culture of our society and also those between the different branches of the subject, and help motivate students by revealing the more human aspects of the subject – its successes and its unsolved problems.

At the present time, the use of history in mathematics teaching is hampered by its lack of an established place in the curriculum, the esteem in which it is held and the credit attached to it. There is a consequent shortage of suitable teaching materials, slides, texts, photographs, etc., and of qualified teachers. This latter deficiency will only be remedied by an increased emphasis on history within teacher-training, and the group concluded its discussions[1] by recommending that such training should always include a study of the history of mathematics, designed so as to enable students to appreciate mathematics in the context of our general cultural heritage and as an aid to their understanding of mathematics itself.

Assessment in mathematics

The increasing attention being paid to the problems of assessment in mathematics – and the way in which this term is now taken to mean so much more than merely the testing and ranking of 11, 16, 18 or 21-year-olds – was indicated by the number of groups which made reference to it. Thus, for example, the pre-school and primary mathematics group discussed Piagetian tests whilst the group on teaching methods in universities considered those particular problems of assessment raised by project work, open-ended essay-type investigations, etc.

In addition to these discussions which took place within more general frameworks, one group chose to study some particular aspects of assessment, in depth. It is significant that it began its work by looking at the development of examination and assessment procedures. The need for some form of independent assessment of

[1] A longer account of the group's discussions is to appear in *Notae De Historia Mathematica* – the Newsletter of the Commission on History of Mathematics obtainable from Professor K. O. May, 'Historia', Dept. of Mathematics, The University, Toronto 181, Canada.

students gave rise to the examination system as we now know it and it must be admitted that this need still seems as widely felt as ever.

With increasing educational opportunities and with the moves to make secondary education comprehensive, examinations at the university entrance level are becoming of growing importance and the group heard of several new initiatives at that level. Two would seem to merit special attention; the experiment now taking place in Sweden in which an attempt is being made to dispense with all written examinations for entry to university, and the establishment of the International Baccalaureate. This latter initiative, which is described more fully in a paper by J. B. Morgan reprinted on pp. 254–61, seeks to provide a university entrance qualification that will be accepted in all countries. It arose from the needs of the substantial number of children who are educated in one country and who wish to receive their university education in another. Clearly, such an international enterprise will not be without problems and the group expressed some concern at the difficulties of recognition of the examination's standards not only between countries but also between universities within a single country. Nevertheless, the project is not only of major interest in its own right, but it also serves as one of the few examples within mathematical education of international cooperation leading to a system which is used in several countries. Its progress will be watched with interest.

Other specialist points discussed by the group included the comparative virtues of multiple-choice and essay-type testing[1] at particular age levels and the use of film in tests for Piagetian conservations.[2]

Mathematical competitions

Closely allied with the problems of assessment were those considered by the group constituted to discuss mathematical competitions. It is indicative of the increasing and world-wide interest in such contests that this small group contained representatives from fourteen different countries and that it included ten leaders of delegations to olympiads.

The use of contests as a means for discovering outstanding talent was mentioned by Academician Sobolev (see p. 185) in his account of mathematical education in the USSR. This aspect of contests – particularly in relation to their use in developing countries – together with such other aspects as their use as teaching aids, as part of extra-

[1] A. P. Penfold, University of London Institute of Education.
[2] G. H. Wheatley, Purdue University, Indiana.

curricular activities, and as stimulators and motivators was considered by the group.

It must be acknowledged from the outset that by no means all educators are in favour of competitions – whether they are conducted as part of ordinary classroom procedure or on a national or international basis – and a divergence of views about the merits of the various types of contests was apparent in the group meetings. Thus, for example, one group member questioned whether competitions did aid the mathematical education of the ordinary child, whilst another explained why, although his country encouraged informal, small-scale contests, they did not compete in the International Olympiad – which they saw as providing special training and opportunities for a few exceptionally talented students and offering little or nothing to the less well-endowed. Clearly, like examinations, contests bring both benefits and possibly bad side-effects, since an atmosphere of intense competition can be harmful for winners and losers alike. It is necessary, then, when speaking of mathematical competitions to spell out what, in the given context, the word 'competition' is to mean.

Many mathematical educators will associate the word with the national contests, first held in Hungary in 1894, and since then established in various countries. The group heard how in Hungary the number of competitions has grown until they now cater for 12–13 and 13–14-year-olds, for older, secondary-school pupils, and for students of the Teacher's Training High Schools.[1] The success of these national contests has led to similar contests being established in many other countries, and to the establishment of an International Olympiad at which students from several countries compete (see, for example, ICMI Report on Mathematical Contests in Secondary Education, *Educational Studies in Mathematics*, **2**, 80–114, which includes an account of the growth of these contests and also an extensive bibliography relating to them).

These national and international contests were given considerable attention and raised such interesting questions as 'Is there supporting evidence that such competitions have some value in the preliminary identification of outstanding students?' and 'What effect has school size on mathematical achievement?' There is clearly concern about whether or not the contests can discover outstanding pupils – or

[1] Examples of the problems set can be found in *Hungarian Problem Books* I and II, Random House, New York, 1962.

do they merely confirm who are the outstanding teachers and which are the outstanding schools? Certainly, pupils from English-speaking private schools have performed much better in the South African Mathematical Olympiad than have those from the Afrikaaner schools, and in Britain it is noticeable that the independent schools stand out – possibly due to their experience at preparing students for Oxford and Cambridge examinations. The group was interested to learn that research into some of these questions is being undertaken in the USA.[1]

Clearly, a key factor in all this is the type of problem set in the contest, and the difficulties involved in framing suitable questions was a major item for discussion. The need to provide easy problems so as to ensure that even the weaker student goes home with some feeling of success clashes with the desire to indulge in 'talent-spotting'. There is also a constant need to find problems which demand original thought without needing a large mathematical experience. (The possibility of setting 'take-home' problems was mentioned by Professor Hódi who said that their use in Hungary had so far given rise to no particular difficulties.) At an international level, questions of syllabus, of limited preparation time, and of varied teaching approaches arose – all these affect the fairness of the contests.

One question which was raised on several occasions and which is frequently posed when mathematical contests are discussed is 'How does one involve more girls?' and clearly this is a matter of some urgency. Perhaps the answer at an international level lies in the suggestion that all national teams should be composed of an equal number of boys and girls.

With the increase of national and international contests, it is apparent that the experiences gained in overcoming the many obstacles to success should be shared and that all such information should be communicated in as efficient a manner as possible. The group recommended that ICMI's assistance should be sought on this score.

As was mentioned above, though, there are those who would argue that local contests involving 'average' pupils from 'average' schools would yield greater benefits to the mathematical community than the more prestigious International Olympiads. This was the view of the Italian mathematicians who decided that, rather than participate in

[1] Professor N. D. Turner, State University of New York, Albany, N.Y.

the international contests which they saw as a means of stimulating a few students already identified as the best, they would concentrate their attentions on informal competitions with modest prizes (such as a copy of Pólya's *How to Solve It*). In this way they hoped to improve the general quality of mathematical thinking and to encourage students to see mathematics as an interesting and amusing way of thinking 'outside the technicalities that usually make it tedious in the schools'. Comparable with this approach was the use of inter-school contests organised between a few neighbouring schools and 'Mathematical Fairs' at which schools took turn at acting as host and in which competitions formed part of the general activities. By all reports, those fairs which end in 'Banquets' are especially popular! At this level the difficulties of problem-setting and of possible pupil discouragement are less marked, since the personal knowledge that local teachers have of their pupils can ensure that problems are asked at the right level, and no feelings of failure ensue. Such activities have also proved to have great value for teachers.

Extra-curricular activities and student journals

The 'Mathematical Fairs' to which we referred above were but one kind of extra-curricular activity considered by congress working groups. Other activities discussed included clubs and journals. There was general agreement on the importance of all these activities which, although they usually occupy a relatively small amount of time, can be a decisive factor in mathematical education. For, in regular classwork the teacher is often cramped by the need to 'cover the syllabus' and cannot follow up the stimulating side issues that can be studied in a club. Again, the student welcomes some mathematical activities that are not compulsory and in which he can pursue his individual interests. As a result, in later life he may remember little of his classroom work but could be greatly influenced by, say, a vivid recollection of something experienced in a club. A further, and less obvious, point in favour of such activities rests on the belief that teacher-training as it now exists is based on a half-truth – that one can significantly influence adult students. It was argued that a student entering college usually has an established philosophy of education and – particularly in times of stress – will revert to teaching as taught (cf. p. 65). To achieve any rapid improvement in teaching practices one has to intervene in the process at a much earlier stage – and it is possible to do so through extra-curricular activities.

It was reported, for example, how in Hungary mathematical clubs are now organised from grade 3 (8-year-olds). The elementary teachers themselves meet and compose problem sheets which are then mailed out to the schools. These may be problems of enumeration, such as 'In how many ways can a total length of 6 be made with Cuisenaire rods?' or of recognising the regularity in some sequence of numbers.

The objective of clubs and journals is to spread the influence of the most enlightened and stimulating teachers as widely as possible. Thus a club drawn from several schools has greater potential than a club within one school. Sometimes a university teacher who has the knack of speaking to younger students, can make a contribution to a club involving secondary schools, or, in a similar way, a secondary school teacher can help at a primary school level. A teacher-training college might provide a mobile club that visits different schools in its locality. This would benefit both the schools and the teachers in training.

Central organisations can help, as in the USA where a federation of clubs, '$\mu\alpha\theta$', sends out a periodical bulletin and such things as leaflets recommending suitable books for club use and individual study.

In some countries, such as Australia, Canada and the USA, centres of population may be great distances apart. In these circumstances, journals, duplicated documents and correspondence provide an alternative to personal contact.

It was suggested that journals help students to form the habit of independent reading, but this was questioned on the grounds that only those already possessed of the habit look at such publications. This led to consideration of how the skill of reading mathematics was to be acquired. It was felt that more attention should be paid to this in the classroom. It was also pointed out that, even if only a minority read a journal, they might communicate some of their interest to their fellows or perhaps later become teachers themselves.

Dr Avital[1] reported on an investigation of his own, which showed that children of nine or ten were more willing to read mathematical material, and to think carefully about it, than older children. It was therefore important to provide material for this age range.

Journal editors usually find that puzzles and problems are an attractive feature. Puzzles (simple thought provokers) promote a use-

[1] Ontario Institute for Studies in Education.

ful attitude of mind – the readiness to attack difficulties and to try different methods of attack. Problems (which involve some element of generality) lead to organized knowledge and open wider horizons. Since stimulating puzzles and problems are not easily devised, it is essential that there is adequate communication between student journals in all parts of the world so that good material can be shared. The group resolved to seek ICMI's help in establishing such channels of communication.

In addition to fostering the development of future research workers and teachers of mathematics, one must also help the great mass of children and adults who say 'I could never do mathematics'. Such people are accustomed to think about things rather than symbols. Several instances were given of ways in which the attention of this wider public had been attracted – and all involved actual objects or situations, such as a room containing puzzle apparatus, or primitive computers, Turing machines and circuit boards. This, clearly, is another type of extra-curricular activity which could repay great dividends for a comparatively small outlay.

The professional training of mathematics teachers

The professional training of teachers is so closely linked with what is happening in schools that it must be immediately influenced by any significant change in school procedures and in its turn must have an impact on the attitudes and objectives of teachers. When changes are as rapid and far-reaching as those that have occurred during the last fifteen years in mathematics education the effect on teacher education must be as profound. Not only is the content of school mathematics courses being enlarged and fundamentally modified, educational purposes and methods are also passing through a period of basic re-assessment. The training of teachers of mathematics at all levels is subject therefore to two strong pressures. It must alter the mathematical knowledge with which it equips intending teachers and it must show them the new insights into how children learn mathematics and how such learning can be induced.

At primary level, mathematics is but one of the branches of learning that teachers must be capable of fostering, whether they like the subject or not. The training must be different from that offered to secondary teachers who can choose the subject, or small group of subjects, which they enjoy and are prepared to teach. But in a period when change is swift and extensive, teachers already in service cannot rely on their own experience either of learning or of teaching mathematics. Their initial training must be supplemented to give them both new knowledge and new kinds of expertise. Hence three different working groups were formed to discuss the three distinct types of course: initial courses for primary or secondary teachers, and in-service courses.

Papers from five different countries were presented to the group which studied *The Initial Training of Primary (elementary) School Teachers* and very different 'models' were evident. Nevertheless there were common elements and the group decided to focus on these common components. Three main strands could be identified as essential: mathematical knowledge; insight into children's learning and its goals; classroom procedures and materials. There was general agreement that teachers should know, in addition to the accepted number, algebra and geometry, something about probability and statistics, functions, mathematical systems and the role of deduction in mathematics. Nothing was agreed on how and to what depth these would be treated in courses for teachers, but it was emphasised that the prospective teacher should be helped to see mathematics as concerned with formulating and solving problems. This involves the characteristic mathematical activities of classifying, generalising, symbolising and proving. The student himself should be placed in situations in which by exploring and reflecting he can identify these processes and so discover the kind of question which would guide the children to similar understanding.

There was widespread support for the use of manipulative materials, apparatus and other concrete aids, to encourage, through early experience of working with physical models, the ability to abstract mathematical relations and patterns. Such materials provide open-ended situations which give enjoyment as well as independence of approach. But prospective teachers need to work with the materials and become familiar with their uses. As Piaget says (p. 85) 'it is often particularly difficult for the teacher of mathematics, who, because of his profession, has a very abstract type of thought, to place himself in the concrete perspective which is necessarily that of his young pupils'. It is to help a teacher to bridge this gap that he needs to experience for himself the dawning of new understanding through handling suitable concrete materials.

Contact with children throughout the course of training was advocated but many different ways of organising this were possible; class teaching could be over-emphasised. A graduation could be devised which would proceed from observations of children, to work with an individual, to taking a mathematical topic with a small group whose individual responses could be observed, and finally to responsibility for a class which could be organised in a variety of ways. It was said that such experience of children's thinking and misconceptions often stimulates students to strengthen their own understanding of mathematics.

The integration of all three aspects of teacher education was thought to give a better understanding of the development of mathematical education but more experiments are required to substantiate this theory.

Integrated investigations of topics which may involve mathematics are popular in primary schools. The question of preparing intending teachers for such work by taking part in integrated schemes at student level caused much controversy. It seemed to be acceptable if it could run alongside specific subject courses. A further topic for future discussion is the extension of mathematical topics into the uses made of mathematics in technology, industry and social services.

Finally the group agreed that just as the programme of primary schooling has become individualised so the training course should provide opportunities for individual development and the achievement of competence and confidence in teaching mathematics. But initial training can never be adequate for a lifetime of service and a greatly increased provision of in-service courses is urgently required.

The secondary school teacher, in contrast to the teacher in primary schools, should be a mathematician capable of creating and organising mathematical ideas as well as disseminating them. His mathematics courses during training should reflect the changes in the subject as a contemporary body of knowledge as well as developing deductive processes and the creative aspects of mathematical discovery. His course should also include didactic analysis of a variety of teaching and learning approaches and the methodological consideration of classroom procedures. We cannot expect an initial course to give a complete training, but the intention should be to develop an attitude in the teacher which would be likely to produce continued growth in his professional insights and objectives. These views were put forward by Professor H. G. Steiner (W. Germany), Chairman of the group studying the *Initial Training of Secondary School Teachers*. The representative nature of this group is shown by the way in which it produced accounts of training schemes from ten different countries including such widely separated places as Austria, Canada, the Congo and New Zealand.

The question whether the mathematics courses for intending teachers should take a special form became the most important issue discussed. One suggestion was the provision of elective courses additional to the basic undergraduate courses in mathematics. Some suitable topics proposed included the history of mathematics (which was strongly supported) and mathematical literature, elementary mathematics from an advanced standpoint, the analysis of new mathematics curriculum proposals and some research enterprises.

Professor Krygowska (Poland) urged the recognition of didactics as a part of mathematics with a status similar to that of analysis or topology. She identified four aspects of didactics: a synthesis of the appropriate mathematical, educational, cultural and environmental ideas; an introduction to research; the nature and situation of the child; practical experience. For 'didactics' the United Kingdom, South Africa and others would use the term 'mathematical education'. The questions raised showed the difficulty of separating methodology from didactics, and the problem of placing a didactics course in a mathematics department rather than in a department of education. In the ensuing discussion on methodology and 'field work' in schools, it was evident that many of the topics included in 'methodology' were identical with those proposed for 'didactics'. The formulation of a recognised subject called 'didactics' (or 'mathematical education') was felt to be an important task offering opportunities of interesting and valuable work.

Two further points were raised but not adequately considered. Intending teachers should be asked to compare the axiomatic deductive approach with the intuitional approach and discuss their relative roles. Models and problem-solving should find a place in the course. It was pointed out that whereas the mathematician is trained to move from model to structure the teacher must learn to move from structure to suitable models.

The environment has been mentioned several times and particularly its role in mathematical education but its place in training courses was not developed. The effects of local conditions on curricula and teaching methods could well be put on a future agenda.

In the final session resources which should be available were listed. The library should have a good reference section including a retrieval system. Periodicals pertaining to mathematical education and applications should include material from associations throughout the world. A well-equipped laboratory should have do-it-yourself materials and tools, and a small computer or computer terminal; and there should be a media centre with equipment for films, tapes and cassettes. In common with other subjects mathematics needs the use of a demonstration classroom where students can experiment, be video-taped and have their attempts analysed by their peers and supervisor. Of course the constant help of local schools is invaluable.

Both the groups that considered the initial training of teachers urged the provision of *in-service courses* because, they held, a teacher could not be completely prepared for his various and complex tasks merely by his pre-service training. It needs supplementing when experience with pupils learning mathematics has made the possibilities and difficulties clearer. This was widely confirmed, but the chief reason for the remarkably large number of mathematics courses organised all over the world for serving teachers is the rapid change in content and method. Entirely new mathematical ideas have been encountered and have had to be mastered by teachers and then interpreted by them for their pupils.

These courses have introduced teachers to new curricula and given them new understanding of how children learn mathematics. The working group which chose to study the purposes of such courses, ways of organising them, and the possible kinds of presentation of new ideas which would be most helpful, was intent on finding solutions to the problems that have arisen. Members from several countries gave ten-minute talks on their experiences of such courses and started discussions, for instance, on whether mathematics for teachers should be different from mathematics for children and how teachers can be helped to see what is involved in 'discovery' or 'individualisation'.

The group then saw two samples of lessons to local children which could have been shown to teachers at a course. One lesson, for nine-year-olds, illustrated the experimental use of geoboards; the other, for twelve-year-olds, showed a class lesson on rational numbers, using ordered pairs. Immediately deeper questions were asked. What is the effect on a teacher of watching lessons given in such conditions? Because the children were in an investigation situation, independent individual responses could be seen with evidence of new thoughts emerging. Even in artificial conditions the children were absorbed in their explorations. The teacher's part is seen in the way in which the learning situation has been devised and developed. There is an element of drama here in which the teacher-observer identifies with one of the performers (teacher or learner).

It was agreed that such teaching episodes have value, as have films of children engaged with apparatus. But longer courses are necessary if teachers are to become ready to adopt new attitudes. They need time to try out with their own classes some of the new mathematical ideas and new approaches, and to share their experiences with other teachers on the course. In this way they can become convinced of the effectiveness of the new procedures in their own teaching.

Teachers probably need to know more mathematics than they will be required to teach, but it was thought they should experience learning through handling apparatus and experimenting with materials for themselves at their own mathematical level. They should also work with concrete material in the same ways and for the same purposes as their classes will do. It happened that at this time the British National Presentation included a group of primary teachers working under the guidance of Miss Edith Biggs on a typical in-service course. These teachers were engaged actively in using materials which led them to see new mathematical ideas and also the ways in which children could be guided to make the same discoveries. It is through such experiences that teachers come to understand more fully the mathematics they are teaching and its place in the development of children's thinking.

From the vigorous contributions of all members of this group it seems that this aspect of the education of teachers will not be neglected.

Educational technology

Mathematical educators look back on the 1960s as the bringer of 'modern maths' (or, translated into American, 'new math'). In a wider educational context, that decade also brought us 'educational technology' – a term so all-embracing as to be virtually meaningless. On the one hand, it describes an approach to education which makes use of the newer technological *disciplines* – what is sometimes described as a 'systems approach' – on the other, it has come to mean the use within education of the *products* of technology. It was natural that both these aspects should be represented at the Exeter Congress and they can be distinguished in the accounts of the working groups which follow.

Individualised learning methods

There was considerable interest in individualised learning methods, and evidence was presented of grass-roots developments in many countries, especially the USA, Sweden, and the UK. Occasionally a dedicated and inspired teacher would start by working alone, perhaps gradually extending his or her sphere of influence by moving on to become the leader of a creative group working to develop the materials further. In more widely-conceived projects the focus of leadership may not be centred within a participant school. One project had achieved exceptionally close cooperative ties with a commercial producer of programmes.

Most speakers stressed the vital need to involve teachers who use a learning system in some way in the process of prescribing, producing and assessing the materials used. The creative group must feel to a large extent self-determining. This spirit of involvement and commitment can be achieved as much in shaping a learning system from already available materials as in the pioneering of original work. This latter process can prove tedious, time consuming and inefficient in inexpert hands. It is doubtful if teachers have the ability to predict what a student might achieve, or to know in advance the educationally most advantageous means. In an individualised learning system the teacher becomes a divining rod, sensitised to the system, able to make spontaneous compensation and to feed back ideas for improving the system. Thus the system is continually developing empirically.

Advancement in pedagogical sophistication brings a more professional concern for the psychology of individual differences, for ethical, social and motivational considerations and for a more certain gearing of the student's experiences to his needs in the modern world. It is too much to expect a teacher to cope with such complexity alone.

The essence of one's thinking in individualised learning is accommodation to the concept of change. The child is developing and changing within a world which is itself in a state of accelerating change. The educational process must keep apace with all such changes. The design of a learning system subsumes all relevant technologies, such as cybernetics, sociology, management sciences, curriculum development and educational psychology. It is an attainable vehicle capable of adapting to change. It calls for teams of experts continuously re-appraising, re-defining and re-developing the parts of the system and the ways in which they interact.

Taking individualised learning as the central theme, a symposium might be organised to cover modules such as: objectives, especially in the higher order of thinking abilities; variety in modes and media; depth versus breadth; the teacher's role; pupil freedom of choice and self-determination versus controlled and directed learning; analysis and remediation; a continuous mathematical education across the usual horizontal educational structure; flexibility of teacher, pupil and system; responsibility for the building of materials; the affective domain; experimentation or a committed developmental approach, and aspects of evaluation.

The mathematics workshop – the use of apparatus, games and structural materials

The workshop (laboratory) approach is one of many strategies which can be used in the classroom. In order to build images, symbolise, organise, generalise, drill and practise, or apply knowledge to other situations, several modes may be used. For some of these activities the laboratory approach is more effective than for others. In the laboratory the concrete objects (manipulatives) serve as models for the thought images that are moved around in the mind. They serve both as a means of recording what went on in the mind and also to serve as sources of ideas to spark off others. Ideally, if our object is to teach mathematics, the manipulative materials should satisfy the following criteria:

(1) A mathematical fact, concept, or generalisation is the goal.

(2) The material must be appropriate to the discovery of the fact, concept, or generalisation.

(3) The material must be capable of arousing the student's interest.

(4) The directions for the use of the materials must be easy to follow, and must be capable of leading the student to the desired conclusions.

In certain instances it may also be desirable for the directions to be open-ended, enabling different results, perhaps at various levels of difficulty, to be obtained. Tapes, slides and pictures can all be used, although usually the student gains most from apparatus if he can handle it himself.

In the use of manipulatives for learning mathematics, the student is provided with models for concepts. Often he examines the real world for mathematics intrinsic to it, and he is introduced to the relationships between subject areas; since the student has discovered the mathematics himself, his retention is improved.

The laboratory method provides many other benefits in addition to an understanding of the mathematics involved, and it is perhaps because of these benefits that the proponents of the method are most enthusiastic. Students in the laboratory develop a method of enquiry; they are helped to learn to learn. Gathering, organising, recording, and representing data become essential skills. This method also helps develop imagination and creativity, it provides for discovery, it motivates the child and helps him develop interest in further enquiry, it provides for individualisation, it facilitates the use of language, and it often provides for aesthetic appreciation.

Just as the method has its advantages, there are also disadvantages. Time is most often given as an excuse for not using the laboratory method. However, proponents argue that the initial capital time investment of the teacher more than pays off, as classes run more smoothly due to increased interest and alleviation of discipline problems. Research shows that the laboratory method can be as efficient as a traditional teacher-dominated situation and that students learn more than in the latter situation.

Other disadvantages claimed against the method include the difficulties in getting started, in managing the situation, and in evaluating the work; the imprecision which can result, the cost, the possibility that students confuse mathematics with the materials they are using; the lack of transfer from one application to another. One of the greatest problems is one of teacher education. It is necessary to help teachers acquire the organisational skill needed. Organisational patterns vary from those of a local nature, such as arranging the mathematics corner of a classroom, to the problems of organising a large-scale resource centre with branching learning sequences. During training the teacher should be confronted with a variety of experiences, explore many teaching materials, and develop his own resources for working in the classroom. Involvement with children and materials stirs interest and imagination and leads to greater individual development.

The use of manipulative materials and the laboratory method, although well-known in most countries, varies from no-use-at-all to use for a major portion of classroom activity. In some countries, materials, money or space are not available; elsewhere they are available but teachers lack commitment to them. This mode of teaching appears more widely accepted at the primary level than at the secondary level, although this may be because of the lack of knowledge of materials appropriate to the higher level.

Recommendations

Because mathematics is a useful tool in the real world, students need to be provided with real world experiences using mathematics and with such experiences as will help them to develop their own method of enquiry, and to learn how to learn. Because language facility is essential, the experiences provided in school should aim at developing this facility. All of these goals can be met through laboratory experience.

Each lesson should have an underlying framework of objectives: both subject oriented and student oriented. The hardware and the equipment are not the essence; more important than the physical facilities are the attitudes of the children, the atmosphere of the classroom, and the objectives of the teacher.

The style of training of teachers must reflect what we actually wish teachers to do in their classrooms. In this training as in actual teaching, materials must be present and the student-teacher involved with them. To talk about them or to look at pictures is not sufficient.

Just as recipe books are essential to a good cook, references are necessary for doing a good job in the laboratory. Such references need to be prepared. Further discussions on workshops and mathematics laboratories could well concentrate on specific problems, methods and levels.

The use of television and film in the teaching of mathematics

Although the members of the group were those who are deeply involved in the use of TV and film material in education, fundamental questions were asked about the reasons for using it. We use it because it is there, was one strongly held view. This appeared to be supported by the fact that, in the case of TV which is a broadcast medium, an attempt to appeal to a mass audience runs counter to the current trend towards greater individualisation in learning. However, it was pointed out that, although this conflict with current educational thought certainly exists, there is hope that in the near future most educational establishments will have their own equipment to record broadcast material which may then be used how and when the teacher desires.

There is intrinsic value in TV and film material which justify its use. A strong element in this argument is the fact that it is possible to obtain the services of highly skilled people, mathematicians and others, to put ideas across in highly effective ways – better than many teachers will be able to do.

The production of material of the desired quality is a major problem. Certain aspects of mathematics are obviously very visual and producers of TV and film material gravitate instinctively to this. In this respect contributors from various countries showed very convincingly what can be done. However the question was asked whether we should not rather start by looking at the difficult concepts in mathematics, those concepts which students have difficulty in grasping, and try to tackle these. Clearly this is what should be done, but some of the difficulties of this view were demonstrated during a workshop on presenting the concept of 'function' in a visual way.

We should start with a clear understanding of the essential points we want to communicate. However obvious this may be, there is a danger that the mathematicians might push too quickly towards these essential points. Problems and situations should be presented which prepare the way for the ideas to develop. It may be that these problems will contain many extraneous aspects which mathematicians might find irritating, but these are essential for the growth of ideas in the viewer. Real situations are necessary at school, and desirable at a higher level, although university students can go much more quickly to the heart of a concept.

How should these problems be presented? At one end of the spectrum some were presented as inanimate visuals with clinical precision. There was great merit and beauty in some of the presentations of this type which were seen. At the other extreme there were recordings of ad lib situations from which mathematics was extracted. These may have lacked the finesse or precision of the former type of material but they possessed a convincing feeling of reality. Somewhere between these extremes there was material showing the use of puppets, with a presenter, intended for 9–10-year-old pupils. This material raised the question of the value of humour in TV/film material. Humour is certainly a valuable element provided it is expertly handled; but there have been unfortunate mis-uses of humour where it was not appropriate for the intended audience.

In the use of TV material in the classroom there are again two extremes: the situation where all the mathematics being done arises from, or is connected with, the TV material; and the situation where there is no follow-up work at all. Both extremes are undesirable.

The place of the computer in mathematical education

Speakers emphasised the use of computers to motivate students in their study of mathematics and described ways in which such studies were enriched by the use of the computer as a tool. There was general agreement that flow-charts could be omitted unless they aided the logical development of the algorithm, although there is some value in younger pupils starting with non-mathematical flow-charts, the flow-chart being a form of language which most students readily understand.

Model making, in the sense of formulating equations which describe some real situation, is an essential part of mathematics. It is, however, extremely time-consuming, and non-trivial applications may be too difficult for the less-able student; although even for these, models which the teacher has prepared are valuable, especially if the student has the opportunity to amend the model himself. Applied mathematics, which is entirely a model building activity, can be completely changed at school level by the use of computer methods.

Many experiments involving the use of computers were described. These included one concerning teaching statistics to first-year college students (see Wegman and Gere[1]). To avoid students' difficulties with new ideas in computing, packaged programs were used and a visual display was presented of distributions of observed variables, which could be compared with standard distributions.

A particularly interesting experiment was described by Seymour Papert,[2,3] of the Massachusetts Institute of Technology, who had worked with 9–10-year-old children who had previously had little success in mathematics. They were given two hours of instruction per week in a new field, namely, 'turtle geometry'. The aims were for the children to carry out complex projects, to use mathematics where it is needed, to discover it to be logically 'clean', and to learn how to set up a model.

[1] Wegman, E. J. and Gere, B. H., Some Thoughts on Computers and Introductory Statistics, *Int. J. Math. Ed. Sci. Technol.* 3, 1972, 211–21.

[2] Papert, S., Teaching Children Thinking, *Mathematics Teaching*, **58**, 1972, 2–7.

[3] Papert, S., Teaching Children to be Mathematicians versus Teaching about Mathematics, *Int. J. Math. Educ. Sci. Technol.* 3, 1972, 249–62.

Schemes of work intended to give all students some understanding of computers are being developed in many countries, sometimes at a national level. Views vary on the best methods of doing this, and hardware falls into two distinct groups – desk machines which require the use of a machine language and mini-computers or terminals on which algorithmic languages can be compiled. Costs are falling rapidly, and terminals may become cheaper than desk machines. There are educational possibilities in both, and it is necessary to distinguish two groups of objectives, those which are mathematical and those related to the introduction of computer science. The exchange of ideas and experiences on the use of computers in mathematical education could be greatly helped by the existence of an international journal. OECD have established an information centre and it is possible that their newsletter may fulfil this purpose.

Programmable calculators in schools

In this group, a study was made of the projects carried out in various countries, a comparison was effected of some of the available machines, and aims and methods in using programmable calculators in secondary schools were discussed.

Since 1969 extensive work has been done in France.[1] Five or six types of machine have been employed, being used with pupils of average ability in secondary schools (eleven to seventeen years). The main task is to discover which mathematical concepts can be introduced efficiently by the use of programmable calculators. Initially, the aim was to motivate better working in mathematics, and this developed further, leading to ideas of flow-charts, programming, iteration and so on.

Projects have been carried out in several individual secondary schools and colleges of education in the United Kingdom. The broad aims are similar to those in the French project, and the machines are seen both as an aid for the teacher when introducing mathematical concepts and also as a calculating aid for the pupils. Other projects have been started in Holland, Lesotho and Japan. In the USA[2] work has been done with students training to teach in elementary schools. It was found that programmable calculators were more appropriate

[1] M. A. Deledicq, INRDP, Department of Mathematics, 29 rue d'Ulm, Paris 5^e^, France.

[2] Professor M. Sudduth, University of Kentucky, USA.

than computers in the elementary grades, and the main result was that, as the fear of machines was lost, so a new enthusiasm for mathematics developed.

It was found difficult to separate discussion of general aims from consideration of the actual machines, but the main objectives appeared to be:

(*a*) to learn how to program a problem (as distinct from merely gaining an understanding of how the machine operates);

(*b*) to introduce mathematical concepts by means of numerical examples;

(*c*) to simplify the task of calculation;

(*d*) to distinguish two types of human activity: mechanical thinking, which is the way in which machines operate and, secondly, imagination and creativity, which no machine can simulate.

Nine machines from five different manufacturers were available to the group. It is neither possible nor desirable to suggest a 'best buy', but there are several important aspects to be considered by purchasers.

(1) *Input facilities.* Apart from keyboard input, the machines can also be programmed by one or more of punched cards, mark-sense cards, punched tape and magnetic cards. It was agreed that off-line input preparation makes the use of the machines with a class of pupils much easier.

(2) *Program operation.* Machines with a display on which changes of address can be seen, and where the punched cards actually operate the program, enabling loops to be seen, are of value with younger pupils or those at the beginning of a programming course.

(3) *Output.* A printed record is indispensable except perhaps at the most elementary levels.

(4) *Peripherals.* Some machines have further facilities, such as graph plotters, built-in functions and extra memory space. Trends were noticed whereby these machines are becoming more like computers, when indirect address and subprogram facilities are available.

During the discussion about the ways in which the machines are introduced, it was mentioned that flow-charts and a 'match-box' computer could play a useful part in giving the first ideas; use of the machine then follows naturally. Pupils seemed eager to use the machines outside class time and, within a class, appear to work better in groups. A distinct advantage over other types of computer facility is that the machines can easily be transported from room to room.

Some objections were raised that, because a low-level language is used, the machines are difficult to program. Most contributors, however, thought that this was an advantage since pupils were forced to analyse a problem precisely because they had not yet encountered mathematically sophisticated operations; in this way, a feeling for rigour developed. Most participants had noticed considerable enthusiasm among the pupils: it is good psychology for children to be able to give orders instead of merely obeying them; furthermore, it is necessary to think in order to command.

It was generally agreed that programmable calculators are invaluable in aiding the understanding of certain mathematical concepts, such as those of sequences and iterative techniques, and representation of variables, and in giving pupils first ideas about programming. But when the problems become more complicated, the more powerful high-level languages of computers become necessary. However, the elements of many techniques can be taught in spite of the low-level language. Additionally, some concepts can now be taught earlier in the curriculum than was previously the case, and by an experimental approach before the theory is met.

As manufacturing costs reduce owing to improved technology, the choice of a particular programmable calculator, and indeed the choice between them and other computing facilities, will become more difficult.

Curriculum design and evaluation

Reports were received from several projects concerned with curriculum development at both school and college level. These were largely descriptive of the problems that each individual country or project had found in developing its mathematics curriculum, and the steps taken to solve these problems. While many of these problems are dependent on the structure of the society and the educational system of a particular country, a number of the problems implicit in the papers given are common to all nations, and would repay study by a future congress. Some of these points are:

(*a*) *The choice of mathematical subject matter for inclusion in a curriculum*

The approaches of the various projects were frequently based on widely differing goals and it was clear that there was no agreement as far as aims and the comparative weight to be accorded to them were concerned. For example, one project took as a goal the teaching of what mathematics is, as held by mathematicians of the present day, another chose to develop the process of research and to train the students in 'creative activity'. Others argued that mathematical education was dominated by pure mathematics and that new curricula should favour the needs of users of mathematics.

Again, projects differed in the variety of options which they offered to users – one provided a set of optional units which enabled the teacher to build up a suitable curriculum for individual students, others offered only table-d'hôte menus. There is clearly then a need for study of the range of criteria that a curriculum project should take into account, when making choices of subject matter and teaching approach. The state of mathematics, the needs of users, the social context of education, the state of the child's conceptual development and of his interest and creative activity, all these play different parts in the design of different projects. They all need more careful identification and study.

(*b*) *Criteria for evaluating a project*

The problem of how to evaluate the work of a project does not appear to admit any straightforward solution. Some idea of the difficulties encountered was given by Dr J. Hunter[1] who described how students following a modern curriculum had performed less well in first-year university examinations than those who followed a traditional syllabus, but, to counterbalance this, the new syllabus had resulted in a greater proportion of pupils, particularly girls, choosing to study mathematics longer and had increased the general level of interest and enjoyment.

(*c*) *Suitable curricula for a wide range of students*

The increase in educational opportunities at a higher level has already led in the USA to vast numbers of students entering colleges who wish to study the applied sciences but have only a slight understanding of mathematics. There is a need to develop suitable curricula for such students who, of course, will also pose a problem elsewhere as higher education becomes more accessible. The problem of helping those students in higher education for whom the school curriculum

[1] Hunter, J., *Some aspects of syllabus development, evaluation and revision, illustrated by the work of the Scottish Mathematics Group* (copies from W. and R. Chambers Ltd, Edinburgh, EH2 1DG).

has been unsuccessful, is one which has received insufficient consideration.

(*d*) *The advent of the computer*

Several contributors spoke of the introduction of computing in mathematics projects, and raised questions about changed emphasis, subject matter and methods of presentation caused by the increasing availability of computing facilities in schools and colleges.

Research in the teaching of mathematics

When reading the reports of the different working groups one is struck by the frequency with which such phrases as 'much work still to be done on...' and 'a further investigation of this problem seems urgently to be required' occur. There is a general demand for more 'research'. But what do we mean by this emotive word? This was one of the first questions which the group meeting under the above title sought to answer. In this connection, various types of research were defined and the demands of evaluation in these different types of research were discussed. The main role of research in mathematical education was generally accepted to be the improvement of mathematics teaching, and here the value judgements implicit in terms like 'improvement', 'mathematics' and 'teaching' were emphasised.

The role of theory was discussed in the context of (*a*) providing a condensation of what is known, from research, about mathematics teaching and learning, (*b*) a framework in which research studies can be related, and (*c*) a guide to generating hypotheses and thereby showing directions for research. In this connection, it is hoped that theory can play a role in helping teachers to a better understanding of the learning–teaching process in mathematics.

The involvement of teachers in research was a constantly recurring theme and specific reference was made to the desirability of involving teachers in research work during their initial training and in-service education. The idea of 'the teacher as a researcher' was also discussed, as was the communication-gap which often exists between researchers and teachers. It was argued that participation in, or increased knowledge of, research would serve as a strong motivation for teachers in enlarging their knowledge of relationships between goals and means in the teaching of mathematics, that is of the didactics of mathematics. At the same time, there was discussion of difficulties connected with teacher/classroom research. For example, does the teacher have the background training or the time for research? Also there may be design and methodological problems implicit in a 'one-classroom' research setting.

There was a general feeling that more research must take place within the natural setting of the classroom in order to increase our understanding of the teaching process. The need to specify teaching goals as clearly and precisely as possible was emphasised; for without this, proper evaluation cannot be made.

There was a strong sentiment that mathematics education is a developing area (some would say 'science') in and of itself and should be treated that way. Research in mathematics education should be carried out by people competent in the relevant fields of mathematics in collaboration with specialists in other areas such as education or psychology.

Although recognising that different countries may well have different research priorities, reference was made by participants to the need for research on

(*a*) the relationships between topics, and on the sequences of topics within a curriculum,

(*b*) children who have special learning disabilities in mathematics,

(*c*) successful and unsuccessful teacher/pupil interactions,

(*d*) problems of teaching and learning which are not specific to mathematics,

(*e*) pupils' ability to read mathematical texts,

(*f*) the influence of demands for rigour and precision on the attainment by the pupils of creative and aesthetic goals in mathematics.

Mathematics in developing countries

This was one of the largest and certainly the most international of the congress working groups and it was very heartening to note that the Exeter Congress attracted so many more educators from developing countries than did its predecessor. In recognition of the importance of the work of this group and in an attempt to avoid a bland, anodyne communiqué to which every group member could subscribe, the account of this group's activities differs from that of any other, being somewhat longer and in the form of a personal report from the Chairman and Secretary. As such, it inevitably emphasises individual viewpoints. Nevertheless, the authors assure us that the opinions expressed would have received the general support of the group;

indeed, nearly all the material is drawn from the group's working papers, and the discussions to which they gave rise. Despite the diversity in detail revealed by the papers and discussions, a surprising unity in fundamental aims and problems was apparent.

The present movement for the reform of both content and methodology in the teaching of mathematics at all levels affects the developing countries just as much as those of Europe and North America. Indeed, in many ways it raises more acute problems for those countries whose resources are more limited. The group found itself discussing the practical problems of the supply of trained or retrained teachers, and of appropriate teaching materials, but it was even more concerned with fundamental problems arising from the background against which rapid reform is taking place.

1 The social and cultural background

In many developing countries, including most of those in Africa, the following factors arising from the social and cultural background are relevant to the reform of mathematics teaching:

(*a*) instruction has been *oral* rather than visual; not many generations have elapsed since instructors were illiterate;

(*b*) reliance has been placed on *memory* of traditional patterns of interpretation of history, customs and techniques; it has been important for survival to maintain a well-tried and long-established system rather than to make possibly disastrous new experiments;

(*c*) the method of instruction has been *didactic*; where the oldest is the most experienced and respected, the duty of the young is to listen;

(*d*) *spatial* experiences have been quite different from those of the Western world and, in particular, representation of spatial relationships may be almost unknown;

(*e*) *dynamical* experiences will have been few or absent, with consequent difficulty in the alignment of scales and visualisation of movement, and a general lack of mechanical facility.

These factors inhibit many of the methods of investigation and discussion which are prevalent in modern teaching methods in Western countries.

2 The educational background

(*a*) In most developing countries, with the notable exception of India, the length of experience of most graduate teachers of mathematics is short, and of modern mathematics extremely short.

(*b*) There has been a tendency for historical reasons to regard education as first and foremost a means of acquiring a paper qualification which will lead ultimately to better-paid employment; only secondarily as a means of acquisition of a marketable skill. The idea of education as a way of enriching the personality and of increasing man's understanding and control of the world often appears only in a very poor third place. This brings to the developing teacher a great temptation (which is by no means unknown to those who regard themselves as more developed) to measure success by the number of pupils who pass examinations, and to evaluate examination syllabuses by the ease with which pupils can be trained to pass them.

(*c*) Most countries are experiencing a very great increase in numbers of children in primary and secondary schools; this represents a praiseworthy achievement but also creates a situation demanding very serious action if teaching methods and conditions are not to deteriorate.

These are not trivial problems. Teachers in the developing countries themselves are asking questions about such fundamental issues, and there is need for basic research into the relation between teaching methods and the cultural and educational background.

3 *The special needs of mathematics*

While much of the above is common to all subjects, there are certain features which make mathematics a peculiarly sensitive discipline. Mathematics is a subject which demands a quiet, untroubled mind for its proper absorption, as also for its lucid communication. Social uncertainty, political anxiety, examination apprehensions affect mathematical performance more immediately than most other subjects. (We all know how difficult it is to find a mistake on the blackboard when we are concentrating on holding the attention of the class.)

Secondly, mathematics itself has developed in the last ten years rather too precipitately for many teachers, even in well-developed countries. Now of course, if your previous experience has been entirely taken up with simple arithmetic and the uses of ground-nuts, the mysteries of the combination of two reflections are likely to be no greater than those of angles in the same segment. The enthusiasts will say that, provided the pupil can be given a piece of paper to fold, or two pieces of reasonably polished metal (like table-knives), they may even be *less* formidable. But the bulk of the graduates and diplomates in the developing country may include few or none who have ever been taught this at school level, and this is unfortunately what counts. Still worse, they may have regarded mathematics as a terrifying array of data to be memorised, and are now for the first time being confronted with a series of operations to be carried out, systematised, and understood. No progress in teaching method or content can be made unless a teacher is brave enough to do things which are different from what he himself experienced as a pupil; and in mathematics the difference may well be that between memorisation and understanding.

Serious consideration must therefore be given to the content of mathematics syllabuses. Topics relevant to the secondary level of education in an industrial society may be totally irrelevant to a predominantly agrarian country. In the past decade there has been a tendency to transfer unquestioningly syllabuses from Europe and North America to countries in Asia and Africa. The time is ripe for fundamental rethinking as to their appropriateness. This must of course be done by teachers who are nationals of the countries concerned though discussions may be facilitated from outside, for example by the sponsorship of regional conferences and assistance to relevant research projects.

Does this mean that mathematics itself is culturally dependent? The working party for the most part felt that it is not, but that natural aptitudes, the social and economic setting, and the demands of national development should certainly influence both the selection of appropriate mathematics and the methods by which it is taught. While almost every country in the world is moving towards 'modern' syllabuses, far too little thought seems to be being given to the aims and objectives of mathematical education in relation to local culture and needs. Ideally, reform should arise spontaneously from the dissatisfaction of nationals with things as they are, rather than from expatriates' visions of things as they ought to be.

4 *The transfer of teaching materials*

These are transferred between countries at three main levels:

(1) The level of *acceptance*, where materials are transferred directly in their original form for general classroom use;

(2) the level of *adaptation*, either (*a*) small-scale adaptation, often carried out in the country of origin, consisting of little more than alterations to place-names, currencies, and other essentially super-

ficial matters; or (*b*) large-scale adaptation, carried out in the importing country, often after trials of draft materials;

(3) the level of *appraisal*, the transfer of influence and ideas, the materials themselves being used maybe only for teacher-training and specialist study.

As a country progresses educationally, so does its level of transfer, at a rate closely dependent on its resources of qualified manpower, of competent pupils, and of budgeted funds. Transfer at level 2(*b*) is a comparatively recent phenomenon in the history of mathematical education, which leads to valuable savings in time and money, but there is need to assist developing countries to progress through the various levels as rapidly as possible. In particular, indigenous textbook writers should be encouraged and trained by all possible means.

5 *Primary education*

Every developing country would like a niche in the hall of academic fame – an Einstein, a Crick, a Heisenberg. But this is the apex of a pyramid which rests on a very broad base; probably what it needs far more is a properly numerate and literate labour force and electorate. This means a primary school population which is receiving a well-rounded and thorough education. Educationally, socially, morally, this is worth far more than prestigious names or even applied research, for no research project can contribute effectively to development without soundly educated technicians possessed of skill, adaptability and integrity.

Unlike the situation in developed countries, primary education is terminal for the majority of children. In the past, syllabuses have usually been directed towards preparation for secondary education, but their content urgently needs reconsideration in the light of the needs of those who will never progress beyond primary school. Here the developed countries have little relevant experience to offer.

The crucial question is the provision and training of primary school teachers, who often have no more than secondary education themselves, and sometimes not even this. Too rapid innovations will undermine their confidence and arouse their hostility. Large classes demand that the problem be approached with realism and sympathy. This is not purely a mathematical problem. Social, political, and economic changes are necessary to improve the status and pay of the primary teacher, to encourage diplomates to enter primary teaching, and to allow better use to be made of the available manpower (including that of the pupils themselves) in primary schools.

The question of the language which is the medium of instruction arouses strong feelings, but there is widespread agreement that mathematics should be taught first, in the early primary years, in the child's mother-tongue which will lead to greater understanding of basic mathematical concepts. Many countries, however, have a multiplicity of languages so that there comes a point, perhaps during the primary years, and certainly by the secondary stage, where the medium of instruction cannot be the mother-tongue of all the pupils concerned. The working party urged that fundamental research should be undertaken on the relation between the learning of mathematical structures, and the structures of the language through which they are learned.

Account also needs to be taken of the use of simple teaching materials and apparatus and the training of teachers in their use. Suitable aids costing little or nothing can often be collected by the pupils themselves or improvised from material readily available locally. Local crafts may reveal geometric patterns, and traditional games can be a rich source of mathematical ideas. The natural environment may also be rich in illustrative material, but all this will be useless unless the teacher is persuaded that it is important, not because it helps the teacher to teach the syllabus, but because it helps the pupils to understand what they learn.

6 *Secondary education*

Here again, secondary education is terminal for the majority of those selected to receive it. In addition, despite the selective system, there is usually a wide range of ability in the secondary class. Unlike many developed countries, there is only one educational path to be followed, and this is determined by the needs of the few who will proceed to tertiary education. There is therefore a crying need to provide alternative courses in mathematics for different groups of secondary pupils. Again at secondary level the influence of examinations is at its most baleful, with unmodified transfer of Western examination methods. Alternative methods of assessment, appropriate to the pupils' cultural background, must surely be devised, and syllabus content reviewed in the light of each country's needs and the pupils' future opportunities for employment.

Little serious evaluation of the long-term effects of changing from a traditional to a modern syllabus at this level has yet been undertaken. To be effective, such a research programme needs to be supported by the Ministries of Education and the universities of a number of countries in cooperation, perhaps on a regional basis.

7 University education

Just as schools should serve the needs of the society in which they are set, so universities in developing countries should not merely be pale copies of older institutions elsewhere in the world. In some countries of Africa a university intake corresponding to the British 'O' level at 16+ precedes a four-year course leading to a first degree. The content of the course work in such cases needs to be formulated with reference to the projected manpower needs of the country, and not just by reference to the specialist interests of the Department of Mathematics at the time. Teaching methods, too, must be geared to the educational level of the students rather than modelled on traditional methods in Western universities. Such considerations apply even more strongly to the topics of mathematical research supported by the university. The limited nature of resources available demands that such research projects should be relevant to the needs of society rather than simply serve to advance the career of the researcher.

8 Curriculum development and teacher-training

In many countries the educational system is so constructed that teacher-training, curriculum development and classroom practice are three separate activities. We are coming to realise that change can only be effective when the three are seen as aspects of a single process. It is one thing to prescribe a new series of mathematical textbooks for classroom use, but quite another to ensure that the mathematical education of the pupils is thereby improved. It is naïve to define curriculum as the content of the textbook, or its development as the introduction of a new one. It is both more realistic and more constructive to define curriculum as what actually takes place in the classroom. This immediately gives the teacher a key role in curriculum innovation. Many developing countries are already acting on this principle, by giving teachers a major share of responsibility for developing new teaching materials, and by recognising their crucial role in the evaluation of them in the classroom.

This view of the unity of the process of educational change has important implications for the planning of curriculum development projects. Writing-teams must include teachers and not be dominated by university personnel. Only teachers, and particularly those who are nationals of the country concerned, are aware of the practical realities of the school situation, of the pupils' attitudes, capabilities, and responses to proposed changes. At the same time the fact of being a trained national does not of itself make a teacher a good textbook writer. The arts of teaching, and of developing new materials, are ones that the good teacher goes on learning throughout his career, and more particularly through corporate activity with others who are similarly engaged. Mathematical associations have often been found useful in developing this, and in breaking down the traditional isolation of the teacher in his classroom. Local teachers' centres can act as a venue for informal meetings and in-service courses, and as libraries for the study and loan of new materials and resources.

The training of teachers is the key to the whole programme of mathematical education, and different countries are handling it in different ways. Some seem to have no difficulty in ensuring a flow of mathematics and science graduates into teaching, while others find it almost impossible to recruit any. Some put faith in concurrent education and degree courses, others in post-graduate education certificates. But all agree that more ought to be done to help their primary teachers, that teaching needs to be made more attractive, and above all that the training of new teachers will never solve the problem by itself. The school population is increasing so fast (in some countries the primary population has increased tenfold since most of the primary teachers were at school!) that it is like trying to climb an escalator which is descending always faster than you can climb; or, as the Red Queen said, 'it takes all the running you can do to stay in the same place'.

Every teacher is a developing person, and in this self-development lies the greatest hope for the future. Every encouragement must be given to teachers actually on the job to grow in understanding of children and of mathematics, and in efficiency in bringing the two together in an environment in which genuine mathematics can be learned. This cannot be done in a hurry. A cycle of development is not complete until a teacher begins to teach the topics and methods by which he himself was taught at a similar level; only then is a firm base established on which the next cycle of reform can be built. For the university teacher the cycle may be as little as five years; for the secondary teacher it will be nearer ten, and for the primary teacher fifteen to twenty years; and the primary teacher is the most important.

9 *General conclusions*

(*a*) Mathematics teachers in developing countries should be encouraged themselves to develop and modify in the light of their own classroom experience curricula and syllabuses which are imaginative in their outlook but sensitive to the habits of a culture and pattern of education which may be very different from that of the Western world. In this the paramount needs of development will have to be kept in mind. Too abstract an approach is to be deprecated, and the incentives to accurate arithmetical facility provided by commercial activities will need to be respected and directed. The farmer must be able to cope with his accounts, but alongside him the future graduate must be experiencing the all-pervasive pattern and power of mathematics. Both teacher and pupil need the confidence which will enable them to carry out simple arithmetic mentally in less time than it takes to write it out on slate or paper; at the same time they need the spirit of enquiry which will drive them to understand fundamental processes so that they can apply them in a variety of situations.

(*b*) There is need to encourage interest in mathematics as an intellectual exercise which authenticates itself and can bring enjoyment and interest to those engaged in it. The increasing popularity of the mathematics contest helps to do this by provoking logical thought in reasonably simple problems which may be remote from the normal school curriculum.

(*c*) Emphasis must be placed on that part of mathematics which depends on visual imagination: the drawing and interpretation of graphs, the recognition of curves, the appreciation of pattern, the visualisation of motion and of three-dimensional relationships. These are matters which have often been neglected with the excuse that they are time-consuming, but probably because the teacher feels insecure in handling them. There is no doubt of their importance in the world of today.

(*d*) There is a danger in too great reliance on paper qualifications. The pay of a teacher may depend too closely on them, and too little on his responsibilities or suitable experience; indeed, they may be too easily equated with an experience which has not been part of the courses which led to them. This is particularly dangerous when a diploma in education by itself, without teaching experience, is thought to be sufficient qualification to train teachers.

(*e*) At all levels of education, educators in developing countries should be encouraged to pay less attention to the apparent demands of academic respectability, as judged by their professional counterparts elsewhere in the world, and more to the alignment of their work with the genuine needs of the people whom they and their institutions serve.

(*f*) We urge upon the governments of developing countries the importance of investing in the education of their own future manpower. If more pupils than can be effectively taught crowd into schools, the effect is likely to be counter-productive; there is evidence to show that the result is relapse into illiteracy and the creation of a problem class whose ambitions have been inflated beyond their capabilities. The status of the teacher must be made more honoured, his salary scales must be handled more imaginatively, and more graduates must be attracted into education. Rome was not built in a day, nor the educational systems of the developed nations in a decade. The development of sound logic and mathematical imagination within the school population of a country may not pay immediate economic dividends, but it is a valuable long-term investment in that nation's future.

National and other presentations

When the Programme Committee took the decision to invite individual countries to mount their own presentations at the congress it had very little idea of the likely response. Certainly it scarcely imagined that seventeen countries, namely the Arab Republic of Egypt, Argentina, Australia, Austria, Eire, the Federal Republic of Germany, Ghana, India, Italy, Japan, Korea, Malawi, the Netherlands, Poland, South Africa, the United Kingdom and the United States of America, would respond to the invitation. Inevitably, since there were no precedents to fall back on, and since the financial and other resources available differed so greatly, the presentations which these countries mounted varied considerably in size and purpose. At one end of the scale the United Kingdom presentation was able to include a large number of activities involving pupils and teachers drawn from different parts of the country, and that of the USA contained a series of lectures that could by itself have formed the basis for an international congress; at the other end, smaller or more isolated countries were given an opportunity to demonstrate their approach to mathematical education, to exhibit typical texts and children's work and to talk about the steps they are taking to solve the many problems that confront them. Some of the countries compensated for their inability to mount 'live' activities by showing films used in mathematics teaching and videotapes of classroom work. There can be no doubt that congress members found the opportunities to learn about developments and thought in countries other than their own most valuable, and that, offered within the confines of a national presentation, the ideas, activities and materials exhibited a coherence which would have been lost had they been presented piecemeal in a variety of discussion groups.

These benefits were demonstrated also by those exhibitions which were independent of, but nonetheless a valuable part of, the congress. The work of the Open University has aroused world-wide interest and it was fitting that congress members should have been able to see a comprehensive demonstration of the unique teaching methods of this institution and of the materials in several media that it has produced. Again, at the presentations of the School Mathematics Project and the Nuffield Project congress members could see a range of activities typical of a curriculum reform project. Thus, for example, the SMP, through a series of demonstration classes (in one of which each pupil had his own console attached to an advanced time-sharing computer), was able to give visiting delegates a vivid impression of the scale and character of its work.

5 THE CONGRESS IN RETROSPECT

One hopes that members attending a congress on mathematical education will leave with some new thoughts on 'mathematical education'. One can, however, be certain that they will leave with new ideas on the planning of 'congresses on mathematical education'. Clearly, there are lessons to be learned from every congress. Many of these are of a technical nature and, as such, are better left for the consideration of future programme and organising committees. Some, however, would seem to be of wider interest and worthy of consideration and comment by those who attend, rather than plan, such congresses. It is unusual perhaps for such matters to be discussed in a congress report but the precedent is not necessarily a bad one.

Writing so soon after the end of the congress, it is difficult to see its work in perspective, but talks with a variety of congress members suggested that the programme committee was right to reduce the number of plenary sessions and to place emphasis on working group discussions and national presentations. Such criticisms as there were, indicated that further progress is likely to come by improving this 'tripartite' system rather than by replacing it with yet another system.

The feeling that there was altogether too much happening at the same time was to be expected. Perhaps the significant factor here was the length of the congress – it was noticeably shorter than that at Lyons, yet it attempted to cover so much more ground. Clearly, any future congress must be longer and should contain more 'unprogrammed time' for visits to exhibitions, informal chats, or merely 'getting one's breath back'.

Again, with increasing membership the value of the plenary lecture diminishes. The difficulties of holding meetings in large halls with all the paraphernalia of simultaneous translation are manifest: the listener's problems are not only mathematical – they are psychological and physiological! Admittedly there is value in seeing and hearing a certain number of outstanding speakers and in bringing all congress members together for this purpose in one place on at least a few occasions during the congress. But possibly, in place of one or two of the plenary lectures, invited papers might be circulated (in translation where necessary) at the commencement of the congress. Members would then have the opportunity to discuss these with their respective authors during the duration of congress. Such an arrangement would, however, bring further administrative and printing problems in its wake. Already, it is apparent that the complexity of an ICME is as much as can be coped with by what is almost entirely voluntary labour. Any extra administrative commitments will almost certainly necessitate professional assistance and this, together with any major increase in the amount of multilingual printing needed, will inevitably mean a much higher congress fee.

Problems of administration and printing also affected the work of the discussion groups. The amount of preparatory work undertaken by these groups varied enormously and it is no surprise that those which were best prepared turned out to be the most rewarding. Clearly, although much depends on the group chairman and secretary and the facilities available to them, it is the ordinary members who, by their contributions and the interest they display prior to the congress, are ultimately responsible for the success or failure of the groups. It is to be hoped, therefore, that if similar working groups are to be a feature of future congresses, then members will make a contribution not only *at* the congress, but also *before* it. This should enable the groups to move still further from the pattern of 15-minute contributions, often unrelated to each other, to a genuine 'workshop' with more active participation, from which collective conclusions emerge.

As mentioned earlier, the national presentations and other exhibitions were a most popular feature of the congress; the opportunities they presented being welcomed by visitor and exhibitor alike. There could be difficulties if these presentations are allowed to grow in an uncontrolled manner, for more emphasis might be placed on 'selling' particular points of view and less on listening and learning; and, in an endeavour to mount ever more impressive national presentations, less energy and time might be devoted to the corporate workings of congress. It is to be hoped that these hazards will be avoided. Certainly, the principle of national and other presentations was successfully vindicated at Exeter, not least because the activities, displays of texts, etc., served as constant reminders that mathematical education is a *practical* activity involving pupil and teacher, learner and expositor, and they thus acted as a corrective to a dangerous tendency to treat mathematical education as an academic, abstract structure in which 'pupil' and 'teacher' become 'undefined terms'. It is important, though, that such activities involving pupils and teachers should not be viewed merely as 'demonstrations' – as 'method' classes – but that they should be seen as providing opportunities for *shared* observation of the way in which learners and teachers can work together and as a basis for subsequent *discussion*, for only then will they reveal their true potential.

Above all, the lesson of Exeter is that mathematical education is now a matter of great, world-wide interest and that future congresses are assured of a large membership. If these even larger congresses are to generate ideas and to be of significance in the development of a discipline of mathematical education, then they must be prepared for diligently – not only by the committees appointed to plan them, but by the members themselves.

II

THE INVITED PAPERS

As I read them

George Pólya

Some of the following passages are literally quoted or translated, others are paraphrased (condensed, modernised, ...). [Square brackets are used to indicate inserted words in the quotations and comments following the quotations.] I tried not to distort too much the meaning intended by the authors. At any rate, as I read them, these quotations greatly helped me to clarify my opinions and they may find responsive readers.

1 The ideas should be born in the student's mind and the teacher should act only as midwife. Socrates

2 ...we should give no small share of the credit to Democritus who was the first to state the result though he did not prove it [just guessed it]...The method I used did not furnish an actual demonstration [just a suggestion, a guess...Yet] I foresee that this method, once understood, will be used to discover other theorems which have not yet occurred to me, by other mathematicians, now living or yet unborn. Archimedes
[*First guess, then prove – that's the way to do it.*]

3 Intuition is the conception of an attentive mind, so clear, so distinct, and so effortless that we cannot doubt what we have so conceived. Descartes
[*Beauty in mathematics is seeing the truth without effort.*]

4 The chains by which the logicians imagine to be able to control the human mind seem to me of little value. Descartes
[*When introduced at the wrong time or place, good logic may be the worst enemy of good teaching.*]

5 Nothing is more important than to see the sources of invention which are, in my opinion, more interesting than the inventions themselves. Leibniz

6 Mathematics is the science that yields the best opportunity to observe the working of the mind...[and] has the advantage that by cultivating it we may acquire the habit of a method of reasoning which can be applied afterwards to the study of any subject and can guide us in the pursuit of life's object. Condorcet
[*Commenting on Euler's work.*]

7 Thus all human cognition begins with intuitions, proceeds from thence to conceptions, and ends with ideas. Kant
[*Learning begins with action and perception, proceeds from there to words and concepts, and should end in desirable mental habits.*]

8 What is good teaching? Giving opportunity to the student to discover things by himself. Herbert Spencer

9 The object of mathematical rigour is to sanction and legitimate the conquests of intuition, and there never was any other object for it.
J. Hadamard

10 If Euclid failed to kindle your youthful enthusiasm, then you were not born to be a scientific thinker. Albert Einstein

Department of Mathematics,
Stanford University, Stanford,
California 94305, USA.

Comments on mathematical education

Jean Piaget

The orientation one would consider giving to mathematical education depends naturally on the interpretation adopted of psychological development or the acquiring of operations and logico-mathematical structures; this interpretation depends equally on the epistemological meaning given to those things, the two questions of their psychogenesis and their epistemological significance being very closely related. If Platonism is right and mathematical entities exist independently of the subject, or if logical positivism is correct in reducing them to a general syntax and semantic, in both cases it would be justifiable to put the emphasis on the simple transmission of the truth from teacher to pupil and to use, as soon as possible, the language of the teacher, that is, the axiomatic language, without worrying too much about the spontaneous ideas of the children.

We believe, on the contrary, that there exists, as a function of the development of intelligence as a whole, a spontaneous and gradual construction of elementary logico-mathematical structures and that these 'natural' ('natural' in the way one speaks of the 'natural' numbers) structures are much closer to those being used in 'modern' mathematics than to those being used in traditional mathematics. There is, therefore, a body of facts which are, in general, little known to the teacher, but which, once he has a better psychological knowledge, would be of considerable use to him and would help him rather than make things more complicated. This would also favour the realisation of creative vocations in pupils rather than treating them simply as conforming 'receiving' instruments.

However, in order to arrive at this stage it is necessary to revise our ideas about the relation between language and action. It would seem, in fact, psychologically clear that logic does not arise out of language but from a deeper source and this is to be found in the general coordination of actions. In fact, before all language, and at a purely sensori-motor level, actions are susceptible to repetition and then to generalisation thus building up what could be called assimilation schemes. These schemes organise themselves according to certain laws and it would seem impossible to deny the relationship between these and the laws of logic. Two schemes can be coordinated or dissociated (reunion), one can be partially nested in the other (inclusion), or only have a part in common with the other (intersection); the parts of a scheme or the coordination of two or more schemes can allow either an invariant order of succession or certain permutations (types of order), as well as one-to-one correspondences, one-to-many or many-to-one (bijections etc.), and once a scheme imposes a goal on an action it is contradictory for the subject to go in the opposite direction. Briefly, there is a whole logic of the action that leads to the construction of certain identities and these go beyond perception (for example the permanence of the hidden object) and to the elaboration of certain structures (the practical group of displacements already described by Poincaré in his epistemological essays).

Therefore, it would be a great mistake, particularly in mathematical education, to neglect the role of actions and always to remain on the level of language. Particularly with young pupils, activity with objects is indispensable to the comprehension of arithmetical as well as geometrical relations (as was the case with the empirical mathematics of the Egyptians). The mathematics teacher's aversion to activities involving material experimentation is quite comprehensible. They probably see a sort of reference to the physical properties of objects and might fear that empirical verifications will harm the development of the deductive and purely rational mind which characterises their discipline. But this is, in fact, a fundamental misunderstanding and psychological analysis allows us to dispel these fears and reassure mathematicians with regard to their essential demand that the deductive and formal aspect of the mind should be educated. There exist, in fact, two types of 'experience', one very different from the other, which are related to the subject's actions. In the first instance, there is what is known as 'physical experience' (in the broad sense) which consists in acting on objects in order to discover the properties of the objects themselves, for example, comparing weights or densities, etc. But there also exists, and this is generally not known, what could be called 'logico-mathematical experience'; this type of experience gathers its information, not from the physical properties of particular objects, but from the actual actions (or more precisely their coordinations) carried out by the child on objects – these two types of experience are not equivalent. A friend of mine and a well-known mathematician says that the beginnings of his interest in mathematics were triggered off by an experience of the second type which happened to him when he was about 4 or 5 years old. Seated in his garden, he started to amuse himself by placing some pebbles in a straight line and counting them, for example, one to ten from left to right. After this he counted them from right to left and to his great surprise he still found ten. He then put them in a circle and, with enthusiasm, counted them – again ten so he counted them in the opposite direction and he found there were ten in both directions. He went on arranging the pebbles in all sorts of ways and finished by convincing himself that the sum, ten, was independent of the order of the pebbles. It is evident that neither the sum nor the order are physical properties of the pebbles until such time as the child has actually arranged them or put them all together. In this instance the child has discovered that the action of uniting the pebbles gives results and these results are independent of the action of ordering the pebbles. He could have observed this with any solid objects as, in this action, the physical properties of the pebbles played no particular role (apart from the fact that they 'let themselves' be acted on; their nature, however, remains unaltered, that is, it is conserved, but conservation itself also gives rise to logico-mathematical experience).

Thus this initial role of actions and logico-mathematical experience, far from hindering the later development of deductive thought, constitutes, on the contrary, a necessary preparation and this for two reasons. This first is that mental or intellectual operations, which intervene in the subsequent deductive reasoning processes, themselves stem from actions: they are interiorised actions and once this interiorisation, with the coordinations it supposes, is sufficient, then logico-mathematical experience in the form of material actions is no longer necessary and interiorised deduction is sufficient. The second reason is that coordinations of actions and logico-mathematical experience, whilst interiorising themselves, give rise to the creation of a particular variety of abstraction which corresponds precisely to logical and mathematical abstraction: contrary to ordinary or Aristotelian abstraction which derives its sources from the physical properties of objects and for this reason is called 'empirical abstraction', logico-mathematical abstraction would be referred to as 'reflective abstraction' and this for two related reasons. On the one hand, this abstraction 'reflects' (in the same way as a reflector or projector) everything that was on a lower plane (for example, that of action) and projects it to a higher plane, that of thought or mental representation. On the other hand, it is a 'reflective abstraction' in the sense of a reorganisation of mental activity, as it reconstructs at a higher level everything that was drawn from the coordinations of actions.

However, between the age where material actions and logico-mathematical experience are necessary (before 7/8 years old) and the age where abstract thought begins to be possible (towards 11/12 years old and through successive levels until about 14/15 years), there is an important stage whose characteristics are interesting to the psychologist and useful to know for the teacher. In fact between the age of 7 and 11/12 years an important spontaneous development of deductive operations with their characteristics of conservation, reversibility, etc. can be observed. This allows the elaboration of elementary logic of classes and relations, the operational construction of the whole number series by the synthesis of the notions of inclusion and order,[1] the construction of the notion of measurement by the synthesis of the subdivision of a continuum and the ordered displacement of a chosen part which serves as a unit, etc. Although there is considerable progress in the child's logical thinking it is nonetheless still fairly limited. At this level the child cannot as yet reason on pure hypotheses, expressed verbally, and, in order to arrive at a coherent deduction, he needs to apply his reasoning to manipulable objects (in the real world or in his imagination). For these reasons, at this level we refer to 'concrete operations' as distinct from formal operations. These concrete operations are, in fact, intermediaries between the actions of the pre-operational stage and the stage of abstract thought which comes much later.

Thus, having established the continuity between the spontaneous actions of the child and his reflexive thought, it can be seen from this that the essential notions which characterise modern mathematics are much closer to the structures of 'natural' thought than are the

[1] Several authors (Freudenthal, etc.) seem to have understood that I think the ordinal number is more primitive than the cardinal number, or the opposite. I have never made such a statement and have always considered these two aspects of finite numbers indissociable and psychologically reinforcing one another in a synthesis that goes beyond both the inclusion of classes and the order of asymmetrical transitive relations. If order is necessary it is because units which have become equivalent by the abstraction of their qualities can only be distinguished from one another by their ordered position. But the order of the elementary units is relative to the number (cardinal) of units which precede each of the units thus ordered.

concepts used in traditional mathematics. First, the importance should be pointed out of the spontaneous role of operations which allow the establishment of correspondences between sets and thus the construction of morphisms and in particular when these can be combined with recurring sequences. We have, for example, with B. Inhelder, asked children between 4/5 and 7/8 years old to put a bead from one hand into a transparent cylinder and simultaneously with the other hand put another bead into a second transparent cylinder which was, however, hidden behind a screen. The questions were designed to find out whether or not the child understood that the two sets, thus constituted, were equivalent and also to discover whether if this action were to be continued indefinitely, this equality would be conserved. All the children questioned admitted the equality of the two sets whilst the action was going on, however the youngest children refused to generalise to the case where the action was continued indefinitely. From about 5 or 6 years onwards they admit this generalisation and one small boy of $5\frac{1}{2}$ found the following very amusing formula: 'When one knows for one time, one knows for ever.' However this same child, after having seen a set of ten red counters in a one-to-one correspondence with a second set of ten blue counters, refused to admit the conservation of this equivalence once the elements of one of the sets had been spaced out a little and the correspondence between the two was no longer visible. This example demonstrates the constructive role of the establishment of a correspondence combined with the idea of recurrence.

An extremely striking example of convergence between theory and the spontaneous development of the child is that of geometric intuitions. Historically these intuitions appeared in Euclidean geometry, the structures of projective geometry were not discovered until much later and topology only in the nineteenth century. Psychologically children of 3 and 4 years old, who do not yet know how to draw squares and tend to compare them to circles – shapes such as rectangles and triangles etc. being assimilated to simple closed curves – are very careful, however, to make the distinction between closed and open figures, and they are able to draw with as much care a circle inside a figure, outside a figure, or on the frontier of a large figure. From these early topological intuitions arise, later and simultaneously, projective notions (with verification by 'taking aim' or 'sighting') and Euclidean notions according to a process which is nearer psychological theory than history.

From the level of concrete operations – at about 7/8 years – another interesting convergence can be found, that is the elementary equivalent of the three 'mother structures' discovered by Bourbaki, and this itself shows the 'natural' character of these structures. First of all there is the construction of structures of an algebraic nature, in as much as their laws of composition have an inverse and an identity element $+A-A = 0$. This can be observed particularly in the system of logical classes (classifications, etc. with quantification of the inclusion $A < B$ if $B = A+A'$ – and neither are empty sets). Secondly, order structures can be found whose laws of composition are based on reciprocity and this characterises the system of relations (ordering). Finally, topological structures based on ideas of continuity, neighbourhood and separation can be observed. These elementary structures later combine with each other. In particular, inverses (or negations $(-A)$) and reciprocities, which do not combine with each other at the concrete operational level, can be composed with one another from the 11/12 formal level onwards, in a four-group which renders possible such compositions: in this case the beginning of propositional logic with the combinatorial (set of all sub-sets) system, superposes itself on the elementary structures of logical classes and relations. The subject is then capable of handling systems that have four transformations. Let us take, for example, the propositional operation $p \supset q$ and define the four transformations:

1. (I) the identify or 'null' transformation $I(p \supset q) = p \supset q$,
2. (N) the inverse transformation $N(p \supset q) = p \cap \sim q$,
3. (R) the reciprocal transformation $R(p \supset q) = q \supset p$,
4. (C) the correlative transformation $C(p \supset q) = \sim p \cap q$.

In this case $RC = N$, $RN = C$, $NC = R$, $NRC = I$ which ensures finally the coordination in a unique system of inverses and reciprocities.

Many other examples, in particular the construction of elementary and 'trivial' forms of categories, could be given. However, it is now the moment to describe how these convergences between the spontaneous thought of the child in his 'natural' development and certain fundamental theoretical notions can be of use to the teacher. It can, of course, happen that certain people will try to teach young children 'modern' mathematics with archaic teaching methods, based exclusively on verbal transmission from teacher to child with a premature use of formalisation. With such methods there are bound to be a certain number of failures and these help to explain the scepticism of certain great mathematicians such as J. Leray.[1] However, it is not the 'modern' character of the mathematics programmes that is at fault but the methodology and psychology used in such cases. In fact, it is often particularly difficult for the teacher of mathematics, who, because of his profession, has a very abstract type of thought, to place himself in the concrete perspective which is necessarily that of his young pupils. However, from the developmental point of view and in relation to the progressive assimilation of the structures already mentioned, there would seem to be no contradiction (as we have seen above) between the initial concrete phases of structures and the final stage when they become formal and abstract. The teacher can only be aware that there is no contradiction between these two levels of thought if he is fully acquainted with (and this is the difficulty for the teacher) the details and functioning of these successive spontaneous thought structures. Briefly, the practical problem that is difficult to solve is to graft these general types of notions which the teacher understands in his language on to particular cases of these same notions constructed and used spontaneously by the children, without these yet being for them objects of reflection or sources of generalisation.

In order to make this necessary conjunction between the logico-mathematical structures of the teacher and those of the pupil at different levels of his development, certain very general psycho-pedagogical principles should perhaps be mentioned. The first is that real comprehension of a notion or a theory implies the re-invention of this theory by the subject. Once the child is capable of repeating certain notions and using some applications of these in learning situations he often gives the impression of understanding; however, this does not fulfil the condition of re-invention. True understanding manifests itself by new spontaneous applications, in other words an active generalisation supposes a great deal more: it seems that the subject has been able to discover for himself the true reasons involved in the understanding of a situation and, therefore, has at least partially re-invented it for himself. Naturally, this does not mean that the teacher has no role any more, but that his role is less that of a person who gives 'lessons' and is rather that of someone who organises situations that will give rise to curiosity and solution-seeking in the child, and who will support such behaviour by means of appropriate

[1] See the very critical report presented by Leray for Académie des Sciences de Paris (Report No. 276, p. 95, Session of 13 March 1972).

arrangements. Should the child have difficulties in his attempts to grasp a certain idea, the procedure with an active methodology would not be directly to correct him, but to suggest such counterexamples that the child's new exploration will lead him to correct himself.

A second consideration should constantly be present in the teacher's mind: that is, at all levels, including adolescence and in a systematic manner at the more elementary levels, the pupil will be far more capable of 'doing' and 'understanding in actions' than of expressing himself verbally. In other words, a large part of the structures the child uses when he sets out actively to solve a problem remain unconscious. In fact, it is a very general psychological law that the child can do something in action long before he really becomes 'aware' of what is involved – 'awareness' occurs long after the action. In other words, the subject possesses far greater intellectual powers than he actually consciously uses.[1] Consequently, once the teacher has had the opportunity of becoming acquainted with the psychological research mentioned above, and knows the subjacent thought structures the child possesses, he can more easily help the child to become aware of these either by appropriate discussions between the child and himself, or by the organisation of the work in groups where partners of the same age or similar ages (an older child acting as leader of a small group) discuss between themselves, which in turn favourises verbalisation and 'awareness'.

A third remark would seem important: in traditional mathematics it was often necessary for children to solve quantities of problems, some of them quite absurd, and this would mean a huge number of numerical or metrical calculations. In this case, the only way to succeed with children who were not particularly talented in mathematics was to proceed in two stages (but this was often forgotten): the first stage was purely qualitative and dealt with the logical structure of the problem and only afterwards in a second step were numerical or metrical facts introduced with the additional difficulties this type of calculation would create. With modern mathematics programmes the problem is less acute as they are basically qualitative. However, in this case, the problem can be found at another level – the teacher is often tempted to present far too early notions and operations in a framework that is already very formal. In this case, the procedure that would seem indispensable would be to take as the

[1] Euclid himself was not aware of all the operational structures he used in reality, for example, the group of isometries.

starting point the qualitative concrete levels: in other words, the representations or models used should correspond to the natural logic of the levels of the pupils in question, and formalisation should be kept for a later moment as a type of systematisation of the notions already acquired. This certainly means the use of intuition before axiomatisation and the scorn of logicians for all intuitive or 'naïve' thought is well known. However, once it is remembered that mathematical intuition is essentially operational and the nature of operational structures is to dissociate 'form' from 'content', then the final formalisation would seem to be prepared and becomes progressively necessary by the construction itself of these initial intuitive structures. We do not believe with Pasch that formalisation goes in the opposite direction to that taken by 'natural' thought, but so that there may be no conflict between the former and the latter, formalisation should be allowed to constitute itself in its own time and not because it is forced to by premature constraints.

Faculté des Sciences,
Centre d'Epistemologies génétiques,
52 rue de Paquis,
1211 Geneva 14,
Switzerland.

Presidential Address

Sir James Lighthill, F.R.S.

1 Introduction

It has given me profound pleasure to be able to welcome such a very large and such a very distinguished audience to this opening session of the Second International Congress on Mathematical Education. Although records of discussion about mathematical education go back at least 2500 years, to the days of Plato's Academy, it seems that the twentieth century brought a new tempo and urgency to such discussions, while we have during the past *decade* seen a great and growing ferment of activity in the field all over the world. Prominent in discussion of the subject throughout this twentieth century has been our International Commission, founded in 1899 by H. Fehr and C. A. Laisant, while this past decade of intensified and increasing recognition of the importance of mathematical education and of the new approaches and opportunities within it, coincides with the first decade of existence, as a fully-fledged Commission within the International Mathematical Union, of the International Commission on Mathematical Instruction, ICMI.

Up to 1960, the energetic study of mathematical teaching methods and curricula within individual countries was supplemented and strengthened by the holding of meetings arranged by our Commission, by its review journal *L'Enseignement Mathématique*, and by international discussion every four years in the educational section of the International Congress of Mathematicians. Those useful discussions were, nevertheless, rather limited in scope and in the number of interested persons involved. In 1960, the International Mathematical Union (IMU) took the decision to accept the affiliation of ICMI under its wing as a separate Commission of IMU, with separate National Sub-Commissions in member countries: the International Commission on Mathematical Instruction, which could conduct more intense activities in the educational field and supplement those pursued at IMU's regular congresses. The aim of ICMI, as then laid down in terms of reference, is 'to further the sound development of mathematical education at all levels, and to secure public appreciation of its importance'.

In 1962 Professor Lichnerowicz was elected by the General Assembly of IMU as the first President of ICMI appointed under the new constitution. He launched ICMI at once on a valuably extended programme of symposia and publications. It soon became clear that such increased activity was very necessary, to match in the international sphere what I referred to earlier as the 'growing ferment of activity' that was manifesting itself simultaneously in so many different countries.

At the Moscow Congress of IMU in 1966, Professor Freudenthal was elected the new President of ICMI and he brought about a further intensification of activity. In particular, he went beyond specialised or regional symposia to organise the first international congress in the field, held at Lyons in 1969 with over 600 participants. This was a big step forward which brought general recognition that no educational topic is more suitable for international discussion than education in that unique way of thought and that unique language – a language of a completely international character – that we call mathematics. It was agreed that international congresses should be held in future every four years, and indeed in years with *dates divisible by 4*, so that they would alternate with those of the international congresses of mathematicians whose dates are congruent to 2 (modulo 4)!

The IMU at the Nice Congress in 1970 did me the greatly appreciated honour of electing me in succession to Professor Freudenthal as President of ICMI. I had previously been Chairman of a small subcommittee of the British National Committee for Mathematics which had in February 1970 determined upon Exeter as a suitable site where ICMI might be invited to hold its second international congress. Our National Committee's invitation to hold the second congress in Britain was accepted by ICMI and I continued, as President of ICMI and Chairman of the Organising Committee for the congress, to aim above all at bringing about here at Exeter this summer a meeting that would combine *width* of scope and of international representation with *depth* of discussion and of exposition.

My colleagues on the Organising Committee and I have been profoundly gratified by the huge international response that has followed upon our $2\frac{1}{2}$ years of labour in preparing for this meeting. We had been bold enough to plan for an attendance twice as big as at the first congress in Lyons but this number of registrations was reached already last May and finally we took into consideration the importance of *comfortable* accommodation and other arrangements for participants within the facilities on this campus when we declined to accept registrations beyond a maximum of 1300 full and 300 associate members. While apologising to those we turned away, may I suggest that those who are here will appreciate the wisdom of our having kept the number of participants within convenient bounds, as well as the rough justice of giving preference to those who were in good time with their applications to attend![1]

All of us can regard the first decade of activity of ICMI in its new form as having reached a fitting climax with the huge intensification of demand for international discussion of mathematical education exhibited by the more than doubled attendance at this second of our international congresses. About seventy countries are represented here at Exeter. This week we shall among other things be giving longer-term thought to the future, looking as far ahead as the third congress in 1976 and to all the specialised and regional activities in which we should be involved between now and then. It will be important to plan all that future activity with wisdom and imagination. Let us, however, devote the next four days, above all, to reaping the greatest possible advantage from the unique circumstance that ICMI has now brought together within this favourable environment leading mathematical educators from all over the world and provided them with a programme so organised as to allow exchange of ideas and opinions and experience on almost every possible aspect of the subject, together with exposition of a wide range of important national developments.

The design of this programme for our congress has been the work of the international Programme Committee under the chairmanship of Mrs Elizabeth Williams; a committee that has, in my view, successfully brought to a focus world-wide aspirations for discussion on a vast range of different topics within mathematical education, and gone on to create the mechanisms for giving them reality. A cardinal principle underlying the committee's work has been the necessity of viewing mathematical education within the context of the total education of the individual. You will see how this consideration influenced the choice of speakers for our plenary sessions: these main sessions

[1] In the end, late consideration of several 'hard cases', where for particular reasons leniency by the Secretariat appeared justified, raised the total registrations to about 1700.

that will bring all congress participants together are intended, not to raise specialised matters within mathematical education but to help all of us see the subject within wider contexts; including the historical, sociological and psychological contexts as well as that of its relationship to the development of mathematics itself. We are truly fortunate in the outstanding distinction of those who have consented to give these plenary lectures.

It has been a further source of great delight that two persons who have had such a seminal influence on the formation of twentieth-century ideas concerning mathematical education and its place in an individual's total education as Professor Piaget and Professor Pólya accepted a year ago our invitation to attend this congress as the honoured guests of ICMI. All of us have been delighted and stimulated by the messages from our two honoured guests circulated with the other congress literature. Ultimately Professor Piaget's doctors advised him not to travel this summer although for other purposes as you will gather from his fascinating paper he remains well and in good spirits. Professor Pólya's personal presence and inspired string of quotations which each of you has received are a great joy to all of us.

The next most important principle underlying the architecture of our programme was that on all the different aspects of our subject active *discussion* must be permitted and encouraged. This congress is above all a congress for discussion, and to this end it has been organised so as to avoid any formal delivery of main lectures outside the periods of the seven plenary sessions. To make general participation possible within manageable areas for discussion, our whole subject matter has been divided up into thirty-eight such manageable areas, and working groups in each of these areas have been constituted, each with its own Chairman and Secretary.

I am most grateful to these Chairmen and Secretaries for the effort they have put into the advance preparation of plans of diverse kinds for the different working groups. These plans will in every case give a framework for discussion but also leave time and opportunity for unplanned controversy and exchange of ideas to come about. I believe that these relatively small working groups, where those involved can really get to know each other and come to appreciate each other's points of view in detail, will prove to be the cement that binds this congress together to give it real strength and effective influence on future world developments.

Reading through the list of working groups is an experience at the same time fascinating and frustrating, in the sense that most of us feel interested in the subject matter of more working groups than we can possibly attend! It is important, however, that everybody makes a selection, as I believe most of you have already done, partly so that each of us may take part in those groups where we have most contribution to make personally, and partly so that the groups may be of manageable size for purposes of active discussion.

Many of you will select groups devoted to education at a particular level (whether primary, secondary or tertiary or certain intermediate levels) and specifically to education in a particular branch of mathematics at such a particular level. Many others will be involved in working groups on particular kinds of teaching method or technique, or on some of the fundamental studies underlying the choice of methodology. The range of possibilities is very great, and I believe that a great range of memorable discussions will get going in these working groups.

In parallel with that complex mechanism for discussion it has been important to enable also a proper detailed exposition by any participating country of those educational developments that it considers most worthy to be brought to the notice of the congress. These national presentations (some seventeen in number) will, I believe, help us become aware of much that is best in the teaching methods and curricula of many of the participating countries. Several different techniques of presentation will be used: static exhibitions, films, talks, and in a few cases demonstration classes with live pupils.

In these remarks I have been trying, not to give you any accurate guidance that could replace careful reading of the congress programme itself, but rather to indicate the philosophy underlying the work of our international Programme Committee and of its devoted Chairman, Mrs Elizabeth Williams. May I also remark how much we owe to the Local Committee which has done such fine work in arranging the effective utilisation of this site for purposes of accommodation and of meetings of both professional and social kinds. The value and suitability of this attractive University campus for helping us all get to know our colleagues from other countries in the most pleasant possible way, in the working groups, in social gatherings of many different kinds, and in the course of various excursions into the lovely Devon countryside, has been greatly enhanced by the devoted work of many members of the Local Committee, including Mr Duller and Mr Hammond-Smith who have been its Chairmen, and last but not least the Congress Secretary, Mr Denis Crawforth, who indeed is the kingpin of our whole organisation. I hope that all of you during this week will become devoted Devonians while you increase still further your expertise as mathematical educators!

2 Integrated pure and applied mathematics

Now I have come to the part of my Presidental Address which represents more of an individual message to this congress. Like those addresses to be given by distinguished lecturers to the six other plenary sessions, this message is concerned with seeing mathematical education within the context of the total education of the individual. It is a message, indeed, about those approaches to mathematical education that are aimed at bringing about its integration with the educational process as a whole.

I emphasise that this middle portion of my address is a personal message which makes no attempt to give any concerted view of ICMI as a whole. It reflects, rather, an individual view, which I offer as just one contribution among those many and diverse contributions that will be made at this congress and, possibly, harmonised within the minds of the participants into something like a concerted view of mathematical education.

My personal emphasis in this message is on *those* aspects of mathematical education that are concerned with communicating a working knowledge of *how mathematics interacts* with other subjects and with the external world; in one word, a knowledge of how mathematics is *applied*. You could say that this theme for an address is what ICMI might expect in a year when its President is British and its congress is held in Britain! Certainly a feature that has specifically characterised British approaches to mathematical education has been a close association between pure and applied mathematics, and a general predilection for teaching mathematics in a way that emphasised at any rate some of its applications.

The older British curricula stressed at an elementary level the application of mathematics in commerce and at a more advanced level its applications in mechanics and/or statistics, which in turn were valuable as foundations for work in engineering, as well as in the physical, earth and life sciences. The newer British curricula at primary and secondary level bring in a still wider range of applications: a development that seems to have grown out of the pragmatic British traditions of integrated pure and applied mathematics, coupled with a recognition of how greatly the uses of mathematics in all the other sciences, as well as in engineering and commerce, have expanded in this third quarter of the twentieth century. This expansion in the application of mathematics, which seems to have an important contribution to make towards solving this world's pressing problems, has of course been connected with the increased power given by high-speed computers to those involved in such application, and to some extent the computer's new importance has been reflected in certain aspects of these curricula.

I am of course making no claim whatever that developments in those general directions are confined to the neighbourhood of the British Isles! There are many countries where modern mathematics curricula reflect the modern trend towards greatly widened areas of application of mathematics influenced by new computational possibilities. I have commented merely that our academic traditions made this trend a natural and easy one to follow.

There are *other* countries where the tendency in modern curricula is towards a still greater abstraction than ever before. These more abstract curricula contain many attractive features; in particular, they may often succeed in imparting an enthusiastic appreciation of the beauty of mathematical structures and mathematical deductions. Many young minds show a keen response to that beauty, and some of you may regard an educator like myself as doomed to failure because in place of beauty all I could offer to those young minds would be utility: prosaic utility!

In reality, however, no such stark contrast is exhibited by the alternative of a curriculum based on integrated pure and applied mathematics. The values in such a curriculum involve integrated beauty and utility: they lie in a space of two dimensions, and this has certain educational advantages. The most obvious of these derives from the observation that a class may contain some pupils who can be induced to respond mainly to the beauty of mathematical ideas and arguments *and* some pupils whose interest can be aroused mainly from realisation of their utility. Possibly a particular vector in the beauty–utility space may produce optimum results for such a class!

Whether for this or other reasons, the trend in modern mathematics teaching projects in Britain and some other countries has been to give continual illustrations of how the mathematics taught can be applied. They bring in constantly the concrete example, and are particularly concerned to emphasise the variety of uses and applications of mathematics.

This personal message of mine is concentrated, however, on a slightly different educational goal. It says: let us go *beyond mere use* of the concrete example as an aid to understanding or of reference to utility as an aid to widening the circle of those in whom interest is aroused. There is a still more important prize to be won: a prize concerned with a *deeper* integration of mathematics into the total education of the individual.

I want to suggest that educators may have most benefited their pupils when they have succeeded in giving a feel for what is involved in the *process of applying mathematics*. This is the process of building a bridge between the *abstract* ideas and inferences of mathematics and the *concrete* problems arising in some field of application. It seems to be increasingly recognised that there may be more skill, more *art*, in that *bridge-building* process than in the associated mathematical *problem-solving*. Computers may be of great value in problem-solving, but apparently the human brain alone is able to tackle the subtler aspects of creating an effective correspondence between the mathematical world and the world of experiment and observation.

As many of you will know, I gave an address on *this* theme last year, speaking as President of the Mathematical Association of Great Britain on the occasion of its Centenary. The title of that address[1] was 'The art of teaching the art of applying mathematics', and I should like to recommend that slogan in my address to this much wider audience, although perhaps laying emphasis here on slightly different aspects of the art of teaching the art of applying mathematics.

One feature of the art of applying mathematics to which I draw attention in my Mathematical Association address, and a feature which makes the word 'art' especially appropriate, was what I called the 'linguistic aspect' or 'communications aspect' involved in applying mathematics. At an international congress with over sixty countries represented, and gifted translators working for us on all the consequent linguistic problems and communications problems,

[1] Published in *Mathematical Gazette*, **55**, 1971, 249–70.

we are specially able to appreciate the skill and artistry involved in effective solution of such problems. Such artistry is not possessed at all by computers! Indeed, the failure of computer programs for translation between languages is an important reminder of the subtle nature of language and of the ways in which it is assimilated by the brain.

One who is a practising applier of mathematics, as I have been for thirty years, finds that the most delicate problems with which he deals are those of a communications and linguistic character. The applier of mathematics has to be able to communicate with the practitioners within the field to which he is applying the mathematics. They have their specialised language for talking about their problems. He has his own specialised language, namely mathematics. These linguistic differences complicate the communications problem, and make necessary some capability of *translation* between the two languages.

Thus if we see mathematics as being essentially a language, as the title of one of our working groups at this congress implies, educators ought to recognise a need for instruction in the arts of translation between that language and other languages. They should *avoid* giving an impression that such translation may be a crude, mechanical, 'computerisable' process (as some writings on so-called model-building may even seem to imply!). They should try to convey what the practising applier of mathematics always finds, namely, that effective application is possible only if one sets out to learn the language of the field of application and master those characteristics special to it.

This is not only because of the need to communicate with the practitioners of that field. It is partly because that language has had to evolve in such a way that it really is quite effective for sharing ideas and drawing inferences within that field of activity. The applier of mathematics must learn to think simultaneously in both languages, and thus to use simultaneously the weapons of mathematical reasoning and the inferential methods typical of the field of application. The terminology of those methods must be clearly understood, and wherever possible an approximate mathematical equivalent of each term needs to be found.

A teacher who bears in mind these aims may avoid certain dangers which can be described as compartmentalisation: dangers of suggesting that mathematics may best make its contribution by a direct conversion of the real problem into a mathematical problem, followed *separately* by solution of that mathematical problem. Allowing such a divorce between the parts of the work conducted in the two different languages leads often to ludicrous errors! It is most unwise during parts of the work which involve solving a mathematical problem to stop thinking about what the different terms in the equations stand for. Such interpretations of their meaning, coupled with common-sense arguments and other arguments of a non-mathematical character, prove to be of the greatest value in *finding* a good solution, as well as in interpreting it when it has been found.

Those processes are what I mean by integration of pure and applied mathematics and I believe that the teacher who discovers how to communicate that sense of integration and of effective bridge-building finds it to have its own beauty: a beauty to which pupils show keenness of response, and which further justifies use of the word 'art' in the expression 'art of applying mathematics'. In my Mathematical Association lecture I illustrated all these points at some length by an extended example drawn from the application of mathematics in mechanical engineering. Such an extended example would be quite out of place in the opening address to an international congress, but I shall refer to just one aspect of it here.

Engineers make widespread and effective use of a special 'picture language', in which diagrams representing systems are used to pick out and identify the features of those systems that are important for particular purposes. To understand relationships between the idealisations in an engineer's diagrams and those involved in mathematical equations related to his systems may be important for the applier of mathematics to engineering. Advantages may accrue from continued recollection of what is the diagrammatic representation of each term in every equation; and, also, from identifying those equivalences brought about between different kinds of diagram through a parallelism between the equations to which they give rise.

How can teachers communicate such points; namely, that the art of applying mathematics is itself centred on problems of communication, as well as of the recognition of bridges between non-mathematical concepts and mathematical ones? My experience as a university teacher of mathematics has led me to one and only one answer to that question: it is that *some* direction of application needs to be studied in depth; that one field at least must be investigated at sufficient length to give an impression of the subtle ways in which applied mathematics succeeds in making its contributions. The language used in that field should be at least partly put over, and its terminology related to mathematical terminology.

I am fully aware that there is a conflict between what I am now advocating (study of a particular field of application in depth) and what I recommended earlier concerning a wide range of different concrete illustrations. The conflict is a real one, and it is because so much skill in communicating and organising material is needed to overcome that conflict, so much artistry on the teacher's part, that I am particularly drawn to my slogan 'The art of *teaching* the art of applying mathematics'.

On the one hand, mathematics teaching should be permeated with concrete examples which give an impression of how widely and diversely mathematical ideas penetrate into human problems generally, including everyday, technical and scientific matters. On the other hand, it *is* necessary to tell at least one lengthy connected story of the application of mathematics in real depth. This will amongst other things communicate the message that no-one can expect to solve the *whole* of any problem mathematically. There must be an integration of experiment and theory; there must be a combination of mathematical investigation with inferences from observation and experiment and from non-mathematical modes of reasoning. The best primary-school teaching is a good reminder of how effectively such integration can be carried out, and can be an inspiration to those of us attempting the same at other levels of education.

3 Conclusion

But now I believe that I have inserted quite as much of a personal and individual message as is proper in a Presidential Address to a great international congress like this where the total experience represented from the huge field of mathematical education dwarfs the significance that any individual views may have. My views can be read in *Math. Gazette*, vol. 55, at much greater length. In the meantime, in the next four days, all the great issues of mathematical education, *including* this one of what should be the extent of integration of pure and applied mathematics in the educational process, will be given that discussion in depth, from the standpoint of the combined experience of those engaged within the educational systems of some seventy different countries, which alone can do justice to the magnitude and significance of those issues.

The concluding remarks which I now wish to make are on a theme which I believe is particularly proper to be pursued by a President, whose main task as the Chairman of the congress must be to seek to bring about the fullest possible representation of different views at our meetings and the fullest possible interaction between different participants, with the aim of fostering movements of opinion which might bring about towards the end of our congress some greater degree of consensus on many important issues than at the beginning. With this in mind, may I encourage each of you to make positive contributions at the working groups you attend and to give your personal views on matters under discussion. We want the maximum participation at those sessions. At the same time may I respectfully request that you speak briefly and concisely so that as many other participants as possible will also have a chance to contribute.

In general, let me encourage you to plan your time in advance so that you may succeed in attending those working groups in whose work you are most interested, and inspect those parts of national presentations that are of most concern to you, and in addition make use of parts of each day to take advantage of those opportunities for personal contact with mathematical educators from countries other than your own which you and all of us have this week from living all together on this campus. Avoid the danger that, out of force of habit, you may find yourselves mixing only with persons from your own country. Seize upon the chance of introducing yourself, and others, to as many people from *different* countries as possible, and of coming to know them and their opinions and practices as mathematical educators. There are marvellous opportunities for all this at meals, on the campus generally and on the excursions, and I should like to encourage you to take these opportunities and thus to make full use of what I referred to earlier as this unique circumstance.

At the same time the members of ICMI itself, and of its Executive Committee, will be making plans for our future meetings great and small. If any of you have ideas under this heading, do please communicate them to an ICMI representative from your own country, who can then ensure that they may be brought into those discussions this week. And finally, may I express my own warm thanks to you all for showing such determination to complete the, in many cases, long and arduous journey here to Exeter so as to make this Second Congress of Mathematical Education still more effective by your personal participation. This congress is now actively in progresss; may all our great hopes from it be more than fulfilled!

Department of Applied Mathematics
and Theoretical Physics,
Silver Street,
Cambridge.

What groups mean in mathematics and what they should mean in mathematical education

Hans Freudenthal

It would be naïve to bet whether or not you have met figure 1 before – for many years this has been the first drawing children perform when they are given a pair of compasses. An eight-year-old girl did this.

Fig. 1

She was quite skilful at handling a pair of compasses which is a difficult thing for children of this age.

Fig. 2

She did even more, she added a second ring of circles as in figure 2. Then I suggested to her that she should colour the drawing, although she would have done so if nobody had mentioned it, because a drawing like this cries out for colours. The most surprising feature of her performance was that it respected flawlessly all the symmetries of the drawing. Of course, the girl would not be able to rationalise her behaviour in a way mathematicians would do, though she firmly grasped all the relevant consequences of such a theory instinctively.

From the decoration of stone age vessels, to the ornamentation of the Alhambra, to Escher's sophisticated graphic art, symmetries have played an important part in painting and sculpture. Science, too, knew and used symmetry as a principle from olden times. Among the few things we know about the first geometer in Greece and the first non-anonymous scientist in human history, Thales of Milete, is that he formulated and used geometrical theorems on symmetry. By a symmetry argument, Anaximander explained why the terrestrial disk suspended in the universe did not tilt or fall – it was at equal distances from all parts of the heaven. Perhaps you know the story of Buridan, a medieval scholar, who imagined a donkey standing between two haystacks of equal bulk and equal smell and let it starve to death because there was no reason why it should eat from the one rather than from the other. By symmetry axioms, Archimedes tackled the laws of the lever, Simon Stevin the laws of the inclined plane, Huygens the laws of collision. Physicists today call it Pierre Curie's law when they argue that a symmetry in the causes is preserved in the effects. Curie applied it in crystallography; today it is a most important principle of quantum theory.

Let us take a closer look at mathematics. What is the beautiful thing about a regular hexagon or about regular figures like those illustrated above? They admit mappings onto themselves that do not change their aspect. How many? Three reflections in diagonals, three reflections in lines joining the midpoints of opposite sides, and finally a number of rotations, all of them through angles which are multiples of 60° (the zero-multiple is included as the identity mapping). How do you know that there are twelve, no less and no more? The answer is not as trivial as you think – I will return to such questions later.

You know what complex numbers are: pairs of real numbers written in the form $a+bi$. They form a number field, with the four operations and the usual laws; i is the imaginary unit, the square of which is supposed to be -1. Changing i into $-$i is called conjugation; it changes $\gamma = a+bi$ into $\bar{\gamma} = a-bi$. Conjugation is an automorphism of this field – it preserves the fundamental algebraic relations of sum and product:

$$\overline{\alpha+\beta} = \bar{\alpha}+\bar{\beta},$$

$$\overline{\alpha\beta} = \bar{\alpha}\,\bar{\beta},$$

and by consequence all algebraical relations whatsoever. By conjugation every true relation on complex numbers passes into a true relation.

From an algebraic point of view the three solutions $\alpha_1, \alpha_2, \alpha_3$ of

$$x^3-x-1 = 0$$

are indistinguishable. What is true of one of them algebraically, is true of any other. In such relations as

$$\alpha_1+\alpha_2+\alpha_3 = 0,$$

$$\alpha_1\alpha_2+\alpha_1\alpha_3+\alpha_2\alpha_3 = -1,$$

$$\alpha_1\alpha_2\alpha_3 = 1,$$

and all other rational relations, they occur in a most symmetric way. The equation

$$2x^3-7x^2y-7xy^2+2y^3 = 0$$

is symmetric in x, y. Does this mean that all its solutions (x, y) are symmetric too, that is, of the form (a, a)? Of course not. But it means that if (a, b) is a particular solution of that equation, then the one that arises from it by interchanging x and y, that is (b, a), is also a solution.

Why cannot

$$(x-y)^3+(y-z)^3+(z-x)^3 = (x+y+z)^3+6xyz$$

be a true identity? Because the right hand member is symmetric in x, y, z, whereas the left hand one changes its sign under an odd permutation of x, y, z.

Why does the ruler not suffice to construct the centre of an ellipse? Because there are mappings which, although they preserve straight lines and map the ellipse onto itself, carry the centre of the ellipse onto any given point not on the ellipse.

Why is it we can solve equations up to degree four by root extractions, yet cannot do this with those of degree five? Because equations solvable by root extractions show far fewer symmetries than fifth degree equations in general – this is what was proved by Ruffini and Abel.

Nowhere do symmetry arguments reveal their power more convincingly than in probability. Why has each ball in an urn the same chance of being drawn? Because the urn and the drawing procedure and hence the probabilities are invariant under all permutations of the contents of the urn. Or a more sophisticated example:

Six persons A to F are put at random in a row. What is the chance of A standing somewhere left of B? Well, the chance of A standing left of B is the same as that of B standing left of A and both together exhaust all possibilities, so each one has the chance of one half. And the chance of

A left of *B* and *C* left of *D*?

The same as that of

A left of *B* and *D* left of *C*,
B left of *A* and *C* left of *D*,
B left of *A* and *D* left of *C*,

so each of them is just one quarter. And the chance of

A left of *B* left of *C*?

By the same reasoning it is one sixth.

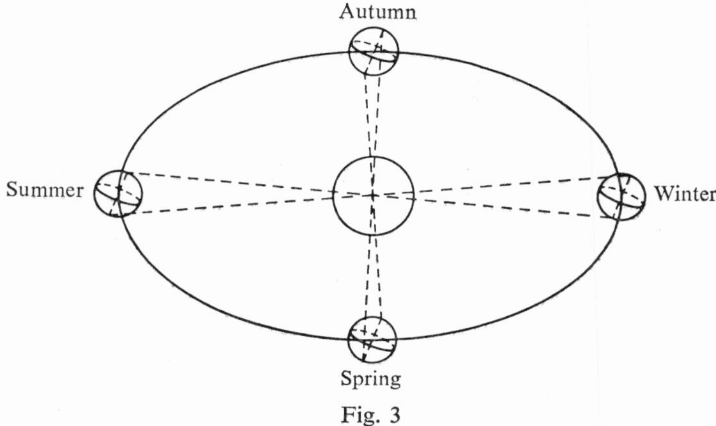

Fig. 3

This is sound reasoning in spite of today's fashionable misgivings about *a priori* probabilities. When interpreting reality by means of mathematical models, I am entitled, nay obliged, to incorporate all symmetries found in reality into the mathematical model, and this is what I have done in the above examples. Arranging people at random means that all statements about those arrangements must be invariant under all shuffling, or as mathematicians say, under all permutations; and from this principle all relevant probabilities can be derived in the problems I just discussed.

From probability let us turn to astronomy. Everybody knows that as to climate and seasons the Northern and Southern hemisphere of the terrestrial globe are mirror images of each other, that while we enjoy the last summer weeks, our antipodes are waiting for spring to come, and that when in the arctic zone the sun does not set, in the antarctic one it does not rise. But why is it so? It is worthwhile to make the symmetry reasons of these phenomena explicit in mathematical terms.

The Earth moves around the sun in a nearly circular orbit, while rotating around an axis, skew on the orbit plane but fixed in space. This system admits a few symmetries (see figure 3). First, the point reflection at the centre (the sun), which displaces the Earth over half a year in its orbit and at the same time interchanges the Northern and Southern hemispheres – it explains the greater part of the geographic phenomena I mentioned. Secondly, there is the reflection in the plane orthogonal to the orbit plane and passing through the summer and winter solstices, which inverts the course of the Earth; and thirdly, the half-turn rotation of the system about an axis joining the spring and autumn equinoxes, which also inverts the course of the Earth but at the same time interchanges the two hemispheres. The last two symmetries explain why the seasons are mirrored by the equinoxes and solstices with respect to such optical phenomena as solar risings and settings and day length. But since these symmetries invert the course of the Earth and hence the direction of time, they break down if applied to phenomena that need time to develop, such as heat distribution and weather, and this illustrates why the terrestrial climate is not mirror imaged by the equinoxes and solstices, why 21 June is not the hottest day and 21 December not the coldest. Notice that of these three symmetries, each is the product of the other two.

Let us look further at mathematics applied in reality. A mass or an electric charge determines a field of force. If I know about some symmetry of this mass or charge distribution, I may be sure that the field will show the same symmetry. For instance, a rotationally symmetric mass or electric conductor will produce a rotationally symmetric potential and field of force. It is sound mathematics to profit from this symmetry before attempting to calculate the potential and the field of force.

On the other hand, if a harmonic oscillator is vibrating under the influence of an exterior force $f(t)$ with period T, that is

$$x''(t)+\alpha x'(t)+\beta x(t) = f(t),$$

I am not entitled to claim that all its vibrations will have the same period T. What is invariant under the mapping $t \to t+T$ is not each particular vibration, but the set of all of them; which means that by shifting one solution $\phi(t)$ over T, I get a new one, $\phi(t+T)$.

Solving differential equations arising from physical problems can be an arduous job. Often qualitative information on the symmetric character of solutions is all we can obtain and precisely the thing we need. Symmetries of space, of interchanging particles, of inverting charges, spins, magnetic fields play a paramount role if differential equations arising in quantum mechanics are to be interpreted.

In the examples I have displayed, experts will have recognised a common feature – each of them shows in its particular way how groups arise and are used to study regularities in nature and in mathematics. Why did I refrain from using the word groups? If systematics is pursued, one starts by defining a group, continues by proving a few general theorems about the group concept, then develops the general principles according to which groups can be applied, and finally arrives at some applications of groups according to these principles, provided, of course, that sufficient time is left for this minor concern. Yet mathematics develops systematically only in an 'objective mind'. In the individual it takes the path from the particular case to the general principle, from the concrete to the more abstract, and so it happened in history, too. Groups and group theory methods preceded the conscious organisation of this complex of investigations in terms of the explicit group concept by at least half a century. This is a common way in mathematics. In order to organise a field of knowledge you have first to acquire knowledge about it by exploring it. Fundamental definitions do not arise at the start but at the end of the exploration, because in order to define a thing you must know what it is and what it is good for.

Camille Jordan's celebrated codification of group theory in 1870, the *Traité des substitutions*, made explicit what mathematicians had instinctively been doing for half a century: analysing geometric and algebraic systems by means of groups and developing the principles of group theory.[1] The most striking example of this instinctive group theory during those fifty years is Hermann von Helmholtz' extensive use of Lie groups in his famous space problem, long before Lie discovered them – even the term 'group' is lacking in this paper on group theory and it may be taken for granted that Helmholtz did not know about groups when he wrote it.

It is instructive to see how groups arose in the paper, which is an enquiry into the foundations of geometry. Space is viewed by Helmholtz as a manifold gifted with a metric and as such it possesses a group of autometries, that is, mappings onto itself leaving the metric invariant. Euclidean and non-Euclidean space are characterised by free mobility, that is by the existence of an as-large-as-possible group of autometries. According to more recent investigations the geometry of a space will be Euclidean or non-Euclidean provided that for some positive α any two triples of points a_i, b_i $(i = 1, 2, 3)$ with

$$\operatorname{dist}(a_i, a_j) = \operatorname{dist}(b_i, b_j) = \alpha \qquad (i \neq j)$$

can be mapped upon each other by autometries of the space.

[1] It is true that, as early as 1854, Arthur Cayley defined groups in a formal abstract way, but this was a premature act with no consequences for either Cayley's investigations or those of others.

Helmholtz did not mention groups but he used all kind of group-theoretical tools in his investigation. The first mathematicians who, influenced by Jordan, made group theory explicit in geometry, were Felix Klein and Sophus Lie. The latter opened up the whole field of what is now called Lie groups, whereas the former restricted himself to subgroups of the projective group as subject matter and to classical theory of invariants as working method. He took his rough material from Cayley. Cayley had derived a metric from a conic in the plane by the requirement that it should be invariant under all projective transformations leaving the conic invariant. Unknowingly, by this procedure he had constructed the first model of the up-to-then abstract hyperbolic geometry. It was Klein's great achievement to make this model explicit and, by the same discovery, to create the concept of 'model' which was in our times to become of major importance within mathematics and beyond.

Through this example, Klein learned to appreciate and to use the automorphism groups of a geometry. He hit upon the idea that groups can be tools to classify geometric properties, and he applied this idea to the projective group and its subgroups. Indeed, recognising whether some property, proposition or definition is metric, affine, projective is an effective means of creating order in the chaos of geometry.

This is the leading idea of the so-called *Erlanger Programm*. It is often expressed in a brilliant aphorism that stems from Klein himself: geometry is the theory of invariants of a certain group. Klein himself was the first among the large number of mathematicians who were misled by this aphorism. There is a lot of geometry that cannot be fitted into this frame, and there are many geometries for which groups are irrelevant. Klein's restricted view of the projective group and the algebraic theory of invariants was broadened by Lie, and later on by Elie Cartan who interpreted the *Erlanger Programm* better than Klein ever did.

On the other hand by stressing groups as a formal means of classifying geometries, Klein forgot about groups as a working tool *within* a geometry. This was the reason why school geometry was never influenced by the *Erlanger Programm*. Not unlike Klein's book *Elementary Mathematics from an Advanced Standpoint*, his *Erlanger Programm* hovered too high above school mathematics to be able to influence it.

Not until the most recent reforms did geometric groups enter school geometry. Geometric mappings were instrumental in the beginning of geometry and still played a part in the last Elements before Euclid. For some – probably philosophical – reasons, Euclid purged geometry of transformations. His surrogate method of chains of congruent triangles became a dogma which for centuries nobody dared to question. Take, for example, the theorem about the cube, that the endpoints B, D, E of the three edges through the vertex A define a plane orthogonal to the diagonal AG (see figure 4). The

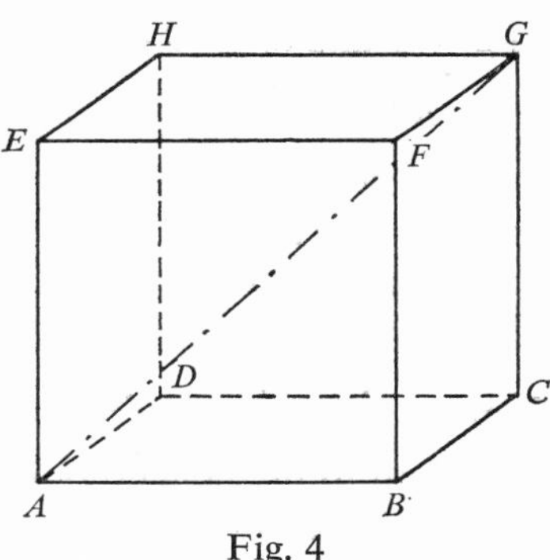

Fig. 4

traditional proof is a complicated one involving a chain of artificial congruent triangles. By means of mappings the proposition is obvious. The cube admits rotations about the diagonal AG; since these interchange B, D and E, they leave invariant the plane BDE, which consequently is orthogonal to the axis AG – a most natural and lucid proof compared with the artificiality and obscurity of the Euclidean method.

A few days ago I happened to check in several textbooks how they prove that the intersection of two spheres is a circle: it is still according to the Euclidean method of congruent triangles. After quite a few years of lipservice to the group idea, the natural way using rotations about the axis joining the centres is still barred.

Groups are now formally admitted at school but I doubt whether the spirit of group theory has also penetrated school mathematics.

After so many examples of what groups mean in mathematics and beyond, it is time to single out the factor common to all of them:

Groups are important because they arise from structures as systems of automorphisms of those structures.

What is a structure and what are its automorphisms?

Examples. Euclidean space with its straight lines and circles – the mappings carrying lines into lines and circles into circles preserve this structure; they are its automorphisms.

A salt crystal, that is, a lattice with Na and Cl atoms alternating in the lattice corners – translations, rotations and reflections carrying Na atoms into Na atoms and Cl atoms into Cl atoms preserve this structure.

The field of numbers $a+b\sqrt{2}$ with $a, b \in \mathbb{Q}$ with all its sum and product relations $\alpha+\beta = \gamma$ and $\alpha\beta = \delta$ – the mapping

$$a+b\sqrt{2} \to a-b\sqrt{2}$$

and the identity leave this structure invariant.

A structure S is a set M with a relation R or a system Φ of relations. An automorphism of S is a one-to-one mapping f of M onto itself such that for any relation R of Φ,

$$R(x, y, z, \ldots) \Leftrightarrow R(fx, fy, fz, \ldots),$$

in other words, f is required to preserve every relation of Φ, and its negation; the relation should be satisfied by $x, y, z, \ldots$ if and only if it is satisfied by $fx, fy, fz, \ldots$.

Let S be a structure and G the set of its automorphisms. Then obviously the identity belongs to G, if f belongs to G then so does its inverse, and if f and g both belong to G then so does their composition $f \circ g$.

The automorphisms of a structure form a group with composition as group operation.

If groups are introduced they are mostly automorphism groups of certain structures. The way of introduction guarantees that the thing defined *is* a group; rather than by an algorithmic verification, this result is obtained in one conceptual blow, and this is a great advantage. Preferring conceptual to algorithmic approaches is one of the most conspicuous features of what is really modern in modern mathematics.

If the problem is to define the group G, then of course the conceptual introduction of G as an automorphism group of a structure S means a shift of the problem. Now one has to make sure whether the defined group G is in fact the group one intended to define. But in order to check what is the automorphism group of the proposed structure, one can again proceed conceptually and according to certain paramount principles. I prefer to show how this is done by means of an example.

Let S be the square lattice in the plane (points with integral coordinates). What is the group G of congruencies leaving S invariant? The translation t_a by a vector a belongs to G, and so do the rotations d_j through $\frac{1}{2}\pi j$ ($j = 0, 1, 2, 3$) about the origin, and the reflection s in the horizontal axis. How do we find all elements of G?

Let f belong to G. Then f carries the origin onto some lattice point a; thus $f(0, 0) = a$. The translation t_a does likewise, so $f_1 = t_a^{-1}f$ fixes $(0, 0)$. Now f_1 maps $(1, 0)$ onto a lattice point that must be a neighbour of $(0, 0)$, that is onto one of $(1, 0)$, $(0, 1)$, $(-1, 0)$ or $(0, -1)$. The same is done by d_0, d_1, d_2 and d_3 respectively. So if j is properly chosen, $f_2 = d_j^{-1}f_1$ fixes both $(0, 0)$ and $(1, 0)$ and consequently the entire horizontal axis. Thus f_2 is the identity or the reflection s. Working back towards f, one gets

$$f = t_a d_j \quad \text{or} \quad t_a d_j s.$$

This is the most general element of G. The integral translations, the rotations through $\frac{1}{2}\pi j$ ($j = 0, 1, 2, 3$) and the reflection s together generate G.

Groups as taught, or proposed by curriculum designers to be taught, at school, are a different thing. They usually begin with the 2-cyclic or the Klein group. The group elements are exhibited by particular mappings of geometrical or other origin; the four corners of a square are mapped upon each other by a horizontal, a vertical, and a diagonal exchange (see figure 5). Or, the set of a red and a blue triangle and a red and a blue square is mapped onto itself by shape exchange, by colour exchange and by both shape and colour exchange. By explicit computations, it is checked that these three mappings together with the identity form a group. In itself this procedure is sound; what is wrong with it, is that by this prelude the stage is set for generalisations which are wrong – mathematically and pedagogically. And so it continues. New groups are introduced, of 6, 8, 12, 24 elements – all of them by summing up its elements, one by one, usually as mappings of different kinds, with the stress on constructing group tables. Verifying in this frame whether the construct is really a group, would be an endless task unless the number of elements is very small, but even in this case it is not good mathematics to trust algorithms better than insight.

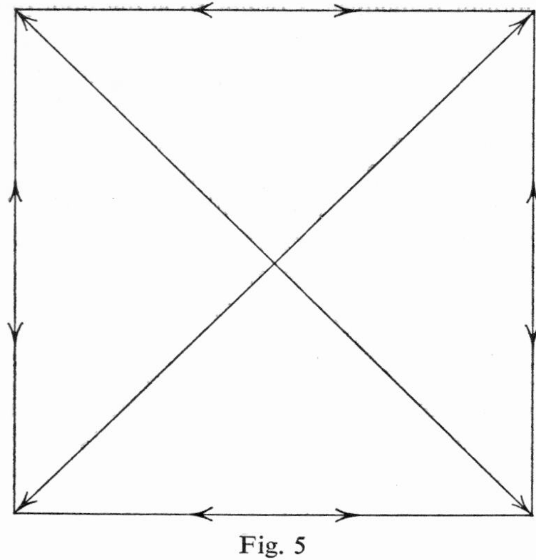

Fig. 5

So what happens is that the young child is led to believe that all systems with a binary operation are groups or at least that the teacher would never present ones that are not. Or the group property is suggested by sham arguments or by correct ones which cannot be

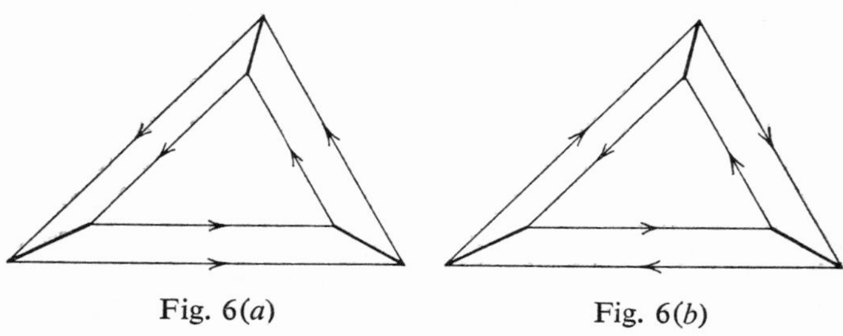

Fig. 6(*a*) Fig. 6(*b*)

grasped by the learner. Group diagrams may play an important part in this method. Consider the two group diagrams above (figures 6(*a*) and (*b*)). The six-point set of the corners is transformed by two mappings, one of order 2 indicated by the thick lines, which interchanges the endpoints of every thick line, and the other of order 3, indicated by the arrows, which maps the tail of each arrow on its head. These two mappings generate a group G of permutations of the six corners. It is now suggested that G is simply transitive on the set of the corners (that is, the element of G mapping one corner onto another, is unique), thus that G is a group of order six. This is indeed true. In the case of the first group diagram it is obvious. This evidence is falsely transferred to the second where it is not at all obvious. The correct way to deal with the second case is to consider it as a graph rather than as a group diagram and to find out its automorphism group. Group tables and group diagrams are devices to make groups explicit or to visualise them, but they are utterly inefficient tools to introduce groups or to prove that some system is a group.

It is true that in such school group theory things are finally put straight if one lands in the safe harbour of algorithmics. It is algorithmics in a finite set of at most twenty-six letters each of which means a constant group element. It is a particularly dangerous kind of algorithmics because if it comes early it may frustrate the interpretation of letters as symbols to denote variables – a dangerous tendency which is today very strongly felt in set theory at school.

Are there valid arguments to teach a school group theory, different from the genuine one? I would doubt it.

According to a famous 'hypothesis' of Jerome Bruner's

> 'every subject can be taught effectively and in an intellectually honest form to any child at any stage of development'.[1]

In fact Bruner at this place was citing Bärbel Inhelder who, however, cautiously had added a proviso:

> 'provided they are divorced from their mathematical expression and studied through material that the child can handle himself'.

There are sounder arguments for teaching some subject matter than our ability to do so. But even if this argument is accepted in teaching mathematics, we must not at the same instant invalidate it by a proviso that requires transforming a mathematical (teaching) subject into non-mathematics.

We have to be careful and honest if we want to adapt some piece of high mathematics to a lower level. Simplifying is a good thing but wrong elementarisations are a danger, and so is imitating superficial features while destroying the great ideas of some mathematical theory. If children are taught groups they are entitled to learn genuine group theory rather than a childish version. In the past, mathematics

[1] Bruner, J., *The Process of Education*, Harvard University Press, Cambridge, Mass., 1960, p. 33.

has seriously suffered under the falsifying tendencies in adaptations of mathematical subject matter to school level. Let us be more cautious in the future. Honesty is a cardinal virtue in education. Nothing is lost if some subject matter cannot be taught prematurely and much is gained if it can in an honest way.

I.O.W.O.,
Tiberdreef, 4,
Utrecht,
Holland.

Nature, man and mathematics

David Hawkins

Several years ago, when I had brought home a new microscope designed for children's use, we had opportunity to observe the first recognition, by a five-year-old, of the world of size and scale. Or perhaps it was not the first, beginnings are hard to catch; and this fortunate young girl was already deeply involved with fragments of that world, at least – with dolls and furniture to scale, with pictures and maps of her own and others' drafting, and much else besides. But the *world* of size and scale is something else again, it is a recapitulation and a surmise; a glimpse of generality and of closure. At that young age the eyepiece of a microscope is first a shiny object and then, with luck, a sort of peep-show or television screen in miniature. At any rate we did what we all three, Christa, my wife, and I, called 'looking at' various objects. Some, which Christa brought for this new occupation, were ten or fifty times too big to fit between object and stage, and one saw a young child's perceptual unreadiness to make use of what might be called the transitivity of congruences.

But one evening Christa brought to the microscope a tiny bit of lint from the floor. Here for the first time there seemed to be recognition, the lint was seen as lint though transformed a hundred-fold in scale. But the next day confirmation came in full measure, pressed down and running over. Our young friend came trotting from our bedroom carrying a small souvenir of London, a red Corgi double-decker bus. Halfway to the microscope she hesitated, then smiled at us a rueful smile. Touching the outside steps with her finger, she said, 'Wouldn't it be nice if there were little people going up and down?'

It was not a statement one could call theorematic in the usual sense, but it took us suddenly to the world of Leeuwenhoek and Robert Hooke, of the life cycle of the flea, and of Jonathan Swift and Voltaire. In all previous history we find no evidence of such liberation of imagination and even today it is known only to some happy few.

In our work with children and teachers you and we have had many opportunities to observe how poorly developed, in most humans today, are the intuitions of variation and invariance to scale. I suppose this is because we and the things around us are often undergoing translations and rotations, but very seldom shrink or expand. Confronted with the question whether a jar full of pebbles or a jar full of sand will absorb more water, even most adults are in the kind of trouble which Piaget has made famous concerning children's perception of invariance in number, area, and volume. This one concerns invariance to scale, one of numerous topics which should be proposed for similar investigation.

E. T. Bell once observed that while we might admire the ingenuity which led historically to more and more accurate approximations of pi, the greatest admiration should go to that unknown genius who first gave this ratio meaning by recognising that it was a pure number, invariant to scale.

Lacking well-consolidated intuitions which could bring alive the space-groups of transformations, we also seem to lack the conceptual means for getting to a zeroth approximation understanding of natural phenomena on the scale of the very large, the very small, and the very complex. Conversely, our failure to assign dignity to children's exploration of this world of scale robs us of a powerful resource in the teaching of mathematics.

I thought to begin this talk with the example of scale transformations because they are, perhaps out of the whole of mathematics, among the most simple and most illuminating in their relevance to the diversity and nature of the material universe, and to the habits of thought with which mathematical education sometimes is and more often ought to be concerned.

In the United States at least one finds that this glorious topic of size and scale comes first into students' ken only when they are struggling with the equations of a physics text. My own first-year university students have almost uniformly been amazed to discover that a two-centimetre cube has four times the surface area and eight times the mass of a one-centimetre cube, a discovery I have often shamed them into with a gift of sugar-cubes. And even this discovery left them unprepared for the argument that single cells cannot in general be as big as bird's eggs or Lilliputians as small as mice. Dimensional relations in general are black magic to most students, mainly I think because such topics have never been considered to be proper mathematics – despite Hassler Whitney's elegant demonstration of the formal simplicity of dimensional numbers. But even if such topics had been woven into the earlier curriculum they would almost certainly, I fear, have been effectively divorced from the simple empirical and practical sources of their appeal and power. Yet (as I shall argue) such matters as dimensional analysis, whether at the level of five-year-old Christa or at the level of theoretical physics, are very nearly ideal examples of mathematical art.

From such examples one is led toward two questions which I wish to raise in this paper. One concerns the teaching of mathematics. The second, intimately connected with the first at a philosophical level, concerns the nature of mathematics itself.

The first question has to do with the range and repertoire of a teacher who knows success in leading children into the mathematical domain. If such teachers are rare they are all the more worthy of support and study if we hope to make them less rare. Let me therefore say a little more of what is involved in their art.

There are two aspects of this art which are inseparably connected, and this connection leads me from the consideration of teaching to the nature of mathematics as a teacher must grasp it. It commits me, I find, to the view that such a rare teacher has within his grasp a privileged source of information concerning the nature of mathematics. I think this view might scornfully be rejected in some circles. Before the present audience I count at least on a generous initial reception, not least because of the presence of Professor Pólya, who has done so much to illuminate the nature of mathematical art.

The working perspective of a teacher allows him – though unfortunately it does not always compel him – to make many observations of those acquisitions and transitions in intellectual development upon which the growth of mathematical knowledge depends. But such a teacher is of course not only an observer, he would indeed be less of an observer if he were not also a participant; one who, because of the way he shares in and contributes to that development, can earn the privilege of insight into its details and pathways. The ideal work of a good teacher has then these two aspects inseparably combined, that of diagnosis and that of providing in accordance with the indications of his diagnosis. As a diagnostician the teacher is trying to map into his own the momentary state and trajectory of another mind and then, as provisioner, to enhance (not to replace) the resources of that mind from his own store of knowledge and skill.

It is clear to all of us, I think, that teachers who approximate this ideal are rare indeed. We do not educate most of our teachers very relevantly to such a way of teaching, and we hamper their potential fluency of performance in a hundred ways, not least the incredible burden of managing active children in too large numbers and in too sterile surroundings. So my ideal teacher is approximated only as we get out to the tail of the distribution of teaching opportunities and teaching styles which prevail today. Circumstances which allow and encourage good teaching are rare, though we can make them less so. At any rate the teacher I speak of is a presupposition of my argument and does exist, though rarely. He is, so to say, a kind of existence theorem.

For such a teacher a limiting condition in mapping a child's thought into his own is, of course, the amplitude of his *own* grasp of those relationships in which the child is involved. His mathematical domain must be ample enough, or amplifiable enough, to match the range of a child's wonder and curiosity, his operational skills, his unexpected ways of gaining insight. David Page once remarked that when children are seriously attentive they seldom give wrong answers, but they often answer a question different from the one we think we are asking. A teacher–diagnostician must map a child's question as much as his answer, neither alone will define the trajectory; and he must be prepared to anticipate something of what the child may encounter further along that path.

It is obvious, I think, that in many respects a teacher's grasp of subject-matter must include far more than what we conventionally call mathematics. It must include what a child sees, handles, plays with; miniatures, for example, such as cars, lorries, bricks, dolls and dolls houses; more generally the great and the small. It must include finished materials and raw, sand and water and clay as well as batteries and wire and globes. It should include rocks, plants and animals, mirrors and crystals. It should include all those things which in serious play with them contribute to children's grasp of orderings, of number and measure, of pattern and structure.

It goes without saying, of course, that mathematics as conventionally understood may include, on the other hand, a great deal which a teacher of children need not have mastered. Otherwise we would ask the impossible. But a teacher of children, of the kind I postulate, must be a mathematician, what I would call an *elementary* mathematician, one who can at least sometimes sense when a child's interests and proposals – what I have called his trajectory – are taking him near to mathematically sacred ground. There is a delightful report of Edith Biggs concerning a ten-year-old who noticed and became intrigued by the fact that in the graph he had made of area against linear dimension, the curve was *locally* a straight line. That child then was supported in extensive investigations along what one can only call the trajectory of Isaac Newton. A teacher who lacked any feeling for the calculus would almost certainly have failed him. In the same way one has seen children's curiosity about the individual properties of numbers leading straight toward the great problems of number theory, but likely to miss them without a teacher's recognition and support.

If a teacher's grasp of subject-matter must extend beyond the conventional image of mathematics, we must then face the question of definition in a new form – what is at stake is not the nature of the end-product usually *called* mathematics, but of that whole domain in which mathematical ideas and procedures germinate, sprout and take root, *and* in the end produce the visible upper branching, leafing and flowering which all we here so value, and which wither when uprooted.

In this way I find myself compelled to extend the domain of mathematics so that it will provide room, provide closure, for all the mapping operations of a teacher. Mathematics so considered will obviously overlap with other parts or aspects of the curriculum. A child tracing the flow of coloured water through a transparent siphon is not thereby being a mathematician, or physicist, or town engineer, nor simply delighting in the intuition of colour and motion. What he is being is a matter of his momentary trajectory of learning. A good teacher will diagnose the child's involvement as related potentially to all of these or other important educational concerns, but will not identify it as any of these too soon or too simply. In that sense the curricular divisions overlap in all the childhood praxis of learning, as they do in the practical existence of society. The child has not yet chosen a career – except in passing.

So by closure of the mathematical domain I mean not to partition mathematics off from other educational concerns, on the contrary I mean to define the mathematical domain in such a way that it does not *exclude* any situation of learning *merely* on the ground that the latter might also be described under social or scientific or aesthetic categories. I use the mathematical term 'closure' as particularly apt – recognising that as mathematicians use the word, it implies removing barriers, not building them. Ideally any concrete involvement of children, any relationship with the world around them in which they are caught up, will link up with mathematics among other things and in that sense is part of its extended domain.

The extension I propose can be justified, I think, in two ways. The first is that persons called teachers are particularly susceptible to intimidation by persons called mathematicians. Teachers often feel constrained by the opinions of the higher sect, constrained in particular to narrow their own views and their own practice to conform to such opinions, rather than to explore more widely beyond the implied barriers. A deliberate effort to extend the domain of mathematics is inseparable, I believe, from any practical effort directed toward the deepening and enrichment of mathematics teaching. We must aim to convert the higher sect.

We have recently enjoyed a small report of an American teacher, Dudley Hunt, who involved a group of ten-year-olds in an extensive project around the partitioning of regular hexagons. Her original aim was to provide a matrix for experience in the addition of fractions, but as the project ramified, one might equally have described it as a study of the geometry of the hexagon, of symmetry, or of decorative design. This teacher happens to be a mathematician herself and does not need the approval of the higher sect, and indeed many individual mathematicians would be delighted by such work, even though their own 'official' view of their subject-matter, translated in terms of texts and syllabuses and work-books throughout the world, would imply disparagement of some part of it occurring, so to speak, in the wrong part of the syllabus. In my country the only respectable part, I fear, would be those boring, unmotivated work-book pages of symbolic problems, $\frac{1}{3}+\frac{1}{2} = \square$.

It is for such reasons we must speak about the nature of mathematics itself – we will not otherwise give teachers the licence and support they deserve in teaching mathematics, and we will not see the work of serious adult mathematics in its deep inner connections with the world of childhood.

The second justification is therefore that the proposed enlargement gives us the possibility of a view of the nature of mathematics which, regardless of pedagogical motives or implications, may be worth pursuing for its own sake.

In speaking of an extension of the mathematical domain to provide a kind of closure for the mapping of the potential range of children's mathematical learning I am appealing, of course, to a heuristic principle which has been important in the history of mathematics. I shall call it the Principle of the Extended Domain. It is based upon the fact that a problem can arise *within* a domain which nevertheless proves too restrictive to allow an adequate solution of that problem. Indeed I think this principle lies very close to the heart of what might be called the mathematical style, to the secret of mathematics.

The most familiar major historical example of a successful application of this principle is, I suppose, the development of the number system, which only in the complex domain gives full closure to all the elementary operations of arithmetic. In his essay on *The Essence of Mathematics* Charles Saunders Peirce uses chess as a sort of counter-example. 'Chess is mathematics, after a fashion; but owing to the exceptions which everywhere confront the mathematician in this field – such as the limits of the board; the single steps of king, knight and pawn; the peculiar mode of capture by pawns; castling – there results a mathematics whose wings are clipped, which can only run along the ground.' G. H. Hardy, in his *Apology*, uses the example of chess also, as a kind of mathematics which he says is not *serious*; he says of it that its problems cannot be generalised in such a way that their solution links them significantly with the rest of mathematics.

Serious mathematics then must be able, as Peirce says, to fly. And it can fly only as it can generalise. Hence, he says, 'a mathematician often finds what a chess-player might call a gambit to his advantage; exchanging a smaller problem that involves exceptions for a larger one free from them.' That is, he extends the domain. It is interesting in connection with this counterexample of Peirce and Hardy, to consider the rather major gambit later engineered by John von Neumann in the theory of games, by which chess becomes only an example of the most elementary form of game. The mathematical theory of games flies *so* high it can hardly distinguish chess from noughts and crosses.

But the use I wish to make here of the principle of the extended domain is a different one. What I wish to urge is an extension of the domain of mathematics itself, as usually conceived, so that mathematics in the extended domain will provide something like logical closure to the diagnostic mapping and resultant planning of a teacher. I shall argue that this extension, although motivated by a primary concern for learning and teaching, is at the same time entirely consonant with the traditions of Archimedes, Newton, and Gauss. It is dissonant, I think, with dominant pedagogical traditions of the past and present.

In proposing to extend the domain of what we call mathematics and therefore of what teachers conceive their mathematical commitments to be, I have no wish to blur the disciplinary distinctions. Indeed, the challenge is to widen the domain of mathematics with analytical care. We want to make its essence more intelligible, not to dissolve it.

Let me be explicit. The domain is to be consciously expanded to include all those junctures in the lives of children, in their working contact with the great world of nature and of human society, out of which mathematics in the usual restricted sense can be seen to evolve. Only so will educational closure be possible. But it now becomes a question as to how the mathematical treatment of this shared domain can be characterised – what its essence or genius is, what are the invariants across this enlarged domain, of aim and style. Clearly there will be some sacrifices from the point of view of one confined to the restricted domain. Explicitness of symbolic definition and of generality will not be among the invariants, nor will formal argument. Eight- or ten-year-olds working with the Archimedean balance will sometimes come to isolate those moves, those operations, which maintain the state of balance, sorting variables and gradually isolating the underlying relations which characterise the balance. Their discourse will be mostly limited to the concrete context, they will not think to offer formal statements. Their investigation is surely not deductive, but highly empirical. As children continue this process of sorting and isolating, as they come closer to a grasp of regularity and symmetry, they move toward a more analytical and deductive style. Where a teacher can support and provide, can dignify with pertinent curiosity, children will sometimes reach the law of moments empirically, and less easily a simpler fact underlying the famous theorem of Archimedes: the invariance of balance to any pairwise symmetrical displacement of equal weights – the law of the equal-arm balance.

Let us look at these two results, not crammed down children's throats, but supposing each to be achieved with some inner illumination: the law of moments and the law of symmetry. Logically, when put in a proper formal context, these are equivalent, if one supplies a premise which Archimedes failed to state, the conservation of weight. But they are not equivalent in heuristic value. The law of moments for the unequal-arm balance is a part of empirical science, and its formulating could be called 'applied mathematics' if we assumed that the algebra were already available for application. The symmetry principle is on a different footing; its use in characterising the invariance of balance is not applied mathematics; on the contrary it *is* mathematics. It is also theoretical physics, to be sure, but I warned that the extension of mathematics would produce overlap, if not require it. First of all the second formulation, that of symmetry, is simpler and deeper than the law of moments. It is a type of formulation which, in Hardy's term, has more 'seriousness' than the law of moments, useful as this is in many other contexts. It is an example, perhaps the simplest one, of the whole family of logical tools whose nature was first discussed by Leibniz, who related it directly with the principle of causality, of sufficient reason. If we assume that nothing else matters but mass and length of arm, then with equal masses and equal arms, any argument that the left side would descend is *eo ipso* applicable to the right side, and all such arguments will cancel each other by contradiction. It is a deep thing that this symmetry is still sufficient, though hidden, to define the unequal-arm balance, that the special case implies the general one. One should add in passing that with an unstable balance, the symmetry argument gives us equal *probability* for the two possibilities – an example of what Bernoulli called the principle of *non*-sufficient reason. Modern theoretical physics would be unthinkable without such arguments.

But to return to the ten-year-old: much of this is still remote from him, far along on his current trajectory. But even within his own reach a symmetry-argument has seriousness, it relates to his growing manifold of perceptions and intuitions of symmetry and of choice. It provides him with a way of thinking which, though it will not automatically or easily transfer to different situations, will be available as an analogy. It will be a potential cross-link in his intellectual file, when he has worked out what a teacher can recognise as similar patterns of thought in other situations.

That is my reason for dwelling on this example from Archimedes. The symmetry formulation of the balance provides a clear-cut example of something very close to the essence of mathematics – closer than the axiomatic method, closer than the ideal of deductive rigour – and which holds up, I think, across its extended domain. Archimedes showed us something of its power in his argument from the special case of the equal-arm balance to the general case of the unequal-arm balance. And he deepened the demonstration by his use of the balance in those extraordinary extensions of plane and solid geometry which bear his name.

In the essay I referred to before, Charles Peirce offers a definition of mathematics which is helpful, namely 'the study of what is true of hypothetical states of things'. It is not clear to me that this definition as it stands is adequate to my extended domain. In any case it seems also too broad. As a definition it could well apply to the novel, for example, which invents hypothetical states of things and tries to discern what is true of them. Since the nature of the novel is at least as problematic as that of mathematics, it may be well to restrict the definition, while bearing in mind a genuine family resemblance.

Peirce does in fact narrow his definition. Mathematical investigations are distinguished, he says, by resort to what, following Immanuel Kant, he calls a *schema.* A schema is a kind of artifact or model constructed to satisfy the conditions of a hypothesis, about which we then notice that it has thus and such additional properties not obviously entailed by the hypothesis. The kind of schema Peirce has in mind is the use of drawing and auxiliary construction in synthetic geometry. Though the hypothesis may be universal and abstract, the schema which fits it is particular and concrete, produced by the hand and observed by the eye. In the absence of such motor-perceptual transformation no amount of sheer reflection about the hypothesis will produce a mathematical investigation or argument. If you make a triangle out of rigid rods and rotate one of them slightly about some point, you can directly *see* that the sum of angles remains unchanged. Such action and observations are intrinsic to the mathematical style, which thus never loses touch with what Piaget has called the concrete operational *étape* of thought. The symmetry principle applied to the unequal-arm balance is another kind of example. We establish the general case of balance by starting with all mass at the centre and then, by using only symmetrical displacements, produce any arbitrary balance configuration in the general case.

I should like to give two more examples of schematisation at a relatively adult level before proceeding further. Martin Gardiner recently reported the following story of a reader's reflections about a tin of beer, American style. About to put it down at a picnic on uneven ground, the thought occurred to him that if he drank some beer first it would be less likely to tip over. On further reflection he observed that if he were to drink all the beer the centre of gravity would be back up to the centre of the tin. *Ergo* there is a minimum, a liquid level of maximum stability. Now, of course, any mathematician or physicist immediately thinks of expressing the combined centre of gravity of the tin and its contents in terms of the variable amount of liquid, then taking the derivative and finding the point where that derivative vanishes. But the author of this tale thought of another way of finding the answer, which I leave to you, with only a hint that your non-standard solution would delight the heart of Archimedes, who had not yet been taught the calculus. All I need say about this example is that once again the schema of balance is brought into view. In solving the problem by either means one performs an act of abstraction, of cutting away all features of the realistic problem except those that fit the schema provided by the unequal-arm balance – cutting to reveal the hidden symmetry. This is the kind of step which Peirce saw as so characteristically mathematical.

But the first solution is again after all – once one sees it correctly – a standard bit of applied mathematics. The non-calculus solution is more interesting in terms of my general thesis, as I think you will agree when you see that solution.

My last example is of a different kind, but I think it also illustrates the significance of Peirce's thesis. It also comes from chess. There is a stop-rule in chess which says that a threatened king may not simply move back and forth between two squares. In a typically mathematical spirit G. A. Hedlund and Marsden Morse proposed and solved a slightly more general problem. Suppose a king were confined to three adjacent squares *a*, *b*, *c*, from any of which he could move to either of the others. It is assumed that all of these moves would avoid checkmate. Clearly the defensive player could avoid such a pattern as *abab*, which would save him from the usual stop-rule. Morse now proposes a more general rule, namely that the game ends if the player directly repeats *any* sequence of moves – such as *abab*, *abcabc*, *abcacb-abcacb*; and so on. The question arises whether under this rule he can still play an unending game. I do not give Morse's affirmative solution but a different and more special one which Walter Mientka and I happened to find, and of which I therefore know the genesis. Mathematicians seldom let us in on such secrets. In an unending sequence of three letters one must avoid all direct repetitions, double blocks of any length, and those very long blocks get troublesome. It is easy to avoid direct repetitions of pairs or triples, but the farther one goes the longer become the blocks one has to avoid repeating. As with testing for prime numbers, the testing keeps increasing in difficulty.

Now at this point we would all recognise, I think, that a step is needed which does not follow from the hypothesis by any amount of reasoning of the kind outlined in logic texts and it is, somehow, a uniquely mathematical step. The step is, I shall say, a search for a schema. Because one does not find a 'standard method' the problem cannot be called applied mathematics. One does not even know in advance whether this might turn out to be serious mathematics in Hardy's sense. A search for analogies, therefore, is the next step. I happened to find one in the procedure of substitution, as when one replaces a simple element by a complex one, each element in a pattern by a pattern of elements, a noun by a noun clause, a variable by a function. That was my schema. If one replaced each *letter* in a block by a corresponding *block* of letters, each block guaranteed to be repetition-free, one might then have a much longer block which was equally impeccable. The answer is: almost, but not quite. I shall not go on with the details, but with suitably chosen blocks A, B, C the method does work, and the substitution can be iterated endlessly, producing an infinite sequence without repetitions. In Peirce's language, it flies. I still do not know that this is very serious mathematics, although there are many unsolved problems about such sequences and they link up in possibly interesting ways with other parts of number theory. The point of the illustration is that new mathematics – new to a child, new to an amateur such as myself, or new to a professional mathematician – takes off and flies through a successful search for schemata available in one's repertoire, for patterns of construction which one has previously mastered, which *may* provide guidance in building a new variant suited to new situations encountered in nature or in mathematics.

As this process is successful it served also to enrich the repertoire, the store of useful schemata. As is true of all knowledge, the growth of mathematics lies always in some *use* of mathematics – not primarily in providing premises for an argument, but in providing schemata for the guidance of thought.

When we search in our repertoire we sometimes find what we call an algorithm, a standard schema which fits the conditions of a new problem, and leads directly to its solution. In such cases we can speak of applied mathematics, whether the problem is one of everyday life, of science, or within mathematics itself. The implication of the term 'applied mathematics' is often slightly pejorative. You can imagine the other kind of mathematician, called 'pure', offering his discipline for use but not – as mathematician – expecting to learn anything new in the process. *Noblesse oblige.* But as I have suggested, this case of the standard schema shades over into the schema by analogy, where no standard method is available but where those that are available *suggest* ways of looking at a problem which may make it at least partially tractable. This may still if you wish be called applied mathematics but whenever such a problem is solved it does, in principle, add new mathematics to the general repertoire. Finally, there are cases where problems cannot be brought under existing schemas, and where even the power of analogy fails. In such cases we resort to direct induction, to numerical examples, or to various other related, but easier, investigations; and very often the problem waits. If it is a serious problem it waits on a special shelf of fame, such as the list of Hilbert's problems. Whichever case we consider, the general conclusion is clear – that in a proper sense all mathematics grows out of the use of previously schematised knowledge which is itself explicitly or potentially mathematical – in that sense *all* mathematics is 'applied mathematics'.

I have at least sketched the case I wish to make concerning the essence of mathematics. There is a sort of corollary, however, which I would like to develop. Mathematics has evolved historically into a large and richly interconnected system which is not only a mirror of the world of nature but which has many internal mirrors – morphisms of one kind or another – which sometimes generate, in turn, new mirrors for the world of nature, new analogies of structure, new schemata. But running pervasively through this whole system there is a common implicit style which in general human terms is both a strength and a limitation. When Peirce talks about mathematics which can fly, this metaphor refers, I believe, to the generalising power implicit in the structure of the domain, a power which depends essentially upon a certain monotony, a certain iterative character, both in its objects and in its perceptions and arguments. The number system evolves from such monotony, though each step generates novelties which are in turn a challenge to new investigations. The method of Archimedes, like early calculus, depends upon those results of infinite iteration, called infinitesimals, which the great of the eighteenth century used fluently, which physicists have in fact perversely used all along, and which formal logic has recently, after long doubt, declared absolutely rigorous.

From Archimedes to the recent past the assertion that the method of infinitesimals is not rigorous, is now known to be a non-rigorous assertion, indeed a false one! I should mention again the wide sweep and great power of the schema of iterated substitution revealed, for example, in logic, in geometry, in the statistical theory of branching processes, or in the elegant and very 'serious' theorem of Kolmogorov, that a function of many variables can always be expressed by composition from functions of two variables only. This schema, with its imagery of branching trees, has many delightful uses within the range of children's arithmetical explorations – although it seems to find no place within the official repertoire, curriculum, or racecourse.

The iterative or monotonous character of mathematics, so deeply embedded in the nature of its domains and so profoundly exploited in its style of thought, is often noticed by outsiders and given as a reason for a certain repugnance by persons whose special cultivation lies in other fields. Words like 'mechanical' and 'abstract' enter in. Consider for contrast the visual pattern of a painting such as Gauguin's *Maternité* or the thematic patterns of Mozart's Second Horn Concerto or of Beethoven's Eroica. Structure there is, even structure which is repetitive, iterative; but the interesting part typically connects with just that deviation from simple-minded regularity, just that surprising use of ambiguity which mathematics will avoid. Though a computer can compose music which is recognisably Mozartian, it does not compose Mozart which is musically interesting. It does not know when to depart from an algorithm.

So with a great novel, such as *The Magic Mountain*, *The Red and the Black*, *Crime and Punishment*, there is a formal structure but it is never maintained at the expense of those unique non-recurrent or even discordant details which win our trust and convey to us the higher levels of order and significance which lesser works fail to capture. Picasso's Don Quixote presupposes a precision of anatomical knowledge, yet the anatomist despairs of him. To be *that* kind of mirror of the world, a different kind of structure and order is necessary, one which stays far longer in the domain of concrete intuition and which requires a very different, though *not* incompatible, sort of cultivation of education from the mathematical.

Yet structure is never absent, even (at some level) a kind of structure which can be abstracted and schematised. Whereas random music, like Borges' Library of Babylon – to which I shall return – can produce no surprises. Departure from regularity presupposes regularity, and significant irregularity implies order on a higher level. So when we are working with young children we should not be surprised that they wear what may seem to be seven-league boots, and that the cross-connections they can make may go easily from mathematics to science or to decorative or dynamic art. My idealised teacher will not sorrow, but rather rejoice, when the dissection of hexagons leads to crochet patterns or visual fantasy, or when Fibonacci numbers lead to a new interest in rabbits or the growth of trees, or *vice versa*. From the time of Froebel and Montessori to that of Cuisenaire and Dienes, too much of our move toward the mathematics of the concrete, invaluable as that has been, has had such deviant possibilities puritanically designed out of it.

I wish now to return to the perspective of a teacher of children, and consider the extent to which my case holds up. My argument is one which seeks to make it plausible, when mathematics is extended in meaning to include the roots as well as the branch and the flower, that mathematical subject matter is potentially the whole of experience. Its differentiating mark is not primarily one of subject matter, but of style. This style is not defined by reference to the deductive as opposed to the empirical, by the formal as opposed to the concrete, by the axiomatic as opposed to the intuitive, but rather by a characteristic more generic than these, which I have called, following Peirce, schematisation. But let me first reassure you that I intend no disparagement of these admirable, but secondary, stylistic features. I am only saying that as one looks at mathematics in its extended domain, these features are *not* invariant across that domain. As one looks more deeply to the roots one sees these nice distinctions tending to dissolve. They characterise branches of mathematics, or leaves and flowers, but not the whole of it; they characterise these products as finished products. In the process of being born, whether among children or among amateurs or professionals, no mathematics is yet rigorous, or fully deductive, or axiomatic; but its style *is* that of schematisation. In the process of being born, mathematics is a searching out and delineation of structure, guided by those analogies of structure which have already been consolidated within the minds of the searchers. Its final format is intended to convince, but that is only one stable product of mathematicising, not its essence.

I believe that I owe here a further debt to all the modern efforts which have gone into the process of differentiating between mathematics and empirical science. As a young philosopher I was raised up surrounded by the belief of Frege and Russell and the Viennese positivists that all of mathematics is somehow a vast tautology, thus sharply and finally distinguished, and pedagogically separable, from empirical science. Although, they said, our natural language is full of ambiguities and confusions, there is possible a rational reconstruction of that language (we were assured) which will make clear just where the dividing line occurs, and thus rid us of the besetting sin of supposing that mathematical truth owes anything to the nature of the world we live in. This philosophical movement rode partly on great new developments in mathematics going back to Descartes' invention of analytic geometry, to the invention of non-Euclidean geometries, and to the foundations of arithmetic initiated by Peano and Frege. These discoveries revealed the fact that at least major parts of mathematics, and presumably all of it, could be faithfully mirrored within the domain of arithmetic, while arithmetic itself could be reduced to, or mirrored within, a suitably clarified and formalised system of pure logic. Not only was this true of traditional mathematics, but it proved true also of those parts of empirical science which had been sufficiently developed – rational mechanics, for example, the theory of elasticity, or more recently (as in the work of Ulam and Kolmogorov) the theory of probability, long suspect, like the calculus, as to its precise mathematical status.

By such developments, it was hoped, the contribution of rational analysis could be sharply differentiated from all questions of empirical truth involved in the description of nature. What was somehow overlooked or treated arrogantly was the fact that these powerful and impressive mathematical structures had been evolved through constant intercourse with the domains of science, practical life, and engineering. It was also overlooked that they could be *re*applied in those domains only by *informal* rules of interpretation which carried within them all the philosophically interesting problems which had supposedly been banished by the new programme.

What tended to be overlooked also was the fact that this whole development failed in one crucial way to explain the specific content and form of existing mathematics. If we define mathematics merely as a system of propositions organised according to the axiomatic method and the rules of deduction, this is rather like defining a book as consisting merely of a few hundred pages of printed marks; like defining a sculpture merely as any form carved out of stone or cast in metal. Jorge Luis Borges' fantasy, to which I referred before, is about a library which turns out to be the library of all possible books. The inhabitants of this library spend their lives in a search for meaning among its volumes. A book is defined here as – merely – any 400-page sequence of letters (and spaces) from the alphabet. If you calculate the number of books in Borges' library it turns out to be about two to the power 2^{20}. My students and I once estimated the number of the subset of such volumes which consist of recognised words organised grammatically into sentences, and this vastly reduced library, at a few volumes per kilogram, was still incomparably more massive than the known physical universe. I do not quite know how to estimate the number of distinct, self-consistent, formalised axiom sets of not unreasonable complexity, but I would guess it is at least large enough to use up a galaxy or two at the modest rate of 2^{48} kilograms/galaxy of printed paper.

We are in no different position with respect to sculpture or music or any other art. In one way we are in a worse position with respect to the development of mathematics: these axiom sets, though stated in a few pages, will entail an infinity of theorems from which we can in fact deduce only some selected finite number.

The view that mathematics is somehow only a vast tautology, that truth in mathematics has no relation to the order and connection of nature, is thus a misinterpretation of its schematic iterative style. If deductive formulation is necessary to its final formal product, this criterion alone does not enable us to distinguish between deductive sense and deductive nonsense. Defenders of the philosophy of Frege admit this criticism, indirectly, but by adding another criticism, one embedded in a doctrine of art for art's sake. From among the infinity of potential mathematical structures one picks for development only those which are aesthetically pleasing. Mathematics is, so to say, another genre of art, its products free creations of what is somewhat eulogistically called the human mind. No art is free except within the bounds of some discipline; the discipline of mathematics is the deductive mode. But otherwise – the argument goes – it is free. This view has been held by some first-rate mathematicians, notably by Hardy, just as the corresponding view in painting or literature has been held by some first-rate artists. The work of the mathematician may, on such a view, throw light on the world of man and nature, as if by chance. If so, again, *noblesse oblige*. T. S. Eliot produced, as an example of what might engross an artist fully, while lacking all practical utility or moral relevance, the following remarkable image – an eggshell on an altar. Unkind critics might seek to match this from some corners of contemporary mathematics. Surely, Hardy did not go so far as Eliot. His criterion of seriousness precluded that.

I think, however, that we can take one important lesson from this view. Whatever else it may be – and I have argued for much else – mathematics as my ideal teacher sees and lives it is unthinkable except as a kind of disciplined art. It is unsuccessful in the teaching or learning of it without that interplay of aesthetic tension and release involved in all creative activity, and which rewards all the intervening discipline which creativeness requires.

What is wrong with the doctrine of *art pour l'art* is that it makes a mystery of any kind of discipline at all. The essential art of mathematics, if I am right, is that of investigating hypothetical states of things through the discipline of schematisation.

But I have only illustrated this Peircean doctrine, not developed it in detail. In particular I have not discussed the epistemological and historical origins, or the systematics of those basic mathematical structures we know and seek to regenerate in our teaching. Fortunately the subject is very much alive today, thanks in large measure to the work of Professor Piaget. In closing I can only comment on certain aspects of that work. From my own point of view, at least, Professor Piaget has brought about a long-overdue revitalisation of the philosophical framework of Immanuel Kant, who developed the first coherent account of knowledge as the product of a self-regulating synthetic activity.

With respect to the proto-deducting style of mathematical thinking, Professor Piaget has made an important theoretical argument which is thoroughly Kantian in spirit, though grounded also in his own empirical studies of intellectual development. This argument concerns the origin and nature of our sense of logical entailment or necessity. Like Kant (and Hume), Piaget argues that contingent generalisations derived from factual observation can never, of themselves, give rise to this idea of necessity.

This sense of necessity is first operative, Piaget argues, in the habitual use of those schemata by which infants and children develop, with increasing competence, their ability to control and transform their material surroundings by systematic means. In still later intellectual development the distinction between the necessary and the contingent gains recognition by a kind of reflective abstraction; our knowledge can be traced partly to perception and partly to a growing awareness of our own active transformation of that experience into a stable and organised system of intellectual resources. Thus, for example, the space-group of translations and rotations (as Kant also long ago suggested) is developed first through the empirical fact that these are reversible operations whereas other changes, those which we describe only temporally, are not. It is not our direct perception of spatial properties which gives rise to our idea of space, but our reflection upon the operational or manipulatory schema which we have been busy developing since infancy at a motor-sensory level. In the same way our schema for counting and number evolves not from a direct perception of different degrees of numerosity, but from more primitive operations of matching and sequencing. In both cases a process of reflective abstraction, appearing in the fullness of time and experience and education, raises these schemata from the level of use to the level of *objects* for conscious scrutiny and analysis. When we have thus begun to be aware of what are in fact our own operational commitments, we find that they, so to speak, lead a life of their own; the number system or the nexus of geometrical relations as it were imposes its will on us, we are not free to imagine that there is a largest number, that seven has two immediate successors, or that there are spatially unconnected localities. But unlike Kant and Kant's predecessor Hume, Piaget has taken seriously the complex developmental nature of these ideas, and has brought it home to us naïve adults that our obvious necessities of thought are often disconcertingly absent in the thinking of young children, who typically make sense of their world in ways we have abandoned and can retrieve only with great imaginative effort. When I was speaking of a teacher's capacity to map the trajectories of children's thinking, I was referring in part to these way-stations of logical thought, which along with other childish things we have long since, most of us, put aside.

With all due respect to the theoretical perspectives and empirical studies of Piaget, I wish to emphasise what Piaget himself has often asserted, that this developmental framework is not directly relevant or adequate to the practical and theoretical perspective of a teacher. In particular there is a certain danger in the unimaginative use of Piagetian interviews to check off children's conceptual 'attainments' and thus provide a sort of profile of individual developmental level. It would be very poor credit indeed to the thought of a great investigator if such very limited diagnosis became a sort of administrative substitute for the widely abused IQ, which, in turn, was poor credit to the early great investigations of Binet.

But more basically we must reserve judgement about inferences from the average behaviour of groups of children of different ages to the actual pathways of individual growth. As we know from the theory of the comparative method, we can sometimes construct a fair description of the developmental stages of single organisms by observing samples of similar organisms of different ages. The means and variances obtained by this use of the comparative method are however only significant to the extent that we are sampling from populations which are uniform in essential respects – in some degree of approximation, for example, in the case of gross physical growth. If on the other hand we are interested in the common dynamics of growth in populations where individual development pursues different pathways, the means and variances of a composite picture may entirely mask the essential dynamics of the process. When, for example, individual learning is in reality all-or-none, a group average may produce the standard continuous learning curve. And since children are in fact diverging in humanly important ways toward different careers, different competencies and insights, different talents and interests, a method which looks only at those common conceptual nodes which most biographical trajectories sooner or later traverse is likely to miss the most interesting part of the theory of learning and development, and the part most crucial to education. It is likely to observe the fine structure and the dynamics of transitions, differing from individual to individual, under such low resolving power that these are seen as little more than a residual statistical variance, what Piaget calls *décalages*.

None of this is said by way of criticism of Piaget's work, which in common with many others I both admire and learn from. What is at stake is that human creative capacities are only weakly inferrable by testing for the presence of those widely relevant schemata which – *because* they are widely relevant – we all do more or less competently develop, along one pathway or along another. The epistemological perspective of a teacher is one which is closer to the dynamics of developmentally significant learning, whereas this potentially vital role of a teacher is diluted out by the comparative method. In education as in biology the absence of a theory based on detailed study of specific transitions leads away from science toward orthogenesis, toward belief in the automatism of progress. One of the more enthusiastic of Piaget's adherents allegedly once said, 'You don't have to teach, just wait a while.' But that is a remark which cuts both ways; all cats look alike in the dark. On the other hand, the overwhelming mass of studies which deal with the effects of teaching deal with short-run reversible learning, of no particular educational significance. The really interesting problems of education are hard to study. They are too long-term and too complex for the laboratory, and too diverse and non-linear for the comparative method. They require longitudinal study of individuals, with intervention a dependent variable, dependent upon close diagnostic observation. The investigator who can do that and will do it is, after all, rather like what I have called a teacher. So the teacher himself is potentially the best researcher, if only we would offer him strong intellectual support and respect his potentialities as a scientist: lighten his mechanical burdens, join him more frequently in his association with children, argue with him, pick his brains.

In the meantime the very existence of such a teacher as I have described – and he does exist, though all too rarely throughout most of the world – is a challenge to all the narrowing preconceptions and practice of mathematics teaching as that art is usually described and practised.

Mountain View Center,
1511 University Avenue,
University of Colorado,
Boulder,
Colorado 80302,
USA.

Some anthropological observations on number, time and common-sense

Edmund Leach

In 1919, in his *Introduction to Mathematical Philosophy*, Bertrand Russell declared that 'logic is concerned with the real world just as truly as zoology',[1] but in the Preface to the 1938 edition of *The Principles of Mathematics* we read that 'none of the raw material of the world has smooth logical properties, but whatever appears to have such properties is constructed artificially to have them'.[2] Fashions in social anthropology go through similar oscillations. During most of my academic lifetime the bias has been heavily empiricist. Anthropologists have supposed that they were engaged in a kind of social zoology. Human societies have been discussed as if they were organisms. The study of social structure and social relations has been treated as analogous to the study of anatomy and physiology. Anthropology was a social *science*; anthropologists hoped to *discover* an ordered universe of social facts – *objective* facts put there, free from the taint of human intuition.

Broadly speaking, empirically minded social anthropologists of this sort take the view that all unsophisticated pre-literate peoples have a thoroughly practical rule-of-thumb approach to the day-to-day problems of domestic technology. They insist that it is a complete mistake to imagine that the ordinary behaviour of primitive man is dominated by childish superstition. Magical fantasy is never allowed to interfere with common-sense.

That is still the orthodox view but of late there has been a move away from empiricism in the direction of idealism. Many anthropologists would now argue, in imitation of Russell, that 'none of the raw material of our *social* world has smooth logical properties, but whatever appears to have such properties is constructed artificially to have them'.

[1] Russell, B., *Introduction to Mathematical Philosophy*, Allen and Unwin, London; Macmillan, New York, 1919, p. 169.

[2] Russell, B., *The Principles of Mathematics* (2nd edition with new Introduction), Allen and Unwin, London; W. W. Norton, New York, 1938, p. xi.

That is the orientation which has governed my own thinking while I have been preparing this paper.

I started out by asking myself why on earth should a social anthropologist be invited to address a gathering of teachers of mathematics? I came to the conclusion that one possible answer might run something like this:

The subject matter of social anthropology is human custom but mainly the custom of pre-literate unsophisticated peoples living outside (or on the fringe of) the modern industrial world. Such peoples do not engage in mathematical computations as *you* might ordinarily understand them.

But that is true also of the vast majority of those whom we ourselves encounter in our daily lives. For the ordinary 'man in the street', whether child or adult, mathematics is a mystery. *Your* problem, as teachers of mathematics, is to overcome this mystery, and that entails, at least to some extent, changing the way that your pupils think about the nature of things. But part of your difficulty is to be able to understand how your unsophisticated, pre-mathematical pupils interpret their experiences in the first place.

Are there universal aspects of common-sense which the teacher of mathematics, with his special initial prejudices is likely to overlook?

This is the sort of question a social anthropologist *ought* to be able to answer but I am afraid that I must disappoint you. Common-sense turns out to be a much more variable factor than one might have supposed. The only lesson that comparative ethnography can offer in this respect is that what seems obvious to you and me is not necessarily obvious to anyone else.

Let me start with an example from Ancient Egypt which was almost the first of the really sophisticated societies. The Egyptians had only a very rudimentary mathematical understanding but, for purposes of survey and accountancy, they adopted quite elaborate techniques of computation. Some of these seem surprising.

The Egyptians evidently came to the conclusion that in measuring a straight line, the fractions $\frac{1}{2}$ and $\frac{1}{4}$, $\frac{1}{3}$ and $\frac{2}{3}$ could be accurately judged by eye – as indeed is pretty much the case. For the purposes of arithmetical computation they therefore made their number series start, not with the integer 1 but with a fraction – either $\frac{1}{4}$ or $\frac{1}{3}$. The numbers were thus in two series:

$$\tfrac{1}{4}, \tfrac{1}{2}, 1, 2, 3, 4, 5, \ldots$$
$$\tfrac{1}{3}, \tfrac{2}{3}, 1, 2, 3, 4, 5, \ldots.$$

All these numbers were in effect treated as if they were integers. Other fractions were then written as combinations of these natural numbers with unit fractions. For example,

$$\tfrac{2}{5} \text{ becomes } `\tfrac{1}{3}+\tfrac{1}{15}'.$$

What could be common-sensical about that? Well it depends upon one's point of view. The resulting computation procedure is certainly extraordinarily cumbersome yet close inspection shows that it employs repetitive algorithms appropriate to a modern computer program.[1] Evidently in the Egyptian case the advantages of mechanical simplicity involved in the repetitive element of the procedure outweighed the disadvantage that it was very slow.

Incidentally this Egyptian fractional numbering system with its special use of halves and thirds provides part of the answer to another common-sense question which modern children may raise. Since we have a twenty-four hour day why does the ordinary clock face only show twelve hours? The details are complicated but the main point is this. The shadow face of the Roman–Egyptian sundial was divided into quarters, and each quarter into thirds, making *twelve* sections in all. Although *astronomers* had used a twenty-four hour, equal interval, day–night from as early as the *third century* B.C., this twenty-four hour manner of reckoning did not come into *general* use until around the eleventh century A.D. along with the introduction of mechanical escapement clocks. Prior to that period the term *true* hours (*horai kairai*) was always applied to *sundial* hours which vary in length according to the time of year and the latitude of observation.[2] Common-sense, but to *our* thinking rather odd.

With that introduction let me delimit my subject matter. I shall mainly be talking about relatively unsophisticated concepts of *time*. Until I get near the end I shall not be going into any great detail. I simply want to examine the principles of 'common-sense' which these time concepts entail. I shall concentrate on those features which are at variance with the assumptions normally current in the modern, twentieth century, industrial world.

I cannot now remember how my mathematics teachers first introduced the concept of time. I suspect they avoided it. After all at first

[1] Neugebauer, O., *The Exact Sciences in Antiquity*, Princeton University Press, Princeton, 1952, pp. 21, 72–8.

[2] *Ibid.* p. 81. See also Neugebauer, O., Ancient Mathematics and Astronomy in C. Singer, E. J. Holmyard and A. R. Hall (eds.) *A History of Technology*, Vol. 1, Clarendon Press, Oxford, 1954, pp. 785–803, esp. 796–7.

sight it seems an elementary matter. Time is something that we measure and something that we measure with, therefore it is a dimension. And yet surely this is very puzzling, for time, whatever it may be, is something which is experienced quite intangibly. We cannot see it or touch it as we can a footrule. How is it then that we come to think of it as *measurable*? Measurable in relation to what?

When we measure anything the units of scale that we employ – feet, centimetres, hours, ounces, grams and so on – represent numerical quantities of dimensions. This is so much of a commonplace that the dimensions themselves appear intrinsic. It seems *sensible* to measure a quantity of sugar by weight or by volume, but nonsense to measure it by length or by area or by duration. Yet in fact, the dimensions that we employ in any particular case are largely arbitrary and differ according to the social and operational context in which we make our observation. In many parts of the world farmers regularly measure their fields in terms of seed requirements or crop yield; all of us tend to judge journey distance by the time it takes to get there. This implies measuring area by volume and distance by time, procedures which seem to blur the edges between sense and nonsense.

It is consistent with our assumption that dimensions are 'given' facts of the *external* situation that we today tend to prefer scales which have some kind of universal validity. The theoretical standard metre, for example, is not the actual length of any man-made object but 'one ten millionth part of the meridian quadrant', that is to say it is an absolute feature of the cosmos which can be ascertained only by calculation. All other measures of length, in any scale whatsoever, can, in theory, be expressed as a standardised multiple or fraction of this ideal metre. And this relationship is absolute. An English inch *equals* 2.54 centimetres; we could not imagine it to be 2.54 cm today and 3 cm tomorrow.

But standardisation of this sort is not a quality of scales as such. In the world of commerce and international finance, for example, scales of value are shifting relative to one another all the time and we accept this as normal. In a comparable way, in a non-scientific world, *all* scales, including those which are used to measure time and space, are adjustable to circumstance. It is a *peculiarity* of *scientific* society that an ideal scale should be one which is unambiguous and exact; under other conditions people have preferred scales which were easy to use. Where the criterion of a good scale is its convenience, too much precision may even be a nuisance.

All this is relevant to my central theme. In any society the generally prevailing ideas about the nature of time and space are closely linked up with the kinds of measuring scale which are thought appropriate. If we alter the scales and dimensions with which we measure, we seem somehow to alter the nature of that which is being measured. For us distances *consist of* miles or kilometres just as time *consists of* hours and minutes. But in a clockless world there are no hours and no minutes. If we *consistently* measured distance by time, then we should doubtless take it for granted that the topography *consists of* days and nights. It follows that our present-day feelings about the nature of the cosmos are largely determined by the nature of the scales which we use to measure its components. It is therefore very significant that, as compared with *any* previous period of history, our scientific culture operates with *more precise* scales but far *fewer* dimensions than ever before.

We manage to make do with *fewer* dimensions because, having perfected the art of numerical calculation it is convenient to have all values expressed in interchangeable numbers. For example, in the field of economics, the value of land, of goods, of valuables, of food, of labour, and of every type of service can now be expressed in terms of a single numerical dimension 'money'. In primitive society this is not the case. Houses and yams both have value, but there would ordinarily be no possible way of computing the value of a house as a numerical quantity of yams. In primitive economics, in the absence of a general medium of exchange, we have a situation where there is a multiple range of value dimensions.

Space dimensions and time dimensions can also both be multiple in this same sense. Nowadays we usually take it for granted that the three linear dimensions, length, breadth and height, are all measurable in units of the same type. This is because we find it convenient to compute areas and volumes as squares and cubes of a numerical linear scale. Other people, who lack our arithmetical proficiency, may find it more convenient to keep such dimensions apart, to measure height, for example, in different units from length and breadth, or land area in different units from the size of buildings and material artifacts. And so also with time.

In post sixteenth century European mathematics, time has come to be treated as a fourth dimension distinct from, but precisely on a par with length, breadth and height except that every now and again we have to remind ourselves that the arrow of time is not reversible. We now take it for granted that time is continuous and that both past and future have infinite extension. We also take it for granted that there is just one kind of time...that the nano-seconds by which we compute the time lag of computer mechanisms, if magnified sufficiently, will turn into the light years by which we compute the distance of extra-galactic nebulae. We not only think of time as being 'like space' in that it is an attribute of what is 'out there' but we think of duration as a kind of length. We move along the time axis as we might along a space axis; more picturesquely, we float down the river of time as we might travel along a road. All metaphors of this very general kind, which one way or another entail the assumption that time is unitary – all in one piece – and that it exists 'out there', external to individual human experience, are highly artificial. The 'time' to which they refer is a construct which has come to be grafted on to our thinking by the logical requirements of mathematics rather than because of any direct personal experience.

But how do we in fact *experience* time flow? Here I must emphasise again that I am a social anthropologist and not a psychologist.[1] I am not here concerned with the problem of time 'perception' or time 'intuition'. I am talking about cultural phenomena; interactions between man and nature which can be directly described like the sequence of days of the week or the oscillation of a pendulum.

Time experience, in this sense, appears in six quite separable forms.

(1) *Time as alternation:* day–night, day–night.

(2) *Time as sequence:* one thing happens after another.

(3) *Time as distance:* if an individual moves from locality *A* to locality *B* this will use up time.

(4) *Time as delimitation:* any named and identifiable event necessarily has a beginning and an end. Time, in this sense, delimits events, just as boundaries delimit objects.

(5) *Time as repetition:* the sequence of events in one working day is the same as in the day before or the day after; in every annual cycle, productive activities follow one another in the same sequence, and so on. The recognition of such repetitions is universal, but this does not necessarily entail a notion of continuity...today is separate from yesterday. There is often a gap of several months between the end of one working year and the beginning of the next.

(6) *Time as aging:* older people are aware that they and their

[1] For a recent discussion of psychological aspects of this problem see Ornstein, R. E., *On the Experience of Time*, Penguin Books, Harmondsworth, 1969.

friends were once younger; they are also aware that in the future they will all be dead. The end of the world lies ahead.

Now to anyone with your kind of mathematical orientation the last of these six categories of time is simply the notion of entropy while the other five can all be combined into one figure. But a unitary conception of time such as is implied by a wave diagram of this sort does not arise from ordinary experience; it is an intellectual construct imposed on 'the world out there' by the thought processes of mathematicians.

In the world of common-sense, time is fragmented and the fragments do *not* necessarily fit together.

But let me go back to my list of the varieties of time. Most accounts of the history of science give the impression that, from the second millennium B.C. onwards, men were aware of the 'existence' of

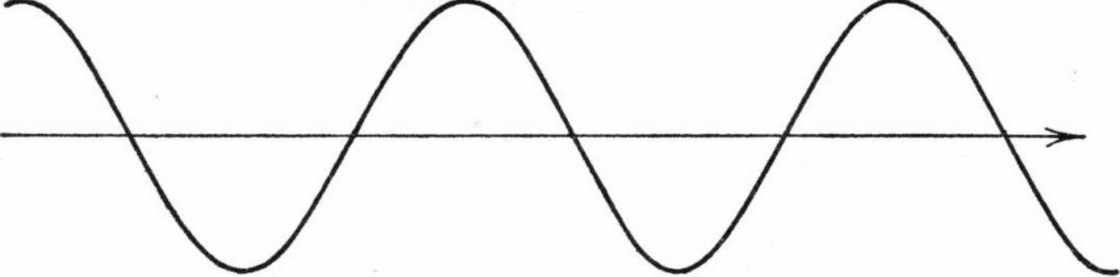

a unitary entity 'time'; and that the progress of astronomy was directly linked up with more and more refined attempts to measure time – by calculating the relative lengths of lunar, solar and sidereal cycles so as to establish the 'true' length of the year. In retrospect this is indeed how it worked out, but that is certainly not what the ancient calendar makers thought they were up to.

We know for example that, from the third millennium B.C. at least, the Ancient Egyptians had two quite different calendars, one for computing official and religious events and the other for organising the agricultural seasons which were linked with the rise and fall of the Nile flood. The civil agricultural calendar was a lunar calendar. The religious calendar was a day-count system which made use of the special number scales to which I have already referred. Each third of a year was divided into quarters making twelve sections; each section was then subdivided into thirds, of ten days each. The whole yearly cycle thus consisted of a symmetrically arranged sequence of thirty-six ten day periods. To this was added a special half section of five days which consisted of religious festivals outside the normal year, giving a full cycle of 365 days. The Egyptians were well aware that this year was not astronomical, but it was convenient. Until very late they did not attempt to calculate its precise discrepancy from the natural year. In effect they behaved as if the two calendars, the secular and the religious, measured two quite separate varieties of time. This was common-sense since the day-count calendar served religious purposes for which astronomical correlations were irrelevant. It is only convention which makes *us* think that the movements of the heavenly bodies constitute a *natural* clock. On the contrary, it is at least arguable that the symmetrical, astronomy-free, Egyptian day-count system was the only completely rational method of reckoning time that has ever been invented anywhere.[1]

For that matter even the Chaldeans and the Greeks who, unlike the Egyptians, really did become interested in astronomical (as distinct from calendrical) problems, were both quite unconcerned with what we should now consider to be the *practical* aspects of astronomy. *Their* concerns were metaphysical. This is a point I must emphasise most strongly. In the history of science, astronomy and mathematics were both step-children of astrology, not the other way about. Astronomy was first developed to serve astrological ends and astrology is just *one* of a vast number of 'para-logical' techniques by which man has, at one time or another, attempted to predict the future.

All these techniques derive from the same basic non-rational yet common-sense belief, namely that every person or animal or thing or event has its own 'destiny' or 'life-time'. In retrospect, after it has happened, this proposition becomes a self evident truth; the *metaphysical* hypothesis is simply that the destiny is 'already there', *before* it has actually happened. But if it is there, it is 'logical' to think that it should be discoverable.

And why not? Suppose I go to Bristol next Sunday. I do not at this moment know the way to get there. But the way from Exeter to Bristol already exists and I can discover what it is. If I go to Bristol I shall make a journey along this road which already exists; if I do this I shall uncover a piece of my destiny; I shall use up a piece of my life-time. Surely it *is* common-sense to think that this *future* life-time already exists *now*?

That anyway is the logic of pre-destination. Each person, animal, thing, event carries with it its own destiny, its own unique 'piece of time'. Part of this time is already past and uncovered; part still lies

[1] Neugebauer (1952), *The Exact Sciences in Antiquity*, p. 81.

in the future and is in shadow; but the whole has 'existed' 'from the beginning'.

Historically, astrology arose when it was realised that astronomical events are computable in advance. Once it was postulated that an association might exist between the time of a particular personal event – such as a birth – and the time of a particular astronomical event – such as an astrological configuration – then it became perfectly 'reasonable' to suppose that the future course of an individual's personal destiny can be predicted.

From our modern scientific point of view this is nonsense, but this is what happened in history. Clockmaking and astronomy did *not* evolve as techniques for measuring an abstract unitary entity, sidereal time, which is part of nature, but as devices for linking together the conjunctions of isolated, very specific, very *personal*, chunks of time.

Joseph Needham and his associates have given a fascinating account of the medieval Chinese version of this ideology which I feel is worth repeating, if only to add an element of light relief. In the eleventh century A.D. the Chinese emperor possessed the most sophisticated clock in the world. It was an elaborate water-driven affair about thirty-five feet high. The function of the clock was not merely to tell the time of day but to compute the positions of the stars and the planets and their conjunctions. I quote:

From time immemorial the large number of women attending upon (the Chinese Emperor) were regulated according to the numinous cosmism which pervaded Chinese Court life...his consorts and concubines comprised one empress, three consorts, nine spouses, twenty seven concubines, and eighty one assistant concubines. The total adds up to 121, which (certainly by no coincidence) is one third of 365 to the nearest round number...The lower-ranking women came first, the higher-ranking came last. The assistant concubines, eighty one in number shared the imperial couch nine nights in groups of nine. The concubines, twenty seven in number, were allotted three nights in groups of nine. The nine spouses and three consorts were allotted one night to each group, and the empress also alone one night. On the fifteenth day of every month the sequence was complete, after which it repeated in the reverse order...The secretarial ladies kept a record of everything with their vermilion brushes.

What was at stake was the Imperial succession...(any one of an Emperor's sons might theoretically be chosen as heir); one of the factors in this choice was the nature of the asterisms which had been culminating at the time of the candidate's conception. Hence the importance of the records which were kept by the ladies secretarial, and the value of a (mechanical instrument) which not only told the time but from which one could read off the star positions at any desired moment.[1]

I cannot help feeling that some of your more reluctant pupils might find mathematics a much more exciting subject if they thought that their calculations could lead to a similar pay off!

The case of the Emperor's concubines illustrates, among other things, the magical property of numbers, particularly of multiples of the number 3. This is no trivial matter; most of *your* pupils will almost certainly have magical feelings about numbers.

Almost universally, even in the most unsophisticated societies, odd and even numbers are recognised as complementary and opposite, often as male and female. By an extension of this mode of thinking, three, reckoned as $2+1$, may be considered the first *complete* number. Hence the recurrent appearance of mystical religious triads – Osiris–Isis–Horus, the Christian Holy Family, the Christian Trinity and so on.[2]

Correspondingly if 3 is perfect and complete it follows that 2×3 is imperfect and incomplete but 3×3 is again perfect and so on. Hence 6 is 'bad' but 9 is 'good'.

But this is taking me far away from my theme of time reckoning so let me go back yet again to my list of 'the varieties of time', in particular to the phenomenon of entropy – the human peculiarity that, of all animals, man alone *knows* that he is going to die.

[1] Needham, J., Wang Ling and de Solla Price, D. J., *Heavenly Clockwork: The Great Astronomical Clocks of Mediaeval China*, Cambridge University Press, London, 1960, chapter 8.

[2] The world-wide magico-religious emphasis on triads and ternary numbers of which a variety of examples appear in this paper has both logical and psychological foundations. Theological disputes about the nature of the Trinity are ultimately concerned with problems of 'truth' just as are the logicians who are able to show that Boolean algebra, when applied to propositional logic, can reduce the sixteen connectives of a standard truth table to three: 'union', 'product', 'complement'. But apart from its logical implications this same numerology evidently strikes a chord which reaches deep into human psychology. At a fairly superficial level, every individual tends to perceive himself as standing at the apex of a triangle of which the two parents form the base, but much more fundamental is the empirical finding that the phonology of language depends upon an innate human capacity to learn how to discriminate between binary distinctive features and then to mediate oppositions.

The kind of dialectical logic by which we first recognise an entity '*A*' by distinguishing it from 'not-*A*' and then synthesise '*B*' as the negation of 'both *A* and not-*A*' to form a new triadic unity, seems to be a universal component of human thought. It can be illustrated in the myths and customs of even the most exotic peoples. This is the central theme in Lévi-Strauss' 4 volume *Mythologiques* (Plon, Paris, 1964–1971).

The nature of religion cannot be summarised in a sentence yet it is fairly obvious that a very large part of all religious ideology is concerned with attempts to deny the fact of death. Death, we are told, is not 'really' death at all, it is a gateway to eternal life. In accepting any such doctrine we reject the inevitability of entropy and the arrow of time.

The forms which such belief can take are enormously varied but most of them fall into just two major classes:

(1) There are systems (such as that of orthodox Christianity) in which the time of life on earth is recognised as subject to entropy... we get older and older every day...but life in 'the other world' is 'eternal', that is time-less. In Heaven and Hell the individual soul does not experience aging.

(2) There are systems which are essentially cyclical and repetitive – the future life is a copy of this one – birth follows death but death still follows birth.

Our modern 'scientific' notion of infinitely extensible entropic time – a universe which is for ever running down hill – fits especially badly with religious ideologies of the first type which postulate an after life of eternal bliss; so let us take a closer look at the time structures which are entailed by such systems.

Christianity, if we accept the Bible as literally true, presupposes a time framework which is similar to that of the Australian Aborigines. Time has a beginning, but thereafter the past falls into two distinct stages.

There was first the period of dream time or myth time in which the first beings existed in a newly created Paradise, in a stationary state without reproducing themselves or getting older. Then, in contrast, there is the waking time of ordinary experience in which entropy operates, events happen one after another, and ultimately everyone is dead.

A characteristic of the first of these periods, the dream time, is that all events are, in a sense, simultaneous; it takes time to tell the story but the story when it has been told is like a map; it is a description of a social topography; it would not really matter if the events had been listed in quite a different sequence.

The other characteristic of dream-time-past is that it is not really 'past' at all. The legendary first beings, who appear as hero figures in the myths, are not 'dead', they exist 'now', and they still operate with potency in our present existence; 'God liveth' as a kind of super grandfather laying down the moral rules.

Now in unsophisticated, non-numerate societies, such as social anthropologists usually study, this dual evaluation of the past does not create any serious intellectual difficulties. Entropic time, in which human beings grow old and die, is current and recent, it relates only to the memory of man – that is to the life experience of individuals who are still alive and their immediate forbears. The timeless eternity, from which the hero ancestors are still controlling events, is close at hand, not chronologically distanced from the present.

But as soon as it becomes customary to measure time by numbers, there is a tendency to use number magic to relate the past to the present. The 'beginning of time' then becomes a base point; the patriarchs cease to be immortal and turn into giants who live to a very great abnormal age but eventually die. The Biblical Book of Genesis exemplifies the general pattern. But it is a great mistake to imagine that people who have developed a chronological sense of the past of this type, have a view of history which closely resembles our own.

To round off I propose to give you in rough outline an example of the point I have just made. It illustrates the main thesis that I have been making all along. Common-sense is a variable; the fact that people act in a way that seems to us sensible, or that they make statements which seem to us comprehensible, does not necessarily imply that they mean what we think they mean.

The areas in which there is likely to be the greatest misunderstanding are those in which we feel ourselves most expert.

All of you in this room are accustomed to the manipulation of numbers, but you also operate within a framework of strict conventions about what sorts of numbers may be manipulated. If, for example, you had a Western style education you will have been taught that the time framework of history is 'a given' which is *not* open to manipulation. But that of course is just a convention and it may be salutary to consider the works of medieval Christian historians precisely because they constitute a class of authors who manipulated the time framework of history quite blatantly.

The justification for my citing this rather complicated and superficially crazy material is that it illustrates a particular, and widespread, way of thinking about numbers. I am not suggesting that *your* pupils think like that; but it is quite possible that they may do so!

But now to my example.

Whenever the past is given chronological depth but is still credited with a mystical influence upon the present, chronology itself becomes a part of the magical apparatus. This readily leads to an obsession with number magic.

The Christian Fathers of the third century A.D. argued as follows:[1]

(*a*) God created the world in 6 days and rested on the 7th day.

(*b*) A day in the sight of God is a thousand years.

(*c*) It is therefore self evident that the world will come to an end 6000 years after the Creation.

(*d*) This impending doom is confirmed by the fact that Noah was 600 years old at the time of the Flood, that the Idol set up by Nebuchadnezzar measured 60 cubits by 6 cubits and that the mark on the Beast in the Book of Revelations is the number 666.

(*e*) The Incarnation of Christ the Redeemer was the recapitulation of the Creation of Adam the Sinner.

(*f*) But Adam was created on the 6th day and had sinned at the 6th hour (i.e. $5\frac{1}{2}$ days after the first Beginning). Therefore the redemption of the World was timed for $5\frac{1}{2} \times 1000$ years.

(*g*) It follows that Christ was born in Bethlehem in the World Year 5500. He was crucified in His 33rd year; 33 being morally good, just as 666 is morally bad.

And so on.

One aspect of this is that the authors concerned were living in the third century A.D. so that by computing the End of the World at A.D. 500 they were bringing the Day of Judgement near enough to be interesting. The exaggerations of the environmental Doom-watchers of today who predict total disaster within the next fifty years have similar motivations. But early Christian numerological calculations could be much more specific than that.

The following characteristic example comes from Hippolytus' *Commentary on the Book of Daniel* written in the early part of the third century.

> The first coming of Our Lord, the Incarnation of his birth at Bethlehem, took place on the eighth day before the Kalends of January (December 25th) on a Wednesday in the forty second year of the reign of Augustus, five thousand five hundred years after Adam. He suffered in his thirty third year on the eighth day before the Kalends of April (March 25th) in the 18th year of Tiberius Caesar in the consulship of Rufus and Rubellion.[2]

[1] *The Writings of Irenaeus* (translated by A. Roberts and W. H. Rambaut), Ante-Nicene Christian Library, Edinburgh, 1969, vol. 2; pp. 118, 132, etc.

[2] Bonwetsch, G. N. and Achelis, H. (eds.), *Hippolytus Werke* vol. 1, part 1, *Die Kommentare zu Daniel and zum Hohenliede*, Leipzig, 1897, p. 242.

On the face of it this reads like an assertion of historical fact such as we might encounter in a modern school history book. It is nothing of the sort. If we are to understand what was intended we have to appreciate that the author's central problem was one of time rather than events. The exact date of the Crucifixion had become an issue of extreme doctrinal significance, but it was unknown. Hippolytus believed that he could *discover* the 'correct' date by *computation.*

As is the case among many much more primitive societies, the early Christians believed that the welfare of their community might be very seriously jeopardised if the various annual rituals were not properly performed on the 'correct' dates. But Christian festivals such as Easter were supposed to be tied to dates in the Jewish *lunar* year. Any straightforward reading of the Gospels for example must imply that the Friday of the Crucifixion corresponded to the Jewish Passover which falls on the fourteenth day of the month Nisan. But how could the lunar date Nisan XIV be identified in the Roman Julian calendar of 365¼ days? The theologians have never managed to solve this problem[1] but in the early centuries of Christendom attempts to solve it led to endless theories about 'time cycles', each of which tended to become the doctrinal banner of a particular schismatic group.

Considered astronomically, *all* the various theories were defective, and indeed, prior to the sixteenth century A.D. astronomical observation was always too crude to decide a disputed issue one way or the other.

In practice the rival theorists ignored astronomy and attempted to give their arguments a mythical authority by projecting them backwards through time. Each author sought to validate the accuracy of his own favoured Easter table by showing how well it fitted with the events of sacred history.[2]

So what about Hippolytus' statements concerning the dates of the birth and Crucifixion of Jesus Christ? They represent a curious amalgam of calendrical calculation, historical tradition and doctrinal theory.

[1] After the Council of Nicaea the Crucifixion was presumed to have occurred on Nisan XV and the tables were redesigned so as to prevent Easter Sunday from ever coinciding exactly with the Jewish Passover. However in 1923 the Paschal full moon fell on the day given in the modern Western Church tables for Easter day. To conform with the post-Nicaean rules Good Friday should have been on the Friday following Easter Sunday!

[2] For a full account see Jones, C. W. (ed.), *Bedae: Opera de Temporibus,* Mediaeval Academy of America, Cambridge, Mass., 1943, chapters 1–4.

All the rival theories about the dating of Easter manage to drag in the names of the two consuls, usually called Rufius and Rebellius. According to modern reckoning they held the consulship in A.D. 29 but their significance for the Christian tradition was that they were supposed to have been twin brothers. By specifying them as *gemini*, the founding of the Church of Christ is linked up with the founding of the City of Rome by the *gemini* Romulus and Remus.

The statement that Jesus was crucified in his 33rd year is an essential detail which distinguishes Hippolytus' theory from rival doctrines which place this key event in A.D. 29. The link with the 18th year of Tiberius is based on Luke 3: 1, 23. On this basis, Jesus would have been born in the 44th year of the reign of Caesar Augustus as ordinarily computed and the reference to the '42nd year' is probably simply a mistake.

The references to days of the week and days of the month are however based wholly on computation and doctrinal theory. The precise details of this particular computation cannot be reconstructed with certainty but they would have been based on some or all of the following postulates.

(1) The World was created at the Spring Equinox, 25 March, on the first day of the week, Sunday.

(2) The moon was created on the evening of the fourth day, Wednesday.

(3) Since it was created to light the night, it was a full moon.

(4) The Annunciation and Conception of the Blessed Virgin was a recapitulation of the Creation of the World and therefore occurred on 25 March, but since it brought light to our (moral) darkness it was a full moon.

(5) The birth of Christ followed, exactly 9 Calendar months after the Conception, on 25 December. It was a Wednesday because it recapitulated the creation of the sun and the moon on the fourth day.[1]

(6) The Crucifixion of Jesus Christ on Friday in Holy Week was the act of Redemption which repeated in reverse the expulsion of Adam and Eve from the Garden of Eden on the sixth day and the ninth hour. It was linked with the full moon of the Jewish Passover. But since this too was a beginning of new time, this event again must have occurred on 25 March.

Apart from these theological assumptions Hippolytus also made

[1] In fact if 25 March is a Sunday, 25 December is a Tuesday.

use of some perfectly straightforward calendrical calculations, such as,

in the Julian Calendar the days of the week repeat themselves in relation to the days of the month every 28 years (4 × 7) so if 25 March is a Sunday in year 1 it will also be a Sunday in year 29, and in year 33 it will be a Friday.

Finally, there is the fact that Hippolytus' Easter tables assume, quite erroneously, that there is a 16 year lunar cycle such that if 25 March is a full moon in year 1, it will also be a full moon in year 17 and year 33.

Putting all this together Hippolytus argues that the Conception of Christ, as the crucial beginning of the Christian era, occurred on a Sunday, at the Equinox, on 25 March, at the full moon. By his (inaccurate) reckoning, 25 March 32 years later was likewise a full moon, but a Friday – the Friday of the Crucifixion. Counting from the Annunciation as base, this is correctly described as 'the 33rd year' of Christ's life.

Far from being a mere artistic flourish Hippolytus' references to month dates and days of the week lie close to the heart of the matter since they serve to justify the table of actual Easter dates which started from A.D. 222.[1]

At first sight this all seems very silly but we need to notice what is going on. Hippolytus first assumes that chronological numbers are no more sacrosanct than other numbers and that they are open to

[1] In Hippolytus' table the cycle begins with the (genuine) full moon of A.D. 222 which fell on 13 April. Easter is allowed to fall on any of the days *luna* xvi to *luna* xxii of the Paschal moon. This implies that Christ was crucified on Nisan XIV and lay in the tomb on Nisan XV. The table assumes that the earliest limit for Easter day was 18 March the day the sun entered Aries according to the Old Roman computation. This would imply that the Paschal new moon corresponding to Nisan I could not retrogress beyond the last hours of 4 March.

A revised Hippolytan table, which appeared in the year 243 under the name of Cyprian, explains this equation of Nisan I with 4/5 March by the following remarkable piece of reasoning:

The World was created at the Spring Equinox, 25 March
The moon was created on the evening of the 4th day, 28 March
Since it was created to light the night it was created as a full moon. The following day 29 March was therefore Nisan XIV. If this moon had existed before it was created full it would have been a new moon on 16 March.

The lunar date falls back 11 days each year in relation to the solar calendar. Therefore the first *actual* Nisan I would be 11 days before 16 March, i.e. 4/5 March, near the end of the first year of the Creation, and this set the earliest limit for subsequent Paschal full moons as 4/5 March + 14 that is 18 March. Q.E.D.

(See Jones (1943), *Bedae: Opera de Temporibus*, pp. 12–13.)

manipulation in a mathematical way. He then assumes that if we link historical events with numbers (i.e. dates), the series will be recursive (i.e. that 'history will repeat itself'). He then treats the repetitive sequences of which his history is composed as interlocking epicycles of varying duration and postulates that the 'important' events in history always occur on dates at which several different epicycles all come into phase. His key dates are those at which the 7 day week, the $365\frac{1}{4}$ day Julian year and the 354 day lunar year synchronise.

This way of using a numerical view of the past as a code for deciphering the present was not a peculiarity of early Christians. Other civilisations have used historical time in a very similar way, notably the Maya of Central America. Granted the primary assumption that history repeats itself it is a perfectly rational way of proceeding and we should perhaps ask ourselves why we are so confident that the assumption is false. But my present point is a different one. The early Christian authors looked upon the writing of history as the application of a general theory of number to practical problems. Dating was not ascertained by reference to contemporary records but by citing 'authorities' and by computation. Moreover, in the correct scientific style of Professor Popper, they recognised that their hypotheses could be falsified by events, in which case they would have to change their theory and this would alter the structure of history. Here is a striking example of the latter principle.

Some 80 years after Hippolytus published his tables the Alexandrine ecclesiastics became interested in the arithmetic of the Kallippic cycle of 76 years. It was noticed that the number 5776 was 76×76 while the reign date of Diocletian, by Hippolytus' reckoning, would be World Year 5787. Arguing that the reign of Diocletian, with its anti-Christian persecutions, must mark the era of Anti-Christ who was to be the forerunner of Christ's true second coming, the Alexandrine church authorities decided that the reign of Diocletian must have initiated a new era of time. They therefore quietly shifted the dates of both the Crucifixion and the Creation of the World forward by 10 years – to the consternation and anguish of later chronologists! In this way Diocletian's reign date became World Year $5776 + 1$, the first year of a new great cycle of time.[1]

Let me emphasise again just why I am giving you these tedious

[1] Mas Latrie, L. Cte de, *Trésor de Chronologie* (Paris, 1889), Col. 30/31: *Encyclopaedia Britannica* XIth edn, article Chronology.

examples of phoney arithmetic. They illustrate the two main ways in which the medieval historian's attitude to time differs from that of his modern successor. In the first place, events are treated as interesting only in so far as they can be seen to be fulfilments of Destiny or omens of the Future. Secondly, dating, though meticulous, is a matter of computation rather than of evidence.

Until this view of the nature of history and of the nature of evidence could be abandoned, the development of modern science was impossible, but, in the context of established Christianity, any such change was liable to smack of heresy.

Writing about A.D. 1267 Roger Bacon reviewed at length the whole of the earlier argument about the date of Easter and then he went on to recommend to the Pope a calendar revision of his own devising. Bacon justified the need for this calendar revision by saying that the existing system made the Christian church a laughing stock in the eyes of Arabic scientists; he justified the revision itself not by referring to historical 'authorities' but by a straightforward astronomical calculation.[1] His viewpoint is thus the exact antithesis of that propounded by the earlier writers whom I have mentioned.

Bacon's proposed revision was broadly similar to that ultimately adopted by Pope Gregory at the end of the sixteenth century but his scientific enthusiasm was three hundred years too early; all that Bacon earned by his proposals was fourteen years imprisonment!

That perhaps is an appropriate place to stop because it brings us back full circle to the uncertainties of Bertrand Russell. Bacon was not thrown into gaol because he was a scientist defying the Church but because he was putting forward the claims of empiricism against the idealist assumptions of established mathematical orthodoxy. Today, as I suggested at the beginning, the movement of thought is going the other way; idealist heresies are tending to undermine the empiricist assumptions of scientific orthodoxy.

Let us beware lest the would-be heretics among our own pupils, by challenging our authority, should tempt us to react as the Pope reacted against Roger Bacon.

King's College,
Cambridge.

[1] Burke, R. B. (trans.), *The Opus Magnus of Roger Bacon*, 2 vols., University of Pennsylvania Press, Philadelphia, 1928, vol. 1, pp. 222–30; 291–306.

Mathematical education in developing countries – some problems of teaching and learning

Hugh Philp

The original invitation to me to address the Conference suggested as a topic 'The Psychology of Mathematics Education'. For two main reasons I have chosen to go off at something of a tangent. First, Shulman's brilliant paper in the 1970 NSSE 'Yearbook' represents so careful and thoughtful an analysis of current Western thinking on the psychology of mathematics education that it would be both presumptuous and superfluous for me to attempt to improve on it. Secondly, my colleagues and I at Macquarie University in Australia have been concerned, over the last five years or so, with some problems related to the education of children in developing countries and I thought it might be more useful, and interesting, to discuss some of our findings with you than to recapitulate what has already been so well described by Shulman.

The central concept in much of our work has been that of 'Educability', operationally defined as 'the probability that children will learn what they are supposed to learn' – and with the factors, both genetic and environmental, which affect this (Philp, 1967). The initial emphasis, although not the only one by any means, has been on factors related to cognitive development, essentially because so much of the current theory and practice of curriculum development and teaching methods is dependent on notions about the nature of cognition. The number of occasions on which the name of Piaget is invoked in other papers in this volume is itself evidence enough of this.

The great bulk of the research on the development of cognitive skills and hence of the derived theory has been carried out with Western children. Similarly most of the curriculum building based on the theories of Piaget, Bruner, Gagné, Ausubel and others has gone on in Western educational systems. Sometimes such curricula have been transferred, almost unaltered, to non-Western societies; in other cases, in the current jargon, they 'have been adapted to meet local needs'. But very seldom, if ever, has their fundamental psychological basis been questioned...do the theories of cognitive development on which they rest stand up in non-Western contexts? Do the children of New Guinea, for example, develop cognitive concepts in the same way as Australian children? If not, what are their modes of concept formation and what are the implications for curriculum and for teaching? Much of our work has been concerned with questions of this kind.

The main purpose of this paper therefore is not so much to discuss the general psychology of mathematics teaching and learning as to describe recent data, much of it unpublished, which suggest that there may be a need for re-examination of current practices, particularly in non-Western societies, and perhaps also of current theories of mathematics curricula and methods of teaching in the schools. I hasten to add that these new data will need further extension and research, for their implications, if verified, are far reaching indeed. My emphasis would be that they are more in the nature of 'work-in-progress' than of definitive findings.

Before going on to describe them it would seem appropriate to make some distinctions and clarify some concepts which are germane to the presentation.

First, there is a real distinction to be made between mathematical thinking and mathematical learning. There is no necessary relationship, in the shape of a one-to-one correspondence, between the logic of mathematics itself and the ways in which children form concepts generally. Piaget (e.g. 1926, 1957) has demonstrated fairly conclusively that children's logic, in the early years at least, is far from being hypothetico-deductive in character and the work of a generation of anthropologists has amply shown, in Bridgman's words (1958), that 'It begins to look as though formal logic as we know it, is an attribute of the group of Indo-European languages with certain grammatical features.' We have been too prone to assume that because the logic of mathematics is pretty much the logic of those Indo-European languages, it must also be the logic of all languages and all cultures. There is a good demonstration of this fallacy in Gay and Cole's fascinating book (1967) on mathematical thinking and learning among the Kpelle people of Liberia. That is, while there may well be a universal logic of mathematics – a subject on which I would not feel qualified to judge – there is almost certainly not a universal logic of the ways in which children form mathematical or indeed any other concepts. Some of the later data bear further on this.

Second there is some point in distinguishing between the structure of mathematical thinking and learning and the functions or processes involved. This is not merely or even the old philosophical distinction between structure and function, for it involves a whole set of procedures related to curriculum and to teaching. It is fair to say that traditionally in Western education we have accepted, at least until fairly recently, 'structural' notions about mathematics learning; we have talked about 'mathematical ability' and have accounted for learning differences among children in terms of this. And indeed there is a good deal of evidence from factor analysis studies that, among Western children and students, there are 'abilities' which are related to performance in tasks of a mathematical character. Whether these 'abilities' are genetically determined, in the sense of D. O. Webb's 'Intelligence A' or whether they represent ways in which people structure their learned world or whether there is a combination of both, is still a matter of speculation. The general assumption has been that there are basic 'mental structures' and that these have some kind of universal character to them. Some of the evidence given below suggests however that different cultural groups exhibit different structures in the factor analysis sense, when presented with apparently identical tasks. For the moment it is sufficient to emphasise that most current curricula, particularly at secondary level, assume 'mental structures' which are more or less isomorphic with curriculum 'subjects'. Put another way, we have been concerned with concepts and not with how they are formed.

Alongside this, since Piaget, we have begun to look at the *functioning* mind, with how people in general and children in particular, go about forming concepts and have begun to frame curricula and teaching methods accordingly. In this, as in the theories of structure, there has been as a rule the assumption that the processes involved are universal: that children, whatever their background, language or culture, form concepts in essentially the same way – and hence that mathematics can be taught, as far as its logic is concerned, in the same way to New Guinea children as to English or Australian boys and girls. I would doubt that Piaget himself, despite his insistence on 'fonctions invariantes' would go as far as to say this, although, as Sigel (1969) writes, he has 'been criticised for underplaying the role of socialization experience as an influence in cognitive growth'. Many educators, including mathematical educators, *have* assumed universality of concept formation however. Some of the data to be presented below suggest that the assumption is unwarranted and may lead to disastrous consequences in learning.

At this stage two points are stressed: (*a*) in our present state of knowledge about the neurology of the brain, any theories about structure are themselves inferences from performance: that is, from function – which raises difficult questions about the nature of the performance tasks themselves; (*b*) that *even if* there are universal structures, these result in a very wide variety of performance under different cultural conditions, so wide in fact that for practical purposes, knowledge of the structures would be largely irrelevant without parallel knowledge about the nature and range of the functions implicit in these structures.

That is, we are on sound ground in our attempts to build mathematics teaching and learning on the basis of the ways in which the child learns to form mathematical concepts: the logic of child development must take precedence over the logic of mathematical development, or rather, we must develop mathematics curricula in order to take maximum advantage of the ways in which the child develops cognitively. The corollary to this is that if cognitive development and/or cognitive functioning is different in different cultural contexts then so must the curricula and probably the methods of teaching be different.

This leads directly to the allied distinction between 'process' and 'product', a distinction admirably stated by J. S. Bruner (1966, p. 72) in his classic little book *Towards a Theory of Instruction.*

Finally a theory of instruction seeks to take account of the fact that curriculum reflects not only the nature of knowledge itself (the specific capabilities) but also the nature of the knower and of the knowledge-getting process. It is the enterprise *par excellence* where the line between the subject matter and the method grows necessarily indistinct. A body of knowledge, enshrined in a university faculty and embodied in a series of authoritative volumes, is the *result* of much prior intellectual activity. To instruct someone in these disciplines is not a matter of getting him to commit results to mind. Rather, it is to teach him to participate in the process that makes possible the establishment of knowledge. We teach a subject not to produce little living libraries on that subject, but rather to get a student to think mathematically for himself, to consider matters as a historian does, to *take part in the process of knowledge-getting. Knowing is a process, not a product.*

Need one say more?

A more difficult problem, however, lies in determining the subject matter of a curriculum which will attain objectives such as these. Shulman, in the penetrating chapter on 'Psychology and Mathematics Education' to which I have referred, contrasts the positions of Bruner and Robert M. Gagné on the issue; 'Gagné' he writes (p. 55), 'has come out in substantial agreement with Bruner on the priority of processes over products as to objectives of instruction. His emphasis, however, is not on teaching strategies or heuristics of discovery; he is much more concerned with the teaching of the rules or intellectual skills that are relevant to particular instructional domains.' And he quotes Gagné himself:

Although no one would disagree with the aims expressed (by Bruner), it is exceedingly doubtful that they can be brought about solely by teaching students 'strategies' or 'styles' of thinking. Even if these can be taught (and it is likely that they can), they do not provide the individual with the basic firmament of thought, which is a set of externally-oriented intellectual skills. Strategies, after all, are rules which govern the individual's *approach* to listening, reading, storing information, retrieving information, or solving problems. If it is a mathematical problem the individual is engaged in solving, he may have acquired a strategy of applying relevant subordinate rules in a certain order – but he must also have available the mathematical rules themselves. If it is a problem in genetic inheritance, he may have learned a way of guessing at probabilities before actually working them out – but he must also bring to bear the substantive rules pertaining to dominant and recessive characteristics. Knowing strategies, then, is not all that is required for thinking; it is not even a substantial part of what is needed. *To be an effective problem-solver, the individual must somehow have acquired masses of organized intellectual skills.*

Shulman deduces from this distinction the view that the objectives of a curriculum determine the methods of teaching, and that therefore, 'psychology has been successful in suggesting ways of teaching only when objectives have been made operationally clear'. The position taken in the present paper is that this does not go far enough, since it fails to take into account the facts that (*a*) some objectives, however clearly stated, are not attainable unless certain pre-requisites are met and (*b*) some methods are inappropriate to the children and the teachers however clearly the objectives may be stated in operational terms. That is, while I would agree that objectives often determine methods, I would also argue that objectives have to be determined as much by the total learning situation, including the capabilities of the child, as by the demands of the subject matter, whether these demands be couched in terms of strategies or in terms of knowledge and skills.

A similar comment applies to the equally important distinction between 'guided learning' and 'discovery learning'. This is not identical with the process–product argument for, as we have just seen, Gagné accepts the objective of 'process' but argues for 'guided learning' as a more effective methodological strategy for teaching. Ausubel, on the other hand, stresses guided learning but dismisses more or less out of hand any thought of 'process' directed curriculum, maintaining that the primary objective of formal education is the transmission of knowledge. Not of course that any of these major theorists on the application of the psychology of development to education – Bruner, Gagné, Ausubel – would wish to argue a black and white case. The question is rather one of emphasis or stress in curriculum and methods and stems from an important difference in theoretical interest: Bruner is concerned with the whole range of issues relating to the cognitive development of children and with the implications of his findings for teaching and learning. Gagné, on my reading, takes his beginnings from the learning process itself and is looking for relationships between this and the content to be learned: he is less concerned than Bruner with the learner. Ausubel seems to focus on the nature of the content and looks from this to the appropriate teaching–learning situation for acquisition of this content. A gross oversimplification of their respective stances on the issues of discovery versus guided learning and product versus process would give a paradigm like that below.

		Objectives	
		Product	Process
Method	Guided learning	Ausubel	Gagné
	Discovery learning	?	Bruner

I have dwelt somewhat overlong on this issue for three reasons: first, to emphasise again that objectives to a large extent determine approaches; secondly, to suggest that current theories do not take into sufficient account the nature of the total learning situation, particularly the nature of children's thinking in different cultural contexts; and thirdly, to point out that although no major theorist, to my knowledge, is concerned with *product* as an objective, that is with the transmission of knowledge – and *at the same time* argues for the use of 'discovery learning' as a basic method, nevertheless this is a far from uncommon strategy among curriculum makers and teachers, particularly teachers of mathematics. That is, they have 'got the message' about 'discovery learning' but are still reluctant to abandon their well-ingrained loyalties to content.

One further set of ideas relevant to this must be outlined here. Bernstein (1971) in a fascinating discussion of curriculum from the viewpoint of a sociologist of education, distinguishes between 'integrated' and 'collection' types of curricula and between 'strong' and 'weak' classifications and 'frames' of instruction. A 'collection' type of curriculum is described as one in which 'the contents stand in a closed relationship to each other; that is...are clearly bounded and insulated from each other'. Against this he goes on to 'juxtapose a curriculum where the various contents do not go their separate ways, but where the contents stand in an open relationship to each other' (p. 186). This he calls an 'integrated curriculum'. These distinctions may pertain within so-called subjects as well as between them; Geometry may be taught as distinct from Algebra as it is from say, History or Bahasa Indonesia in a collection type of curriculum. Clearly there is some relationship between this dichotomy and the product–process one just discussed.

His second distinction, between 'strong' and 'weak' frames is somewhat akin to that between 'guided' and 'discovery learning'. 'Collection' and 'integration' refer to the content of the curriculum, but Bernstein is also concerned with relationships between contents. He uses the concepts of 'classification' and 'frame' for this; meaning by classification 'the nature of the differentiation between contents'. Classification may be 'strong' or 'weak':

> Where classification is strong, contents are well insulated from each other by strong boundaries. Where classification is weak, there is reduced insulation between contents, for the boundaries between contents are weak or blurred. *Classification thus refers to the degree of boundary maintenance between contents.* Classification focuses our attention upon boundary strength as the critical distinguishing feature of the division of labour of educational knowledge. It gives us the basic structure of the message system, curriculum (p. 187).

'Frame' refers to the frame of the *context* in which knowledge is transmitted and received. Frame refers to the specific pedagogical relationship of teacher and taught. In a different jargon, 'frame' would appear to be equivalent to the 'total teaching–learning situation' or, in a more restricted sense, to the 'teacher–pupil' relationship. Bernstein argues that frame, like classification, may be 'strong', when teachers and pupils have a limited 'range of options available ...in the control of what is transmitted and received in the context of the pedagogical relationship'; or 'weak' when the range of options is relatively wide. In this sense 'frame refers to the degree of control teachers and pupils possess over the selection, organisation and pacing of the knowledge transmitted and received in the pedagogical relationship' (p. 187).

The importance of these distinctions from the viewpoint of the present paper, is in his argument that integrated curriculum codes are more likely to be accompanied by weak classification and weak frames and that this combination, to revert to the earlier language, is more likely to go along with process type objectives and with discovery learning.

The pedagogy of integrated codes is likely to emphasise various *ways* of knowing in the pedagogical relationships. With the collection code, the pedagogy tends to proceed from the surface structure of the knowledge to the deep structure; ..., only the élite have access to the deep structure and therefore access to the realising of new realities or access to the experiential knowledge that new realities are possible. *With integrated codes, the pedagogy is likely to proceed from the deep structure to the surface structure.* We can see this already at work in the new primary school mathematics. Thus, I suggest that integrated codes will make available from the beginning of the pupil's educational career, clearly in a way appropriate to a given age level, the deep structure of the knowledge, i.e., the principles for the generating of new knowledge (p. 200).

And he goes on in words which Bruner might have written

Such emphasis upon various *ways* of knowing, rather than upon the attaining of *states* of knowledge, is likely to affect, not only the emphasis of the pedagogy, but the underlying theory of learning. The underlying theory of learning of collection is likely to be didactic whilst the underlying theory of learning of integrated codes may well be more group- or self-regulated (p. 209).

That is, Bernstein, from an entirely different frame of reference, appears to me to finish in the Bruner box of my little paradigm. His distinctions, however, suggest an additional important consideration. In most developing countries – and in not a few developed ones also – curriculum tends to be of the collection type and to be accompanied by strong classification and strong frames: it tends to be subject centred, with few methodological options available to teachers and still fewer to children. This is in marked contrast to the informal out-of-school learning–teaching situation in most developing countries, where socialisation tends to have an integrated curriculum – even though this is seldom explicit; teaching–learning situations may be strongly framed (as in, say, initiation ceremonies) or, more frequently, weakly framed (as in the acquisition of the mother-tongue, including of course, the vernacular number system and its applications). The implication, as Margaret Mead (1943) argued in her remarkable discussion of the difference between 'teaching' and 'learning' societies, is that there may be conflict of learning modes between 'home' in the broad sense, and the formal school system, especially when this is an externally imposed system which has not evolved within the society.

To illustrate most of what has gone before it is proposed now to discuss some data, challenging data, most of it drawn from recent work in the Territory of Papua and New Guinea. The peoples of this Territory, many of whom, until quite recently, have had no contact with any groups other than their most immediate tribal neighbours, live for the most part in remote, isolated villages. Something like 700 different languages have been identified, about 200 of these being Austronesian and 500 or so non-Austronesian, or Papuan (Ward and Lea, 1970) and there is a fairly diverse group of socio-cultural living patterns. Since the war a Government education system has been established alongside a somewhat older mission-based pattern. In the early years and still largely persisting, the curriculum and teaching methods were based on those of New South Wales, in Australia. These may fairly be described in Bernstein's terms, as characterised by strong collection, strong classification and strong frames; or, in terms of the paradigm, as being in the Ausubel-type-cell with the curriculum product oriented and the methods based on guided learning. No comment is offered on the appropriateness of the content. In the last ten years or so, however, under the influence of a new Director, L. W. Johnston, and his successor K. S. McKinnon, there have been major efforts, particularly at primary level, to introduce new, process-based curricula and to train teachers in the use of discovery learning. As part of these reforms the staff of the Department of Education, working with groups of teachers, have developed a mathematics curriculum which makes intensive use of attribute blocks and other materials derived from the work of Zeldon Dienes in Britain, the US, South Australia and the Territory itself. The system, marketed as TEMLAB, has been introduced into many Territory schools, accompanied by a programme of teacher re-education. The fundamental theory of the system has been described in a number of publications, perhaps most clearly in the well-known compilation prepared by Dienes for ISGML and published in 1966 by the Unesco Institute for Education in Hamburg (Dienes, 1966).

There is little need here to give the details of the programme which is an imaginative and consistent development from the theory, but the theoretical principles should be outlined since some of the research to be described has called into question not so much the principles themselves, but some of the assumptions which underlie their application. Dienes appears to accept, with minor reservations of a technical nature, both Piaget's basic ideas about the staged development of concept formation and Bruner's position on the use of strategies. In addition he quotes with approval Bartlett's work on the development of open systems in thinking through some kind of dialectic. Skemp's distinctions between 'rote learning' and 'schematic learning' (which has some affinity to Ausubel's view about learning) and between 'sensory-motor' and 'reflective' intelligence are also seen by Dienes as important in the development of curriculum and methods of teaching–learning in mathematics. He quotes Skemp (1960) as claiming that

> mathematics is essentially a structure of subordinate and superordinate concepts and, therefore, in order to achieve a schema which involves a superordinate, all the subordinates must already have been constructed. So no new schema can be evolved until other schemata which form part of the new schema have also been evolved.

Dienes' own notion of abstraction is related to this:

> it is a process of class formation. Abstract ideas are formed by classifying objects into classes through some common property which, it is discovered, is possessed by these objects. Generalization is regarded as the extension of an already formed class and, therefore, it is more of a logical operation whereas abstraction is regarded as a constructive operation. Abstraction, therefore, is likely to take place as a result of abstracting information from rather a lot of different situations in which one particular aspect, namely the structure to be learnt, is held constant. This gives rise to the principle

of multiple embodiment. On the other hand the need for generality in mathematics gives rise to the principle of varying all the mathematical variables possible. The constructivity principle in its more sophisticated form is the theory of how constructions, abstractions, generalizations and play stand in relation to one another, as regards the process of learning. Another important principle is the principle of contrast. In order to learn something about a relationship, this relationship must be seen not to be necessarily valid in certain other cases (Dienes, 1966, p. 21).

Dienes' ideas about play are also highly relevant to the teaching–learning process and TEMLAB makes considerable use of them.

The central idea of the curriculum method, apart from its concentration on 'process' and on 'discovery learning' is that of abstraction. In 1966 Dienes contended that 'From results up to date, there is no evidence to suggest that native children are in any sense less capable of learning mathematics than any other children' (p. 113). Later statements, principally by the teachers and members of the Department, have been less optimistic and there is some evidence that, although Territory of Papua and New Guinea children are able to manipulate attribute blocks and other structured materials with quite astonishing skill and to convert this performance into paper and pencil situations, many of them are not displaying the appreciation and application of mathematical concepts which might have been expected to follow – and which had followed with Western children. A possible explanation for this derives from the research work of some members of the staff of the School of Education at Macquarie University.

Our interest, which was generously supported by Territory of Papua and New Guinea Department of Education, was as I have said in general problems of cognitive development in the children of the Territory of Papua and New Guinea. For a variety of reasons, some of these related to the TEMLAB project, our theoretical orientation stemmed from Bruner, although a number of studies based on Piaget's work have also been conducted.

Bruner contends that there are three basic strategies for attacking problems – including mathematical problems: indeed much of his earlier work and many of his experimental examples concerned mathematics. These strategies he terms 'enactive', 'ikonic' and 'symbolic'. To quote Dienes (1966, p. 19):

Bruner believes that the child in the beginning thinks in terms of action. His methods of solving a problem are, therefore, severely limited because if he cannot act out the solution, he cannot solve the problem. The next stage is the manipulation of images. This is what he calls the iconic stage. Images are very much more easily manipulable than actions, but nevertheless they tend to have a kind of permanence which makes them not very adapted to transformations. Mathematical thinking in particular abounds in transformations and, therefore, Bruner believes that fairly sophisticated mathematical thinking cannot take place until a child learns to think in terms of symbols and this is the third and last stage of the development of mathematical thinking.

This framework has major affinities with Piaget's notions about developmental stages, but is not identical. An important idea for Bruner is that anyone – adult as well as child – can and does 'operate' in any one of these strategic modes, depending partly on the specific demands of the problem and partly on individual 'preference'. That is, some people who are perfectly competent in the use of symbolic strategies for solving problems 'prefer' to use the ikonic mode – as Bruner writes, they are more 'comfortable' with it, just as some mathematicians are more 'comfortable' with, or 'prefer', to seek geometric solutions to problems they are quite capable of attacking algebraically. There are problems, however, which cannot be solved efficiently or even at all using ikonic strategies and many others in which the symbolic mode is by far the most effective or efficient – in the sense of being more economic of time and resources. Obviously enough, the TPNG mathematics curriculum, as described by Dienes, attempts to capitalise on the Bruner strategies and has as one of its objectives, the development of the use of the symbolic mode. It therefore became of some interest to examine the use of the basic strategies by TPNG children.

Ideas about classification and abstraction are fundamental to the theoretical positions of both Piaget and Bruner; a great deal of their experimental work has centred round the ways in which children classify their world and account for these classifications. The long statement from Dienes which has just been quoted emphasises the importance which was placed on abstraction and classification in the development of the TPNG mathematics curriculum and of course similar ideas underlie most of the curricula in the 'new mathematics'. It was therefore another matter of importance for us to explore the kinds of classification used by TPNG children and to examine, in particular, whether this performance was like those described by the Geneva group and/or the Harvard group. We were also interested

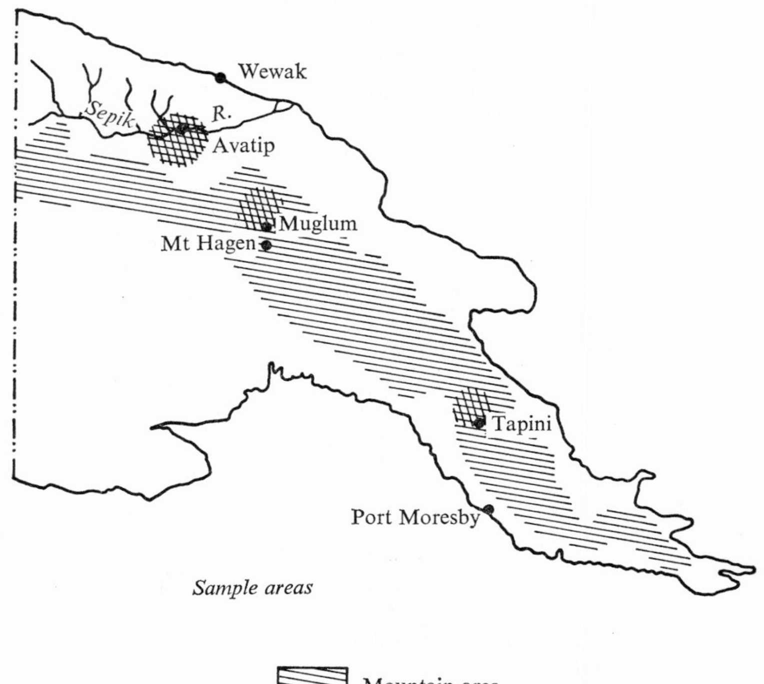

Territory of Papua and New Guinea (to show sample areas). After Kelly (1972).

Avatip:	Avatip speakers
Muglum:	Melpa speakers
Tapini:	Tawaudi speakers
	Kunimaipa speakers

in attempting to determine whether experience of school made any difference, either to the use of strategies of problem-solving or to levels of sophistication of classification.

The education system of TPNG provided an almost ideal situation for such a study. Apart from the remoteness of many villages, which meant a minimum of 'cultural contamination' in a high proportion of them, only about half the children in any one village attend school. Moreover, on such evidence as is available, attendance or non-attendance is determined partly by chance, partly by physical location of the school and only to a minor degree by the social factors which largely determine such things in developed countries. It was possible, accordingly, to obtain groups of attenders and non-attenders reasonably well matched in terms of age and language spoken. We had four such groups from different areas of TPNG, ranging from the remote headwaters of the Sepik River to the mountain valleys of the Western Highlands, as shown on the map.

The final sample is shown in table 1. It will be noted that it is not an ideal matched sample: this was essentially because it was difficult to persuade parents to allow their children to walk for two or three days through rough mountain jungle to play games with mad white men. One important characteristic of the sample, although to be honest, not one for which we planned, is that the four village groups use different number systems; in the sense of different bases. None of them is quite as exotic as those of, say, the Chimbu who use a base of thirty-one, or the Eastern and Western Kewa, whose body-counting system has a base of forty-seven (Wolfers, 1971) but they are sufficiently different from the European system and from each other to merit brief description.

The Sepik people in Avatip use a language which, according to Kelly (1972, p. 113) 'has a quite advanced counting system,...words from one to a thousand were recorded. When counting goods they use a kind of continuous adding process which effects multiplication...They do not rely on one-to-one correspondence.' The Melpa speaking people of the Western Highlands have 'counting words to ten. Larger numbers appear to be counted in base eight, using the fingers of the clenched fist to mark the eights (*ibid.* p. 118). A similar system is used by the Kunimaipa villagers of the Goilala–Tapini area, but their neighbours, the Tawaudi 'appear to (have) only (words for) one, one plus and many...certainly the Tawaudi trade and sell garden produce by a literal one-to-one correspondence of object to object' (*ibid.* p. 124).

For testing the choice of strategies we used an instrument developed by M. R. Kelly from an earlier model devised by Olson and described by him in Bruner, Olver and Greenfield's *Studies in Cognitive Growth* (Bruner *et al.*, 1966). A series of problems was presented to each child on this machine, which demanded a minimum use of language; responses could be classified with considerable reliability into 'enactive', 'ikonic' or 'symbolic' categories of strategy. It is important

TABLE 1. *Age, district, school years and sex distributions of final sample as drawn*

District		Ages 7	8	9	10	11	12	13	14	15+	Total
1. Avatip											
School years	Male	4	6	—	1	1	—	—	—	—	12
	Female	5	5	1	1	—	—	—	—	—	12
	Male	—	—	2	1	3	3	2	1	—	12
	Female	—	—	1	1	3	7	—	—	—	12
	Male	—	—	—	—	—	2	1	3	6	12
	Female	—	—	—	—	1	1	6	1	3	12
	Male	1	—	—	—	—	1	—	—	—	2
	Female	—	1	—	1	2	2	—	1	1	8
2. Muglum											
School years	Male	10	1	—	—	1	—	—	—	—	12
	Female	11	1	—	—	—	—	—	—	—	12
	Male	1	—	1	7	1	—	2	—	—	12
	Female	—	—	8	1	1	1	—	1	—	12
	Male	—	—	—	—	2	—	6	3	1	12
	Female	—	—	—	1	2	1	2	2	4	12
	Male	1	4	3	6	4	8	6	4	8	44
	Female	2	5	6	2	1	2	5	3	2	28
3. Keltiga											
School years	Male	3	2	10	8	3	6	3	3	1	39
	Female	1	—	2	6	1	2	5	4	2	23
4. Goilala/Tawaudi											
School years	Male	2	2	—	1	1	—	—	—	—	6
	Female	1	1	—	—	—	—	—	—	—	2
	Male	—	—	—	2	2	1	—	—	4	9
	Female	—	—	—	—	1	—	—	—	—	1
	Male	—	—	—	—	—	—	2	1	4	7
	Female	—	—	—	—	—	—	—	1	4	5
	Male	3	1	7	7	2	3	3	2	—	28
	Female	2	3	4	5	3	4	4	4	9	38
5. Goilala/Kunimaipa											
School years	Male	3	3	—	—	—	—	—	—	—	6
	Female	2	2	1	2	3	—	—	—	—	10
	Male	—	—	—	—	—	—	—	1	2	3
	Female	—	—	—	—	2	3	3	2	1	11
	Male	—	—	—	—	—	—	1	—	4	5
	Female	—	—	—	—	—	—	—	—	7	7
	Male	—	—	1	3	1	1	—	—	—	6
	Female	—	—	—	—	—	—	—	—	—	0

Avatip 0 School Years (village) + Keltiga 0 School Years = 72
Goilala Tawaudi + Goilala Kunimaipa (school) = 72
(village) = 72
Thus three 'districts' provide 72 school and 72 village each
school = 216 village = 216

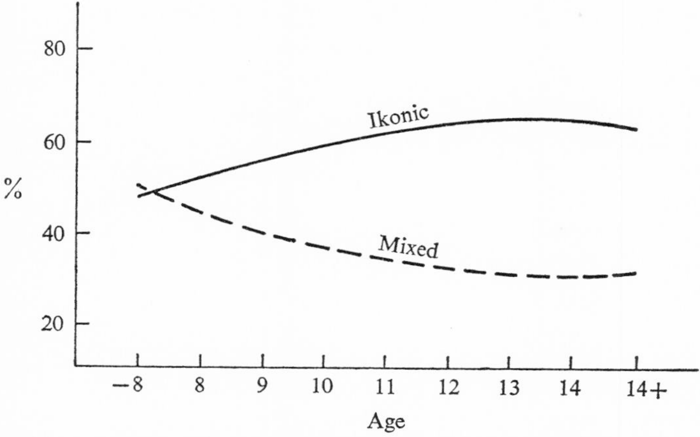

Fig. 1. Trends in use of strategies: summed problems, Series A. All groups: $N = 1668$ problem solutions. After Kelly (1972).

to note that Kelly was not concerned with *correctness* of solution – most children 'solved' all the problems – but with the strategy they employed. Pilot studies showed that many children used a mixed strategy – 'ikonic–symbolic' – and this was introduced as a scoring category in the main study. I should say at once that we found no use at all of the enactive mode in this sample, although with younger children it appeared about as frequently as with NSW children of similar ages. It seems that, as with Western children, the enactive mode is not relevant to our simple problem situation. More surprisingly, none of the children in our sample used the symbolic mode consistently; a very few did solve one or two easier problems using symbolic strategies, but as the tasks became more difficult even these few used mixed or ikonic strategies. The data to be presented, therefore, show proportions of responses categorised as belonging to the ikonic or mixed ikonic–symbolic modes.

In accordance with developmental theory, we predicted an increase in the use of the mixed strategy with age and a reciprocal decrease in the use of the ikonic. Figure 1 summarises the results over all children. We were wrong – and the differences between the curves are highly significant at all ages from nine onwards. There is a slight tendency – which fits a parabola – for the use of the mixed mode to be beginning to increase again about 12–13 years. Now let us break these curves down according to sex and according to attendance or non-attendance

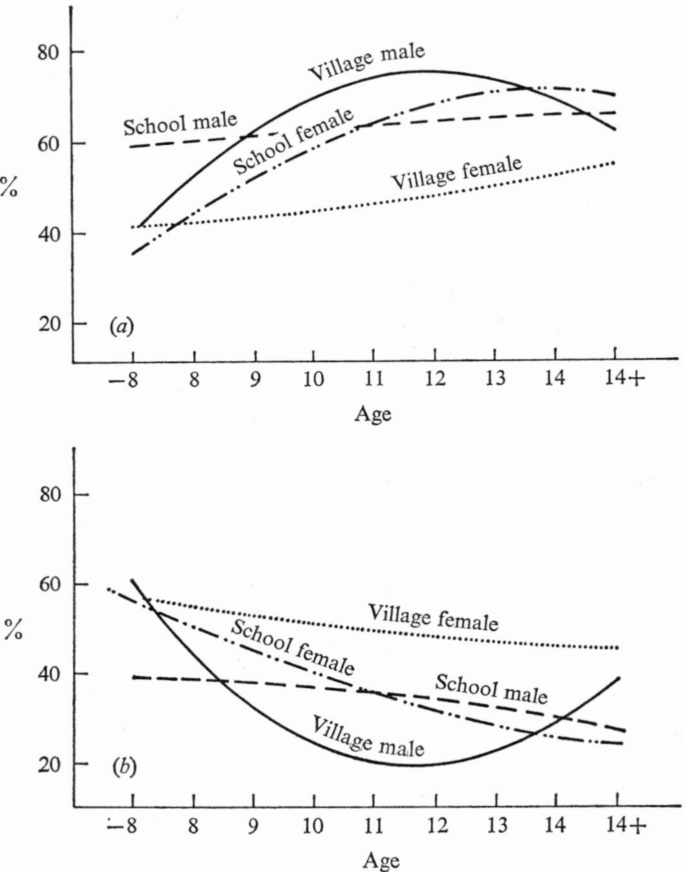

Fig. 2. (*a*) Ikonic mode: trends in use by males and females, in school and village groups. (*b*) Mixed mode: trends in use by males and females, in school and village groups. After Kelly (1972).

at school. Here we predicted no sex differences, and greater use of the mixed mode by school attenders than by non-attenders (called 'school' and 'village' children on the diagram). Figure 2 gives the results: obviously the bottom graph is a mirror of the top. Clearly enough, girls in general use the mixed mode more often than boys but this is much more pronounced in the 'village' group than in the 'school' group. Overall, there is a significant difference between the school group and the village group in favour of the village children in use of the mixed mode, but this is confounded by both sex and age effects. It is worth looking at males and females separately: the village girls, although there is a slight but significant decline with age, make uniformly more use of the more efficient mixed mode than the school girls. The gap increases with age. The male picture is different: the school group, like the girls, slowly falls with age – the difference between the male/female curves is not significant at any point except 8. The village boys, however, decline rapidly in use of the mixed mode until about 10–11–12, when they begin to use it more frequently. Nor are these results an accident of sampling, for they appeared in all four of the groups studied. The theoretical analysis of some of these findings is not the concern of the present paper – fascinating though they are. Here I am interested in pointing out that, contrary to expectation, among TPNG children there is apparently a decrease with age rather than an increase in the level of efficiency, in terms of strategies, with which problems are solved. Further, exposure to school makes little difference; such differences as do exist operate in favour of the village children. The same apparatus and problems have been used with NSW children, both native born and non-English speaking migrants, and Kelly has shown that the results are in the expected direction; that is, there is an increase with age in the use of the mixed and symbolic modes.

It is pertinent in the light of these data, to question the use of a curriculum heavily dependent on the development of symbolic type strategies.

Furthermore, when we used Piaget-type situations similar results emerged. For example, no child in this sample (TPNG) could solve a standard formal operations problem using local materials.

We may now look at some data on classification. For this, with the same sample as before, two sets of tasks were developed from the earlier work of Bruner and his group. The first set of materials was a square matrix of nine blocks which can be ordered according to two criteria of classification, length and area of cross section. This has obvious relationship to the attribute blocks of TEMLAB. The second set of materials consisted of separate sets of objects, drawings of these objects, photographs of them, and sets of words in the vernacular languages. The original objects, which were either full size or scale models, were all of local origin and were familiar to the children – we tested for this by asking each child to identify each object. He was then asked to group them 'in any way' and then for the reasons for his grouping. In accordance with the procedure reported in Bruner *et al.* (1966), the responses were then scored according to 'structure', that is the level of inclusiveness of the grouping, and 'base', the attribute of classification, whatever the level of structure. Identical procedures were used for the objects, pictures and photographs, but, because the 'village' children were illiterate, 'words' were read to them and to the school group by vernacular speakers. In passing, it should be noted that, after pilot testing, most tests were administered by vernacular speakers – often children themselves.

What did we find? First, as we would hope, as well as expect, on the block matrix the school groups, both male and female, had a 'higher' level of performance at each age level than the village groups. The differences were less, however, for tasks which required application of classification, for example, reversal of the matrix, than for those in which straightforward classification was required.

The other classification data, where children had to choose categories, sort materials into them and then account for their classification, gave a less clear picture. There were some differences in the level of structure of objects, pictures and photographs and these differences were in favour of the school as against the village groups. Similar results appeared when the nature of the attributes was examined: the school group made more, though limited, use of nominal, that is 'abstract', classification principles, while the village children almost exclusively used 'functional egocentric' criteria. When it came to classification of 'words', however, there were no significant differences between the village group and the school group in terms of the nature of the 'attribute' of classification. The indication is strong that TPNG children, at least in the areas in which we worked, prefer to use images – to employ 'ikonic strategies' rather than symbols when faced with cognitive problems to solve.

Before going on to discuss possible explanations and implications for curriculum and teaching, particularly in mathematics, it is worth looking at performance on all these tasks in terms of comparisons among the four village groups. It will be recalled that the Avatip people of the Sepik, the people in the Mount Hagen area and the Kunimaipa from Tapini use somewhat more sophisticated number systems than the Tawaudi, whose system is an extremely limited one. On *all* the tasks described, the Tawaudi children performed at a 'lower' level than the children from any of the other three areas – village and school children alike. The Melpa-speaking children of the Mount Hagen area tended to use more high level 'structures' than any of the other groups and the 'base' or criteria of classification was much more frequently on the 'nominal' (abstract) level. This raises some questions of considerable theoretical and practical interest. A possible explanation and a suggestion for curriculum is contained in an extension of a hypothesis advanced by Kuhlman (1960) who writes 'Either the habit of using imagery is suppressed or *it is retained during language acquisition and is adapted to the requirements of complex problem solving*' (italics mine) (quoted by Bruner *et al.*, 1966). What I would add is that the very language structure of some cultures may be conducive to the retention and adaptation of the use of imagery (that is the ikonic or mixed modes) 'to the requirements of complex problem solving'. Western curricula assume the increasing use of the symbolic mode and of 'nominal' methods of classification with the associated superordinate structure. They have usually been 'taken over' or 'adapted' for non-Western groups without any attempt to examine the validity of the assumption.

Considerations of this kind led us to look for further data. An obvious starting point was in the nature of the language systems. I do not want to get involved here in a discussion of Whorf's hypothesis that the structure of the language determines the kinds of classifications available to children and hence to a large extent the nature of the concepts they form, but data recently gathered by Kelly, and as yet unpublished, is very much in support of it. Working with New Guinea anthropologists, he charted the Melpa linguistic dimensions and I quote from a personal communication:

They do not form hierarchies of classification. Their world is a series of intersecting sets. They can perform well on tasks designed from their own system, better than the Australian children at Hagen A school.[1] You can get them to assimilate our objects (for example wooden attribute blocks) to their schema, but can't get them to assimilate their objects to our schema [for example, class inclusion with 'kim' (leaf vegetable) and 'oka' (kau kau) which are both 'rung' (food)]. The lack of ability to handle hierarchies goes through to high school kids and teachers' college students. When you explore English concepts in the vernacular you find that they have been busily distorting them into the vernacular equivalent for years. For example, 'weapon' which is 'mel el ba ng mel kum panda', things designed specifically for killing man or animal (i.e. bows and arrows and spears). A stone cannot be a weapon, even when used to bash in someone's

[1] A Highlands school with the standard Australian (N.S.W.) curriculum.

head. (It is the most common instrument of murder used in Hagen.) A stone is a stone is a stone.

From data of this kind it may be argued that the level and nature of the classification of any given set of material will depend, to some extent at least, on the language of classification. Kelly set out to test this hypothesis in an ingenious experiment. The results are not yet fully analysed, but they seem to me of such interest that I propose to describe them briefly. They were obtained from the Melpa children of whom I have just spoken. Three samples were selected, each of sixty-seven children:

A. a 'school' group: tested in English;

B. a 'school' group, matched in pairs with *A* on age, sex and school performance: tested in Melpa;

C. a 'village' group, matched with the *A* and *B* modules on age and sex: tested in Melpa.

Each group was presented with two sets of classification tasks:

(*a*) attribute blocks, with colour, shape, size and thickness as attributes;

(*b*) leaves from local plants, with colour, size, use (e.g. as food, for construction, for decoration) and method of cultivation as attributes.

Instructions were given, as appropriate to each group, in English or Melpa in the expectation (or hope, rather) that the instruction would produce a 'mental set' for working in the corresponding language. Responses were scored behaviourally as well as verbally, that is, in terms of what the children did physically with the materials as well as in terms of their descriptions of the classifications. In addition to the original classification instructions, the children were 'pushed' to attempt more inclusive hierarchies. The results – and I emphasise that this analysis of the behavioural responses is both incomplete and tentative – show:

(*a*) The level of classification (in the sense earlier discussed) was higher, for both sets of materials, for the group tested in English than for either of the other groups. School group *B*, however, was 'superior' to the village group, that is, in terms of level of classification. Thus $A > B > C$ for both sets of materials.

(*b*) For both groups *A* and *B* the level of classification of the 'Western' materials – the attribute blocks – was much higher than the level of classification of local materials. The difference was far greater for the group tested in English than for the group tested in their native language. No differences appeared in the village group.

(*c*) When 'pushed' to use a more inclusive category of classification, children in all three groups were able to make some shifts, although the amounts were quite small. The group tested in English was again superior to either of the others, while the Melpa-tested school group exceeded the village group in the mean number of shifts made, that is, $A > B > C$ in mean number of shifts on both types of material.

(*d*) No significant differences were found between types of material in terms of the ability to use higher orders of classification.

These data, if confirmed by other studies at present under way in New Guinea and elsewhere, support the earlier findings that it is as if the accessibility of inclusive words in a language in some way affects and restricts the inclusiveness of the classifications which the child is able to make.

And this is to be expected in societies in which classification is built into the language as it is in a number of the TPNG languages as well as in some Asian tongues like Thai. An object is classified according to its linguistic 'classifier' and not according to 'natural' or 'logical' categories, on Western criteria of logic. It is made to fit, as Kelly says, into the child's schema. This would parallel such studies as those of Gay and Cole (1967) with the Kpelle and Greenfield's (1966) with the Wolof children of Senegal. It would seem clear that findings of this kind raise real problems for curriculum construction and teaching methods in non-Western societies.

This is not to say that the fundamental theory behind TEMLAB and other modern mathematics curricula is incorrect and that we should revert to collection type curricula, with strong classification and strong frames or, in other language, to product or subject centred curricula, supported by strictly guided learning. On the contrary, the data seem to me to argue for even greater emphasis on *process* and on discovery methods, but with curriculum *context* carefully designed to take into account the processes the child has already learned to use and which are 'preferred' in his society. Where he has to learn 'new' processes in order to cope effectively with the curriculum, then ample scope has to be given for this. For example, it would appear from what has just been said, that a great deal of specific material will have to be built into the TPNG curriculum, presumably, but not exclusively, through primary school mathematics, on the formation of hierarchies. We cannot assume that, as Dienes wrote in 1966, 'Abstraction is likely to take place as a result of abstracting information from rather a lot of different situations in which one particular aspect, namely the structure to be learned is held constant.' In many languages and cultures the principle of 'multiple embodiment' is not generic. It is, granted, essential for most Western thinking, particularly in mathematics and science: if curricula and methods which will help non-Western children to form and use Western-type concepts are desired then we must help children to learn not only the concepts but the ways of thinking which lead to these concepts. (Incidentally I understand that Professor Dienes and Dr Kelly have been asked to advise on ways of redesigning TEMLAB to include games which will encourage the development of ideas about hierarchies.)

The other evidence I wish briefly to discuss refers to the 'structure' of mathematical thinking, in the factor analysis sense. There is little point in getting involved here in a heredity–environment controversy. My main purpose is to present some data which appear to support the thesis I have been so far arguing, that cultural factors, particularly language, influence not only what is learned, but how it is learned, and how it is applied. That is, *even on the same tests of performance* we should expect a different pattern to emerge in different cultures. This is a somewhat different emphasis from that of Guilford (1971) in his monumental study *The Nature of Human Intelligence* as derived from the results of factor analysis. Discussing some cross cultural work he writes, somewhat curiously: 'There are not many cultural differences in factor structure *where all groups are tested in the same language*' (italics mine) 'and such differences as occur can be accounted for in terms of cultural variables' (p. 40). That is, Guilford seems to be *dismissing*, to some extent at least Piaget's view, which I share, that 'les structures (sont) variables, les fonctions (sont) invariantes' (Piaget, 1968, p. 11). Apart from almost inaccessible Japanese data, there have been all too few studies of 'factor structure' in non-Western societies. Guilford cites Vandenburg (1959) on Chinese students studying in the US and Guthrie (1963) on Tagalog speaking students in the Philippines Normal College. One may add Dunlap (1931) in Hawaii, Biesheuvel (1949) in South Africa, Scott (1950) among the Sudanese and Jahoda (1956) in West Africa as evidence that the picture is not quite as clear as Guilford suggests: what may well be really important are those 'cultural variables', which Guilford dismisses.

Early in 1972 Miss Elizabeth Southwell[1] conducted a factor analysis based study in TPNG. Since it was concerned quite specifically with mathematics her results are of some relevance. She administered a battery of thirteen tests; six of them were specifically of a mathematical character, four others have shown significant leadings on 'number type' factors in Western studies, two were verbal and the thirteenth tested 'general information'. There were four sample groups: European teachers working in TPNG; indigenous teachers; indigenous students in training to become teachers and New Guinea children of high school age. The factor patterns were quite different: that for the European teachers was fairly easy to describe in terms of the familiar Thurstone–Guilford type factors. The indigenous teachers, who had less formal education than any of the other groups, produced a verbal factor, distinct from the Thurstone type *V* of the Europeans, which ran through almost all the tests, including those which used no apparent language. A second factor was concerned with the spatial relationships, but was much more general – that is, it entered into more tests – than the *S* factor for the Europeans and a third, which had something to do with number did not appear at all in the European group. Analysis of the performance of the teacher-trainees and the children produced patterns somewhat like those of the indigenous teachers, but less generalised.

More interesting was a second factor analysis, again on all four samples but this time using the sixty items of her test of 'mathematics understanding'. Difficulty structure, confounded by differential reading speeds, may well have accounted for some of the patterns in the first study, but in this test there were few significant differences in *item* difficulty with the mathematics understanding test, and light is shed on this by the analysis.

For present purposes it is proposed to discuss the differences between the European teachers and the indigenous teachers. In both groups there were four or at best five factors which made 'psychological sense' and among them accounted for about 50% of the variance. Most clear among the indigenous teachers was a general verbal factor – although, it is stressed, this was a *mathematical* test – which took up almost 25% of the total variance. This factor did not

[1] Miss Southwell has just successfully presented this material for a Ph.D. at the University of London. My interpretation of her data, which she generously loaned to me, may not accord with hers. In any event I have not presented it in full since clearly it would be unfair to do so until she has herself published.

appear at all in the European teacher pattern. In the European pattern was clearly to be identified a factor which looked very much like Coombs' (1941) and my own (1951) '*A*' factor, which enters into most mathematical type problems but is distinct from the purely numerical factor *N* identified in many studies. This factor did not appear in the indigenous group. What is of some interest is that items involving sets, whether in the form of braces or Venn diagrams, had significant loadings (> 0.30) on the *A* factor in the European group, but on the verbal factor *and also* on a spatial factor for the indigenous group. The spatial factor also appeared for the Europeans but Venn diagrams had low loadings on it. This would seem to lend support to Kelly's findings about the preferred use of the mixed-ikonic–symbolic mode by indigenous groups in TPNG. Items which were apparently solved by symbolic means by the European teachers were solved, equally well in terms of correct answers, by use of images or a mixture of images and symbols by the indigenes. Similarly the different factor pattern on the items involving sets would seem to imply that different criteria of classification were being used, lending support to the language data discussed above.

What does all this imply? Let me say again that the data are not conclusive. We are still very much in the early stages of our investigations and many questions remain. One intriguing one, which we hope to look at next year, is the effect of different indigenous number systems on school performance. This is part of a much greater attack on the total effect of language: for this we will need the help of anthropologists, psycho-socio linguists and mathematicians interested in education, for it seems important to continue in this general curriculum area.

However, I think that there is already enough evidence to suggest that, at least in non-Western societies and particularly in pre-literate areas:

(*a*) curriculum should be process oriented and methods should be heavily discovery learning based,

(*b*) curriculum should be integrated, in Bernstein's sense with weak classification and weak frames,

(*c*) the learning processes and preferred strategies of each particular culture group should be carefully investigated and the curriculum built and teaching–learning methods devised in order to take account of them,

(*d*) the linguistic structure of the mother tongue should be analysed to determine the classificatory system: this too should be carefully considered when constructing a curriculum, particularly in mathematics.

It is perhaps appropriate to end by quoting the familiar 64th Query of Bishop Berkeley: 'Whether mathematics...have not their mysteries, and what is more, their repugnances and contradictions?' and to ask whether this should not also apply to mathematics teaching and learning?

School of Education,
Macquarie University,
Australia.

References

Bernstein, B., On the classification and framing of educational knowledge, in Hopper, E., *Readings in the Theory of Educational Systems*, Hutchinson, London, 1971.

Biesheuvel, S., Psychological Tests and their application to non-European peoples, in *The Yearbook of Education*, Evans Bros, London, 1949, pp. 87–126.

Bridgman, P. W., Quo Vadis, *Daedalus* **87**, 1958, 85–93, quoted by Cole *et al. The Cultural Context of Logical Thinking*, Methuen, London, 1971, p. 176.

Bruner, J. S., *Towards a Theory of Instruction*, W. W. Norton, New York, 1966.

Bruner, J. S., Olver, R. R. and Greenfield, P. M., *Studies in Cognitive Growth*, Wiley, New York, 1966.

Coombs, C. H., A factorial study of numerical ability, *Psychometrika* **6**, 1941, 3.

Dienes, Z. P., *Mathematics in Primary Education* (ISGML), Unesco Institute for Education, Hamburg, 1966.

Dunlap, J. W., Race Differences in the organization of numerical and verbal abilities, *Arch. Psychol.* N.Y. No. 124, 1931.

Gay, J. and Cole, M., *The New Mathematics and an Old Culture*, Holt, Rinehart and Winston, New York, 1967.

Greenfield, P. M., On culture and conservation, in Bruner, J. S., Olver, R. R. and Greenfield, P. M., *Studies in Cognitive Growth*, Wiley, New York, 1966.

Guilford, J. P., *The Nature of Human Intelligence*, I.S.E. edition, McGraw-Hill, London, 1971.

Guthrie, G. M., Structure of abilities in a non-Western culture, *J. Ed. Psychol.* **54**, 1963, 94–103.

Jahoda, G., Assessment of abstract behaviour in a non-Western culture, *J. Abnormal and Social Psychology* **53**, 1956, 237–43.

Kelly, M. R., The validity of Bruner's Modes in Papua–New Guinea. *Unpublished Ph.D. thesis*, School of Education, Macquarie University, 1972.

Kuhlman, C., Visual Imagery in children, *Unpublished thesis*, Harvard University, 1960.

Mead, M., An educative emphasis in primitive perspective, *Am. J. of Soc.* **18**, 1943.

Olson, D. R., On Conceptual Strategies, in Bruner, J., Olver, R. R. and Greenfield, P. M., *Studies in Cognitive Growth*, Wiley, New York, 1966.

Philp, H. W., The Number factor, *Unpublished thesis*, University of Sydney, 1951.

Philp, H. W., *Some Factors Affecting Educability*, ACER, Melbourne, 1967.

Piaget, J., *Language and Thought of the Child*, Routledge and Kegan Paul, London, 1926.

Piaget, J., Logique et équilibre dans les comportements des sujets, *Études d'Epistémol. Génet.* **2**, 1957, 27–117 (*b*).

Piaget, J., *La Naissance de l'intelligence chez l'enfant.* 6th edition, Delachaux et Niestlé, Neuchâtel, 1968.

Scott, G. C., Measuring Sudanese Intelligence, *Brit. J. Educ. Psychol.* **20**, 1950, 43–54.

Sigel, I. E., The Piagetan System and the World of Education, in Elkind, D. and Flavell, J. H. (eds.), *Studies in Cognitive Development*, Oxford University Press, London, 1969.

Skemp, R. R., Reflective Intelligence and Mathematics, *Brit. J. Educ. Psychol.* **31**, 1960.

Southwell, E. G., A psychological study of the development of mathematical concepts in Papua-New Guinea, *Unpublished Ph.D. thesis*, London University, 1972.

Shulman, L. S., Psychology and Mathematics Education, in *Mathematics Education*, 69th Yearbook of the National Society for the Study of Education, University of Chicago Press, Chicago, 1970.

Vandenberg, S. G., The primary mental abilities of Chinese students: a comparative study of the stability of factor structure, *Ann. N.Y. Acad. Sci.* **79**, 1959, 257–304.

Ward, R. G. and Lea, D., *An Atlas of Papua and New Guinea*, Collins and Langman, Glasgow, 1970.

Wolfers, E. P., The original counting systems of Papua and New Guinea, *The Arithmetic Teacher* Feb. 1971.

Some questions of mathematical education in the USSR

S. L. Sobolev

At this time of unusually rapid change in the mode of life of all mankind, a time when science is being applied with increasing intensity to technology, the demand for scientific personnel – researchers and practical workers – has grown enormously. In particular, the demand for mathematicians has been especially great in recent years. Inevitably, the teaching of the basic sciences has lagged behind in all countries. Of the whole body of mathematical knowledge which I, and those who were students with me at Leningrad University, now require, very little was acquired whilst we were at university. University gave us the basis for something that it is difficult to express in words. Perhaps it taught us to think.

In the same way, what we are teaching young people now, in particular the mathematics we are giving them, will probably no longer meet the demands made on them in fifteen to twenty years time. And it is precisely fifteen to twenty years hence that their time will come. They will create the science and technology of the future.

On the other hand, in every country, and all the time, problems arise which will only be solved, either today or tomorrow, by specialists. These problems change very rapidly, before one's very eyes.

In recent years much has already been said about the necessity of conducting mathematical education from the very beginning on the most abstract level possible, concentrating attention on general mathematical ideas. In a number of countries attempts have been made to introduce children from an early age to set-theoretic terminology and the basic concepts connected with this. The merits and demerits of such early abstraction are now more or less clear. For, although it has been made possible for them to penetrate more easily into some fundamental regions of mathematical science, young people educated in this way sometimes lack the ability to grasp practical mathematical situations, because of their weak knowledge of concrete mathematical material.

The other extreme – teaching principally by the method of solving varied concrete problems – also has its merits and demerits. As a result of such unbalanced education, we often get scientific workers who lack perspective and are unable to be creative when the occasion arises.

All this has been discussed many times in recent years, and one can only argue about the respective weightings we must give to concrete knowledge and general theory in the training of future mathematicians.

I shall not, therefore, talk of these questions, but will attempt instead to talk in concrete terms about the experience of teaching mathematics in the Soviet Union and about those tendencies and opinions which are to be found in our country.

Mathematics is taught in the USSR at two levels of education: in the secondary school and in the higher school.

The secondary school is intended for the education of children from the age of 7 or 8 to 17 or 18 years. This school is a ten-year school in the Russian Federation, and an eleven-year school in some republics of the Union where the Russian language is taught separately but where basic education takes place in the language of that republic.

The final section of the ten-year general-educational school can be replaced by the completion of the eight-year, so-called incomplete secondary school, followed by study in special professional, technical schools, medical schools etc., and also in the evening schools. The curriculum of these schools includes general educational subjects to the same extent as in the ten-year school.

The higher schools are: universities (about fifty in the country), pedagogical institutes, higher technical educational institutions, institutes of medicine and law, musical academies etc. designated for higher professional education.

Students can enter the institutions of higher education from the age of seventeen onwards. The period of study in the higher schools is about five years.

For professional purposes, mathematics is taught in the higher schools in the physics-mathematics, the mechanics-mathematics and the mathematical faculties of universities and pedagogical institutes. Mathematics is also one of the fundamental disciplines in the curricula of other university faculties and higher technical educational institutions.

Until the last two decades the content of mathematical education in the secondary school was very stable. By long tradition, in the classes up to the age of twelve there was a very long and detailed study of arithmetic including the 'arithmetical' solution of rather complicated verbal problems which really required algebraic methods. Then there followed two parallel courses: algebra and geometry. The algebra course was traditional, containing a study of the identical transformations of literal expressions, the theory of algebraic equations and systems, with the application of algebraic techniques to the solution of verbal problems. The course also included the elements of combinatorics and an initial acquaintance with the logarithmic function, including the use of tables. Geometry was based on visual presentations and an axiomatic approach close to that of Euclid.

Only in the last ten to fifteen years has the study of trigonometrical functions and the solution of triangles been distributed between the algebra and geometry courses.

The acceleration of technical progress and the growth of the role of science has necessitated a revision of the content and style of mathematical (and not only mathematical) education in the secondary school.

The basic ideas and concepts of traditional 'higher mathematics': the derivative, the integral, and easy differential equations as a means of describing physical phenomena were needed by almost everybody, whatever his kind of work. It has also become no less important to teach young people some elementary uses of calculating machines.

A broadening of the content of mathematical education, therefore, became essential and syllabuses in mathematics (and other subjects) in the secondary school were radically revised with the participation of wide groups of the scientific public in the country. The resulting changes affected not only content but also the style of teaching.

The primary aim of the changes is to bridge the gaps between arithmetic on the one side and algebra and geometry on the other, and also between elementary and higher mathematics. This is achieved by the early use of letters, first of all for denoting unknowns in solving problems. The concept of a negative number is introduced early. In the very lowest classes pupils meet the elementary geometrical figures and simple problems with geometrical content. As a result the functional point of view is achieved, with considerable use being made of graphical methods. The algebra course is rounded off with the introduction of the concepts of the derivative and integral with various applications, but without developing the complicated technique of differentiation and integration. The concepts of the theory of sets and mathematical logic are introduced *gradually*(!), when necessary, from the fourth class, and these provide a convenient language for the study of systems of equations, inequalities between unknowns, and for the formation of the concept of a function. Greater attention is given to the method of coordinates and to the graphs of functions.

The basis of the geometry course is implicitly the study of groups of motions of the Euclidean plane and space.

The revision of instruction according to the new syllabuses was preceded by long discussion. The mathematical syllabuses, for example, were discussed twice at sessions of the presidium of the Academy of Sciences of the USSR. A competition was announced for the writing of new textbooks, in which several teams of writers took part. Those textbooks that were acknowledged the most successful were accepted. However, we can be sure that in the future it will be necessary to include substantial improvements.

In the revision of the teaching in the secondary school a moderate point of view was adopted which took into account many present-day abstract mathematical ideas and concepts. Nevertheless, it was still considered important that the students should acquire factual knowledge and skills, and familiarity with those concepts mentioned above that are essential for the construction of models of the phenomena of the world about us.

The introduction of the new material is made possible by the extent to which time is saved as a result of its use in teaching traditional mathematics.

In the new syllabus there is a reserve section that permits the teacher to increase the content of the mathematics. This consists of optional activities, beginning from the seventh class, to which special time is devoted (of the order of four hours a week). These optional activities take place in different realms of knowledge, at the student's choice, and this choice often falls within mathematics. In addition, in various towns of the USSR there are schools with strengthened physics-mathematics preparation in the upper classes. Such schools have been in existence for nearly fifteen years and the experiences gained in them were taken into account when the syllabuses for the general schools were prepared.

A particular role is played by the boarding-schools associated with the largest universities of the country (Moscow, Leningrad, Novosibirsk and Kiev). The main purpose of these schools is to attract talented young people from towns and villages remote from the large centres. Such pupils are discovered in the 'mathematical olympiads' – mathematical contests in which very many school children take part. These are organised now in three rounds: first in the schools, then in the large regional centres and finally the all-Union olympiad.

Recently each spring there has been also an all-Siberian mathematical olympiad in Novosibirsk.

The first mathematical olympiad was organised in Leningrad in 1934. From that time these contests have won great popularity.

Until recent years the profession of scientific worker was not very popular, particularly in places remote from the large scientific centres. Now the situation is beginning to change.

The olympiads, the physics-mathematics schools etc., however, are designed not simply and solely for the direct search for talent, but have another important aim – to attract young people to be scientific workers and researchers. Their aim is to acquaint boys and girls with the fascination of scientific enquiry. And in fact, thanks to them, many young people have found their vocation.

The reform of school education in the USSR, which affects not only mathematics, has increased the demands on teachers. Simultaneously with this there was a rise in the salary of teachers both in the secondary and higher schools.

In the higher schools mathematical education has four basic aims:

(*a*) In the technical higher educational establishments and other higher schools and faculties for which mathematics is an important auxiliary subject, the aim is to produce educated engineers who are able to solve difficult technical problems.

(*b*) New branches of engineering have recently been created which are essentially mathematical, for example, control theory, mathematical economics, programming, the construction of new computers, and as a result we can now speak of the 'engineer-mathematician'. His appearance, following on that of the engineer-physicist, means we must change our ideas of what a technical worker must know today. A second aim, therefore, is to produce such engineer-mathematicians.

(*c*) In the pedagogical institutes the aim is to prepare suitably equipped mathematics teachers for the secondary schools.

(*d*) Finally, in the universities the aim is to produce mathematical researchers and teachers in the higher schools.

I will say something in detail about each of these.

The newest thing that has appeared in recent years in the realm of higher technical education in the USSR is the creation in several institutions of the specialism of engineer-mathematician. This specialism has been established both in the technical schools, as for example in the Physics-Technical Institute in Moscow, and also in universities – Moscow, Leningrad, Novosibirsk.

A new specialism like this has been dictated by life itself and the establishment of special engineering-mathematics faculties, both in universities and in higher technical educational institutions, has taken place not only in the Soviet Union but also in many other countries.

The content and style of mathematics teaching in the other faculties of the higher technical schools is subordinate to the requirements of the basic specialism and is therefore rather varied. Recently, there have been moves towards extending this content in certain non-traditional directions. Thus, there are courses on programming, based on present-day computational mathematics, followed by short courses on control theory, the basic concepts of mathematical economics, and so on.

Unfortunately, a shortage of suitably qualified personnel prevents changes being made on a sufficiently large scale.

New mathematics syllabuses have also been developed in the pedagogical institutes. The aim in designing these syllabuses was to bring the mathematical training of their students closer to that of the university, and also to initiate them into the new mathematical specialisms they will have to talk about in school. An important aim of the courses on teaching method is to ensure that future teachers know the new syllabuses and textbooks for the secondary school, which are very different from those from which they learned.

The education of professional mathematicians (in the mathematics-mechanics, mathematics and physics-mathematics faculties of universities) lasts five years. Students who have shown outstanding ability and an inclination towards scientific work can stay for a three-year postgraduate course. In this they will study a chosen field in depth under the direction of a professor and prepare an independent piece of research including a dissertation. They will then obtain the first science degree – candidate of science.

At this time of scientific progress, when mathematical knowledge is developing fast and the role of mathematics is increasing everywhere, there is a need systematically to revise the material studied in the mathematics faculties. Several years ago the growth of applications of mathematical science, precipitated discussion in many universities of the USSR concerning the reforms which would be needed in the teaching of mathematics.

In our country, as it seems in the whole world, up to now the ablest young people, those with a breadth of vision, creativity and deep insight, very often sought to engage in mathematics divorced from its applications. This tendency was encouraged by the fact that in those many parts of mathematics which until now had been little connected with other sciences, it was easier to obtain fundamentally new results and to discover or invent new methods of investigation.

Often also, the value placed by society on concrete and narrow, although also very difficult, results was lower than that it put on wide, though perhaps at times much more banal, generalisations. Young students, therefore, have tended to neglect those problems in which the techniques of research take the lion's share of time and energy and in which the results have a concrete character. This has happened almost everywhere with the exception of some backward conservative educational institutions where concreteness of results was perhaps valued highly, but the results themselves were weak.

Even in Leningrad University, which prided itself on its ancient traditions in applied mathematics, and where in their time worked Tchebishev, Markov (the elder), Liapunov and Steklov, they were not able to avoid this.

Several historical causes also contributed to this separation of mathematics from its applications. Most applications of mathematics in the past were in the field of mechanics: the mechanics of systems, the mechanics of rigid bodies and the mechanics of continuous media. Often mechanics was regarded almost as a part of mathematical science, and the role of experiments was hardly taken into account. In the large universities, such as Leningrad and Moscow, there were combined mathematics-mechanics faculties with the two departments of mathematics and mechanics.

Other applications of mathematics were hardly taught at all and were limited to a course in numerical analysis. The content of this course was reduced to certain largely trivial questions about the estimation of errors and to the enumeration of different computational methods developed historically. It did not touch on such general questions as are to be found in the present-day theory of computation.

In mechanics, after the important discoveries of Liapunov,

Chaplygin and Jukovski, there followed a period of quiet, slow accumulation of facts. Even the appearance of new problems and ideas, such as linear programming, the theory of games, control theory and so on did not help break down the division between mathematics and its applications. Indeed, there sprang up many 'applied' mathematicians who thought of separating the teaching of 'pure' and 'applied' mathematics, and of creating faculties of applied mathematics, engineering mathematics, computational mathematics, cybernetics and so on.

These scientists believed that if students were to receive first a good training in the modern applications of mathematics, and then were to study the more general abstract disciplines, they would be more likely to get a taste for applying their mathematics.

There are not only psychological or sociological arguments for the creation of separate applied faculties.

During a five-year course it is simply not possible to acquaint students with all the new ideas, methods and theories developed in recent times if one preserves all the former material.

After long debate, new faculties were opened in Moscow and Leningrad Universities. In Novosibirsk it was decided after considerable discussion to preserve a united faculty but with two sub-divisions: mathematics and engineering mathematics.

So far few graduates have been produced by the new faculties and they have not worked long enough for us to be able to judge the success of this new venture.

The idea of separating the applied mathematical faculties is not shared by all mathematicians in our country. It has opponents – advocates of the unity of mathematics and its applications. At the same time no-one has serious doubts about the sheer necessity of making changes. Mathematics has grown up. New questions, new problems and new situations have arisen which must find their place in education.

Alongside the creation of new faculties one continues the independent process of refashioning the old faculties of mathematics-mechanics and physics-mathematics. This process began in the strongest universities where the professorial staff included the most creative and active scholars.

Teaching syllabuses are being changed, new courses are appearing, new professorial chairs are being created. The syllabuses of the old established subjects are also being changed radically.

Those mathematicians who insist on the unity of mathematical education base their views on the fact that this unity must reflect the unity of mathematical science itself. In order to be able to cope with the problems they will meet, it is necessary for students to master mathematics in all its breadth. For this reason many would consider it pointless to give students too narrow an education. Mathematicians holding these views believe, therefore, that the creation of applied faculties in universities is unjustified.

The engineer-mathematicians needed to solve the problems of the present day, and also technical programmers, must be trained in the higher or secondary technical school. To meet these new demands the old mathematics-mechanics and mechanics-mathematics faculties of universities, together with applied faculties, are changing, or have already changed, their appearance. These now include new mathematical disciplines on the same basis and with the same justification as such topics as analysis, algebra, geometry, theory of sets, topology and so on.

The syllabuses of the mathematics-mechanics faculties of different universities are basically similar but may differ in detail according to the scientific interests of the leading professors.

In the faculty of which I shall speak, mathematical topics are divided into two classes: those which are obligatory for all students, irrespective of their narrow specialisations, and the special options which are selected by the student.

The aim of the common section is to give the students sufficient knowledge and know-how for them to be able to work independently from contemporary sources should they need to proceed further in the future. This knowledge must be sufficiently wide but not overloaded with details. No professor should regard his own subject as the most important and significant, but should see it simply as an essential part of a united whole; the acceptance of this point of view need not prevent his demonstrating a creative relationship to his subject.

This common core consists of the following disciplines.

(1) Lectures on mathematical analysis are given during the first five semesters. Topics covered include classical differential and integral calculus, the theory of Fourier series, curvilinear and multiple integrals, the theory of exterior differential forms, and the theory of functions of a complex variable.

In addition to the lecture course, there are exercise classes (in groups of twenty-five) which are conducted by assistants, and in which problems on analysis and its applications are set. The style of teaching has been determined over the course of many years by the excellent textbook of G. M. Fichtenholz. In recent years the analysis course has been greatly modernised with the introduction of the ideas of functional analysis and general topology. The works of Bourbaki and Dieudonné's book on analysis have exerted a certain influence.

(2) Algebra lectures are given in three semesters beginning with the first. They include the theory of determinants and matrices, the theory of divisibility of polynomials, theorems about the distribution of the roots of polynomials in the complex plane and on the real axis, elements of the theory of groups, the theory of linear transformations of finite-dimensional vector spaces (including Jordan's canonical form), and elements of the algebra of tensors. The simplest facts in the theory of numbers are also introduced, such as the theory of divisibility and congruence arithmetic, and these are blended with algebraic material.

(3) Lectures on geometry are usually given in four semesters beginning with the first. In the first semester there is a short course on analytic geometry and vector algebra, the largest part of which consists of exercises. In some places there are attempts to unify analytic geometry and linear algebra.

In the second semester one studies the differential geometry of curves and surfaces. Sometimes this section is included in mathematical analysis. The third and fourth parts are not given in all universities. These are the elements of general and combinatorial topology and the theory of Riemannian spaces.

(4) Ordinary differential equations are covered in lectures in the third and fourth semesters. Here, together with traditional material – the study of methods of integration of different classes of equations – are given the elements of qualitative and analytic theory and the theory of special functions.

(5) Functional analysis is covered in lectures in the fifth and sixth semesters. The content of the course is metric spaces, linear normed spaces, Hilbert spaces, including the spectral theory of bounded operators.

(6) The equations of mathematical physics (sixth and seventh, sometimes fifth and sixth semesters) includes the basic study of partial differential equations together with applications to problems of mathematical physics. Great use is made of the methods of functional

analysis, and several of its sections closely connected with the theory of equations are expounded.

(7) The theory of probability (fifth and sixth semesters) is a short course including the theory of random quantities, the limit theorems and the basic concepts of the theory of random processes.

(8) Computational mathematics is sometimes carried out in two parts. First of all, in the first course (first and second semesters) the elements of programming are given and students learn Algol. They do exercises in programming the solution of problems in algebra and analysis. Later (fifth and sixth semesters), methods of computation are studied and, in a special practical class, solutions and programs are composed for problems connected with differential equations, the theory of probability and so on. In addition, a short course on optimisation, devoted to linear programming, the theory of games and other methods of solution of optimisational problems, is also given.

(9) Short courses on theoretical mechanics and physics are given in the fourth to eighth semesters. These enable one to make greater use of mathematics in later expositions of these disciplines.

These common courses end basically in the seventh semester. From the fifth semester (and sometimes earlier) students begin to attend special courses organised by the faculty board and take part in special seminars. Here there is a great choice. In Leningrad University, for example, a student must attend three special courses and take part in the work of a special seminar extending over two years. The faculty boards usually organise a large number of courses and seminars, and students are able to make a choice.

The fifth year (ninth and tenth semesters) is devoted to specialised courses and seminars, and pre-diploma practical and written work, which usually is a short independent investigation. It is by no means unknown for such diploma work to merit publication in scientific journals.

In addition to this considerable theoretical preparation, the students of the mathematics-mechanics faculties also receive an acquaintance with applied questions.

The department of engineering-mathematics has always belonged in the mathematics faculty of Novosibirsk university, where its basis had been the department of mechanics. Its curriculum has been broadened by the inclusion of new disciplines with syllabuses resembling those of the department of mathematics.

The faculty has preserved the unity of mathematical education which corresponds to the unity of mathematical science. The syllabuses of the two departments resemble each other in the first half of the course. In both of them basic mathematical analysis is taught for two years. This course is followed by one on the elements of functional analysis, earlier called analysis III. In both departments computational mathematics plays an essential part. The study of this begins in the first course and continues to the fourth. The syllabuses in algebra differ somewhat, being wider and beginning earlier in the case of the mathematicians. Because of this, more applications can be considered in the engineering departments, and the study of mechanics of continuous media, comes earlier and is more detailed. More attention is given to concrete methods of calculation in the solution of problems in mechanics and physics.

Some of the special options are common to both parts of the faculty. Thus, for example, both departments treat problems in the theory of computation (each has its own section of computational mathematics), aerodynamics and cybernetics. The differences which occur are determined partly by the professorial and lecturing staff of the two parallel departments.

The other specialist options are different. Within the mathematics department there are departments of functional analysis, algebra, topology, differential equations, whereas engineering mathematics includes, for example, departments of aerodynamics, elasticity and plasticity, and geophysical applications of mathematics.

Throughout the world mathematical education is in a ferment, and everywhere there is a search for new ways. Probably there are many different solutions to the basic problem of how new generations of mathematicians are to be educated and the optimisation of these solutions is at present humanly impossible.

In the Soviet Union, as in other developed countries, varied attempts are being made to construct a new and fully up-to-date system of mathematical education.

I have already spoken of different methods that are realisable and are already partly realised, for attaining a harmony between school and life. It is hard to say at present which will prove to be the best way to reach this goal. In my view the most successful will probably prove to be some 'mixed strategy', in which there will be a place for special physics-mathematics schools and special optional courses in the general schools, and also mathematical olympiads. The universities and the higher technical schools will benefit from the mathematics and engineering-mathematics faculties which have been reconstructed in a modern spirit.

The optimal relations must be found between all experimental forms of mathematical education now existing and these will depend upon local requirements. And of course these problems will be solved better by the young people whom we introduce successfully – or even with less than total success – into the temple of mathematical science.

Novosibirsk University,
USSR.

Modern mathematics: does it exist?

René Thom

The future historian of mathematics will not fail to be amazed by the extent of the movement of the 1960s known as Modern Mathematics. This movement now appears to have reached its zenith, and the first signs of waning, a justifiably healthy reaction, are beginning to make themselves apparent. I should like, perhaps somewhat prematurely, to set forth in the manner of a balance sheet those things associated with this movement which should be retained, put in their proper place, or purely and simply eliminated. It is useless in such an issue to conceal the existence of preconceptions and of personal bias which cannot avoid influencing one's judgement. It is a question, not of knowledge nor of pedagogical technique, but of a field where the personal feelings of the mathematician cannot fail to play an essential role. Only dogmatic spirits (and they are not lacking among 'modernists') can believe that there is in these questions a truth capable of being logically established and before which one needs must bow. Consequently, I see this article as a 'speech for the defence' to be contributed to the debate and not a proof which one knows very well to be non-existent.

'Modern Mathematics' has a very complex origin and composition. One can say, broadly speaking, that it seeks the two fundamental objectives:

(a) The pedagogical renewal of mathematics teaching

Exception is taken to the didacticism of traditional teaching, even its dogmatism, which is particularly evident – so one is assured – in the teaching of Euclidean geometry. It is proposed to replace it by teaching which is less directed, more free, constructive, oriented above all to a heuristic approach, and by its nature, more able to arouse the pupil's individual interests and activities.

(b) The modernisation of syllabuses

Mathematics having progressed, so we are told, considerably since Cauchy, it is strange that in many countries the syllabuses have not done likewise. In particular, it is argued that the introduction into teaching of the great mathematical 'structures' will, in a natural way, simplify this teaching, for, by so doing, one offers the universal schemata which govern mathematical thought.

One will observe that neither of these two objectives is, to be precise, 'modern' nor even recent. The anxiety about teaching mathematics in a heuristic or creative way does not date from yesterday (as Professor Pólya's contribution to congress thought shows). It is directly descended from the pedagogy of Rousseau and one could say without exaggeration that modern educators could still be inspired by the heuristic pedagogy displayed in the lesson that Socrates gave to the small slave of Menon's.[1] As for the advancement of mathematics which would necessitate a re-organisation of syllabuses, one needs only point to the embarrassment and uncertainty of modern theorists in dating the alleged revolution which they so glibly invoke: Evariste Galois, founder of group theory, Weierstrass, father of rigour in analysis, Cantor, creator of set theory, Hilbert, provider of an axiomatic foundation for geometry, Bourbaki, systematic presenter of contemporary mathematics, so many names are called forth at random, and with no great theoretical accuracy, to justify curricular reform.

It is hardly possible to deny objectives (*a*) and (*b*) a certain validity. However, one can scarcely hope to attain either of these aims absolutely. I shall not discuss objective (*a*) (pedagogical renewal) at length: I am aware of having no competence in pedagogy – in which I find difficulty in seeing anything more than an art. I shall restrict myself, therefore, in this field to crude, common-sense arguments.

In order to satisfy himself that his pupil is participating fully in the investigation in hand, the teacher must keep a continual check on the student's reactions, so that he may guide his own steps and those of his ward. This is scarcely possible, ideally, except in a *tête-à-tête*: moreover, this was the case in the example of the Socratic dialogue mentioned earlier. As soon as a teacher must handle several pupils simultaneously, he cannot keep check of the often divergent

[1] See, for example, Plato, *Five Dialogues*, Everyman's Library, Dent-Dutton, London, 1910.

reactions of all his pupils, and he is forced to neglect some of them. The next stage, and the anxiety about efficiency, will induce him to adopt the attitude of guide and soon revert to teaching *ex cathedra*. Also, efforts directed towards a freer pedagogy are necessarily costly: they demand more teachers, and better trained teachers with originality. Society will only be able to permit such efforts within the bounds fixed by the financial budget. In another connection, to make a theory of mathematical creativity is almost a contradiction in terms, for nothing can be less easily described in terms of techniques or recipes than creative originality. As soon as one uses a textbook, one establishes a didacticism, an academicism, even if the book be so written as to promote individual research. What is one to conclude other than that efforts at improving pedagogy will always be unfinished?

Point (*b*) on the *Modernisation of Syllabuses* also seems very justified. But let us observe that despite recent progress in our technical civilisation, the stages of a young child's development (physical or intellectual) have not been altered. There is always a stage of necessary apprenticeship, genetic constraints to respect, in order to learn to walk, to speak, to read, to write, and it does not seem as if progress in psychology has been able to modify in any way the normal calendar which governs the acquisition of such knowledge. This is why one can legitimately ask whether the same kind of constraints are not operating in the learning of mathematics. If this is the case, then the hope of arriving, by means of a general reorganisation of curricula or methods, at an accelerated awareness of the great theories of contemporary mathematics, could well prove illusory. Now it is indisputable that a number of 'modernist' educationists have expressed this hope and supported these illusions.

I personally believe that these genetic constraints do exist, that they form an integral part of the pupil's temperament and personality, and that, among many of the pupils (probably most of the children entering secondary education) they will, by their nature, completely prevent the understanding of mathematics at the level of the rudiments of the differential calculus – the goal which would have to be attained by those wishing to enter higher scientific education. This is why it is not obvious that an advancement in recent knowledge must, of necessity, be reflected in syllabuses, especially at the elementary and secondary levels.

But let us admit, for the time being, the validity of points (*a*) and (*b*) taken separately. What is strangest – and most arguable – in the modernist position, is the way in which it believes that these two objectives can be synthesised. Two arguments have been put forward in support of this claim.

(i) The first argument is of a tactical nature: I have heard it expressed *in petto* by French modernists, and I do not know if it expresses the general attitude of reformers elsewhere. For pedagogical reform to succeed, one must overcome inertia, the routine of teachers; with this object, one must change syllabuses. In changing the content, one will more easily be able to change the methods.

This tactical argument only has validity if it becomes evident that the new materials introduced into teaching definitely encourage a constructive, heuristic approach. Now it happens that the reformers (at least those of Continental Europe) have been induced, by their philosophical bias, on the one hand to abandon that terrain which is an ideal apprenticeship for investigation, that inexhaustible mine of exercises, Euclidean geometry, and on the other hand, to substitute for it the generalities of sets and logic, that is to say, material which is as poor, empty and discouraging to intuition as it can be.

(ii) The second argument is more serious. The psycho-pedagogues, aware of the vagueness of their doctrinal position, believed that they had found the key to their problems in the assertions of logicians and formalist mathematicians. Since it was acknowledged that the progression of mathematical thought was modelled by those great formal schemata that are the structures – structures of sets and logic, algebraic structures, topological structures – teaching the child, at an early enough age, the definition and the use of these structures would suffice to give him easy access to contemporary mathematical theories.

This argument merits a searching discussion; beneath its convincing appearance a basic psychological error is made which utterly invalidates the modernist endeavour. One should first realise that most of these great abstract structures – set theory, Boolean algebra, topological structures – are present, here and now, in the infant psyche in an implicit form, when one propounds them explicitly in teaching. (In the case of algebraic structures there are grounds for making distinctions: some, such as the group, exist implicitly, those of the ring and the field are much more artificial.) The whole modernist argument rests essentially on the assumption. *By making the implicit mechanisms, or techniques, of thought conscious and explicit, one makes these techniques easier.*

Now this raises a great psycho-pedagogical problem which is by no means peculiar to mathematics. One meets it, for example, in the teaching of modern languages: must one teach a language to a pupil in an explicit way, from books, instilling into him the grammar and vocabulary of this language? Or, on the other hand, should one teach him the language by direct use, as an alien child would naturally learn it if immersed into this linguistic society? The answer is not easy, but, from the point of view of effectiveness, the direct method is often preferable. In the early development of a child, explicit and deductive learning play absolutely no part: when learning to walk, it would be more of a hindrance than a help to understand the anatomy of the leg; and to have studied the physiology of the digestive system is no help at all when digesting a too-heavy meal. No doubt objections will be raised that I have used very crude examples that have nothing in common with that supremely rational activity, mathematical thought. But this would be to forget that reason in man has, itself, biological roots, and that mathematical thought is born of the spirit's need to simulate external reality. We shall return to this point later.

Another example, typical enough of transfer from the implicit to the explicit, is provided by psycho-analysis which has sought to make this transition from the subconscious to the conscious the essential tool of its clinic. Now in this case, it seems that the results, in the treatment of mental disorders, have turned out to be somewhat disappointing. Knowing the theory of Freudian slips will not necessarily prevent you from making one.

Moreover, this movement from the implicit to the explicit, often useless, can have a bad influence. At times the pupil cannot see the connection between a mental activity already present in his mind, and the abstract, symbolic description which is offered to him (especially if this presentation is permeated by formalist thought); in such a case, this teaching will remain a dead letter for him. At times, the child suspects the connection without reaching a clear understanding of it. In this case, the explicit knowledge of the formal definition of the activity can upset this activity, which, up to that point, was functioning very efficiently without theory: in the manner of those conscientious individuals who hesitate to speak a language because they know too much of its grammar and are afraid of making mistakes.

Finally, it should not necessarily be thought that by knowing the standard structures of mathematics one knows mathematics; on the contrary, they only represent its most superficial aspects. When a biologist wishes to study the physiology of walking, his attention is immediately drawn to those striking structures: the bones and the joints; but he will neglect, for want of understanding them well, all the functional aspects bound up with the synchronisation of muscular contractions, their mechanical effects on the entire equilibrium, the nervous systems which control them, etc. Thus our analysis of the processes of thought only displays the crudest 'joints' of reasoning – while neglecting the fine interactions due to sense, which are difficult to explain or formalise. These crude joints belong to the domain of logic, of propositional calculus. This corresponds to the 'surface' structures of linguistics which in common speech are constantly upset, bent, by the demands of the 'profound' structures of meaning. (See the examples which I gave in [1].) No doubt, as a rule, it is not the same in mathematics, where the combinatorial rules of structures do not permit any exceptions. Not so obvious: the paradoxes of set theory clearly originate because one does not wish to admit exceptions to the validity of certain axioms; and in ordinary mathematics it is by a leap into the infinite and the continuous that the exception materialises. (Cf. what is said in [1] about 'semantic breakdown'.)

But let us return to our problem: is it of any value to transform into an explicit knowledge a mechanism already present in an implicit form in the mind? Before putting the question of knowing whether such a transfer is useful, one must first ask oneself if it is possible. How can the thinker in some way detach himself from his own thought, visualise it abstractly, independent even of the content of the thought? Certainly, this detachment is a necessary step in the process of mathematical advancement: but the inverse operation, which is the reabsorption of the explicit into the implicit, is no less important, no less necessary. This second stage, which amounts to treating as 'existents', as legitimate objects to be treated globally, equivalence classes extracted abstractly as a result of the preceding process of making explicit, corresponds to what logicians call an 'ontological requirement'[1] for the operation in question. Now everything leads one to believe, that this operation of detachment, this splitting of the semantic field, carrying the mental activity that one wants to abstract, is only possible if, to be precise, the object generated by this operation is recognised as the bearer of a stability,

[1] See, for example, Quine, W. V., *From a Logical Point of View*, Harvard U.P., Cambridge, Mass., 1964.

of a 'sense', as strong as that recognised in primitive elements. Let us illustrate these difficult thoughts with an example. It is permissible to define a rational number abstractly as an equivalence class of ordered pairs of integers

$$(p, q) \sim (p', q') \quad \text{if and only if} \quad pq' = p'q.$$

But this definition will only convey meaning if one has shown that the equivalence class so defined behaves like an integer, that it has the same operational properties (and even more, since division by a non-zero rational is always possible), and that, in addition, the set of these new numbers contains in a natural way the set of the integers with which one began. Thus the quality of existence that one attributed at the outset to integers will extend naturally to the rationals which contain them. When one has clearly understood that it is the *result* of the abstraction process which justifies the abstraction and makes it possible, one sees how the formal and axiomatic presentation runs contrary to the natural order. In good teaching, one introduces new concepts, ideas etc. by using them, one explains their rules of interaction with primitive elements one has assumed to exist, one makes them familiar through handling these rules. It is only later that one will be able to give the abstract definition which allows one to verify the consistency of the theory extended in this way. Mathematics, even in its most elaborate form, has never proceeded otherwise (except perhaps for certain gratuitous generalisations of algebraic theories).

In the paper which he wrote for the congress, Professor Piaget gave an excellent description of the process of extracting conscious structures from schemata of unconscious activity: this is what he calls the process of 'reflective abstraction' (see p. 81). He nevertheless expresses his conviction that the explicit teaching of the great abstract structures opened up by contemporary mathematics is a very effective factor in facilitating this process. Ought I to say therefore that it seems to me that the psychologist places excessive trust in the virtues of mathematical formalism? And that he credits deductive, abstract reasoning with a power that it can scarcely have in a young child's mind.

Let us try to give this process of 'reflective abstraction' a geometric image: let us represent the set of human activities (sensori-motor and mental) by the x, y-plane, and let us suppose that the upper half-plane $y > 0$ represents the conscious part of these activities, the lower half-plane $y < 0$ the unconscious part. A schema of unconscious activity, S, will be represented by a geometrical shape (S) in this lower half-plane. Reflective abstraction consists of the creation from (S), emanating out of S, of a form (S') in the conscious half-plane $y > 0$: (S') is a kind of mirror-image of (S), eventually impoverished and purified. This process of the formation of a 'conscious offspring' S' starting from the mother-structure S is at all points analogous to the process of biological reproduction, by which a living being produces a descendant isomorphic to it; the process having

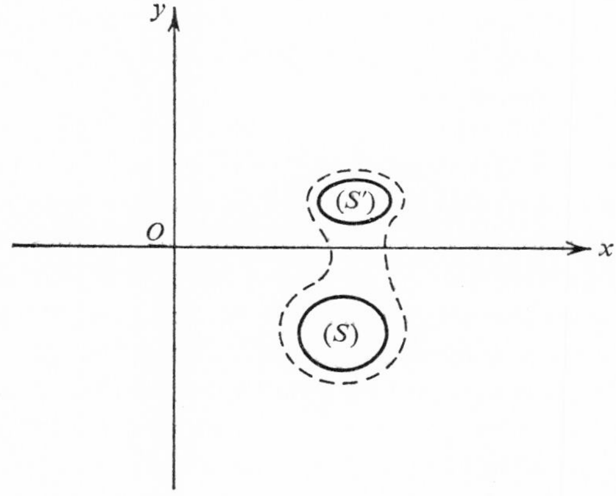

continued, there will always be at the onset the formation in S of a bud, of a foetus, which develops in S and, having come to maturity, detaches itself. This is – as the word indicates – a true 'conception', which permits the formation of S' out of S. The teacher's task is to bring the foetus to maturity and, when the moment comes, to free it from the unconscious mother-structure which engenders it, a maieutic role, a midwife's role – as Socrates has it (cf. p. 77). But, in this analogy, the great abstract logical structures, such as, for example, the notion of equivalence relation, powerful, detached means of abstraction, bear a strong resemblance to the brutal tools of the surgeon, such as the forceps or the caesarian operation. And if one undertakes a caesarian operation with a premature foetus, one loses the infant and one runs the strong risk of killing the mother. If, on the other hand, one had left the child to develop, if one had left him to come to full term while supplying him with a suitably nourishing milieu, the separation from the mother-structure would take place naturally and without the aid of those powerful but feelingless tools – abstract, logical notions. Our fathers (and, in point of fact, the mathematicians of my generation) did not know 'modern mathematics': that has not hindered them from learning mathematics, and I do not hesitate to say it, in a manner much more *natural* than that of the modernist presentation. To leave the embryo to mature, this is in fact to lead it to consciousness, thus to give it a *meaning*, and importance either operational or conceptual. It is to this primordial task of conferring on it *existence* in the mental world, that teaching must be dedicated.

The real problem which confronts mathematics teaching is not that of rigour, but the problem of the development of 'meaning', of the 'existence' of mathematical objects.

Formalisation, axiomatics and rigour

This leads me to deal with the old war-horse of the modernists (of the Continental European variety): rigour and axiomatics. One knows that any hope of giving mathematics a rigorously formal basis was irreparably shattered by Gödel's theorem. However, it does not seem as if mathematicians suffer greatly in their professional activities from this. Why? Because in practice, a mathematician's thought is never a formalised one. The mathematician gives a meaning to every proposition, one which allows him to forget the formal statement of this proposition within any existing formalised theory (the meaning confers on the proposition an ontological status independent of all formalisation). One can, I believe, affirm in all sincerity, that the only formal processes in mathematics are those of numerical and algebraic computation. Now can one reduce mathematics to calculation? Certainly not, for even in a situation which is entirely concerned with calculation, the steps of the *calculation* must be chosen from a very large number of possibilities. And one's choice is guided only by the intuitive interpretation of the quantities involved. Thus the emphasis placed by modernists on axiomatics is not only a pedagogical aberration (which is obvious enough) but also a truly mathematical one.

One has not, I believe, extracted from Hilbert's axiomatics the true lesson to be found there; it is this: one accedes to absolute rigour only by eliminating meaning; absolute rigour is only possible in, and by, such destitution of meaning. But if one must choose between rigour and meaning, I shall unhesitatingly choose the latter. It is this choice one has always made in mathematics, where one works almost always in a semi-formalised situation, with a metalanguage which is ordinary speech, not formalised. And the whole profession is happy with this bastard situation and does not ask for anything better.

One has, moreover, very probably overestimated the importance of rigour in mathematics. Of all the scientific disciplines, mathematics is the one where rigour is *a priori* least necessary. When a mathematician X publishes the proof of a theorem, his reader Y is in a position to check his assertions. He can say: the proof seems correct to me and I am convinced; or else: I do not understand such and such a point, this lemma is not very clear to me, there is a gap in the argument. On the other hand, in experimental disciplines, the situation is entirely different. When an experimenter A presents the result of tests carried out in his laboratory, he can give all the details he wishes concerning the procedure followed, all the desired guaranteed data on numerical results, but I have no way of checking the accuracy of his statements and I am compelled to trust him. As a result, error is ultimately a negligible phenomenon in the evolution of mathematics. It is more frequently a happy accident in the progress of a theory, than a catastrophe which is going to deflect science from its normal course. The mistake is only annoying for its author, not for mathematics itself. The advocates of axiomatics would do well to reflect on the following philosophical problem: why is ordinary language not axiomatisable? (Perhaps the nearest approaches to a formal language are those of the law and theology.) It is that, in everyday situations, members of the same linguistic community have practically the same semantic universe, the same vision of the universe through their own language. Although a name – a concept – is realised in extension[1] by an equivalence class which is not formalisable, nevertheless everyday speech functions with remarkable efficiency and an almost total absence of ambiguities. (If a phrase should be ambiguous, then the ambiguity is generally resolved by the context.) The meaning in ordinary language rests in the main on criteria of a topological character: the identity of an object, or of an individual, expresses itself in the connected character of the space–time domain occupied by that object (or that individual). And the syntax of ordinary language, relatively poor from the structural point of view, describes the most frequent dynamic interactions between

[1] For a definition of this technical term see, for example, Quine, *From a Logical Point of View*, p. 21.

space–time objects. On the other hand, in mathematics, amongst professional mathematicians (and, *a fortiori*, amongst students) semantic universes are very different: an expression which makes sense to X is incomprehensible to Y, etc. This is because 'meaning' in mathematics is the fruit of constructive activity, of an apprenticeship, and there have never been two mathematicians (or even two students) who have had the same history of mathematical experiences. It is this fundamental diversity of semantic universes which explains the need for formalisation – at least in part – in mathematics. At best mathematicians base their universe on a kind of common stem made up of objects and theories which occur in standard teaching (for example, real and complex numbers, analytic and differentiable functions, manifolds, groups, vector spaces, ...) and all proof, other than the more specialised, must proceed from this mathematical vernacular common to all. A proof of a theorem (T) is like a path which, setting out from propositions derived from the common stem (and thus intelligible to all), leads by successive steps to a psychological state of affairs in which (T) appears obvious. The rigour of the proof – in the usual, not the formalised, sense – depends on the fact that each of the steps is perfectly clear to every reader, taking into account the extensions of meaning already effected in the previous stages. In mathematics, if one rejects a proof, it is more often because it is incomprehensible than because it is false. Generally this happens because the author, blinded in some way by the vision of his discovery, has made unduly optimistic assumptions about shared backgrounds. A little later his colleagues will make explicit that which the author had expressed implicitly, and by filling in the gaps will make the proof complete. Rigour, like the provision of supplies and support troops, always *follows* a breakthrough.

In fact, whether one wishes it or not, all mathematical pedagogy, even if scarcely coherent, rests on a philosophy of mathematics. The modernist tendency is grounded essentially on the formalist conception of mathematics – that which was classically expressed in the famous aphorism of Bertrand Russell, 'Mathematics may be defined as the subject in which we never know what we are talking about nor whether what we are saying is true'. Its opponents, on the other hand, insist on anchoring mathematics in reality. One gladly accuses them of Platonism. But there are without doubt shades of difference. With Plato the world of Ideas constituted the supreme reality, and the concrete world of our perceptions was only a kind of degraded image of this Ideal world. But man has always the naïve illusion that he has access to the ultimate reality; more humbly, it must be asked whether mathematics has not played a role in the evolutionary separation of man, if it has not constituted a decisive factor in the superiority of man over the animal. In external reality, certain local processes, of a biological or physical nature, are subject to a very strict determinism; others, however, are aleatory, that is to say cannot be foreseen with precision. Very rapidly, the animal nervous system, then the human, has specialised in the simulation of well determined external processes; it is useless, in fact, to simulate the aleatory processes, since these, by definition, have an unforeseeable outcome. Very quickly, the mind has isolated a certain number of typical dynamic situations with a foreseeable outcome, because they were subject to a rigorous determinism (dynamically *stable*).

These patterns of conflict, organised in a classification of effective processes, were the first situations 'understood' by man (for example, the capture by a predator of its prey); these have formed the 'nuclei of the intelligibility of reality', in the words of J. Ladrière [2]. But having assimilated a formula which works, the mind has a tendency to extrapolate the conditions of application of this formula and to repeat its use (like Pavlov's dog which salivated at the sound of a bell). From this comes the tendency to isolate the repeatable processes, which can then be combined with each other as many times as one wishes. Such is the source of mathematics: it is the science of the simulation of automatisms. To this end, of being able to repeat and combine a configuration of objects, the mind is led to simplify, to purify reality. There is, in principle, the same relationship between the formal and the intelligible, as between a derived function and its primitive.

In the operation of derivation of a germ of a function, one pares away a good part of the information contained in the germ in order to permit a more ready extrapolation. In the same way, in the perception of an intelligible situation the mind schematises, simplifies, so that it can repeat and combine this situation. Thus, setting out from one such nucleus of intelligibility, the mathematical mind engenders by combination the whole of an abstract structure which aims at spreading the conditions of applicability of the formula which results, at extending its domain of validity. But there is between reality and this mathematical construction the same relation as that between the tangent plane and a point of the embedded manifold which it touches; as soon as one moves a little way from the point of contact, the validity of the abstract model diminishes and disappears in general, because this 'tangent plane' strays away from reality. To be sure, it can happen, rather exceptionally, that the mathematical theory be entirely valid empirically. It is that, as Dostoyevsky says, 'reality often lacks a sense of humour'. Certain areas of nature – essentially the field of classical natural philosophy – are entirely governed by rules of an automatic character. Hence the existence of quantitative, physical laws – and their 'unreasonable precision', according to the so accurate expression of E. Wigner. Only in so far as nature is stupid, does she allow herself to be put into mathematical terms...

Such a conception of mathematics clearly goes against the traditional point of view. It makes geometric continuity of premier importance. A discrete algebraic schema only derives its formal effectiveness because it has an empirical realisation in the space–time continuum. Pedagogy must strive to recreate (according to Haeckel's law of recapitulation[1] – ontogenesis recapitulates phylogenesis) the fundamental experiences which, from the dawn of historic time, have given rise to mathematical entities. Of course this is not easy, for one must forget all the cultural elaborations (of which axiomatics is the last) which have been deposited on these mathematical objects, in order to restore their original freshness. One must forget culture in order to return to nature. The modernist tendency represents, on the contrary, an increase of culture to the detriment of nature; it is – in the strict meaning of the term – a preciosity. But if preciosity in art and in literature sometimes has a certain charm, the same may not be true in mathematics...

These considerations – hazardous as they seem – have their importance when one comes to discuss a crucial point in the modernist reform, the place of elementary geometry in teaching.

Comparison of ordinary language, that of geometry and that of algebra

It is interesting to compare normal language with those of Euclidean geometry and (formal) algebra from the three following points of view.

(1) The 'meaning' of an element: can one formalise the equivalence class (in extension) defined by an element of the language?

[1] See, for example, Storer, T. I., *et al.*, *General Zoology* (5th ed.), McGraw-Hill, New York, 1972.

(2) Is this meaning intuitively clear?

(3) The richness (or poverty) of the syntax.

One then has the following answers.

Ordinary language

(1) The equivalence class defined by a word (a concept) cannot usually be formalised (it is often of a topological nature – the invariance of a *gestalt*).

(2) Nevertheless, the meaning of the word is clear.

(3) The syntax is poor. (There are few kinds of nuclear phrases in grammar, and the setting of phrases one inside another as subordinates rapidly ceases: at the most there are three or four possible stages of subordination.)

Euclidean geometry

(1) The object defined by a word, a geometric figure, is formalisable (that is, susceptible of description in a few words as a function of the elementary 'beings', namely points). Equivalence is defined by the Euclidean group, a group of finite dimension.

(2) The meaning of a word is clear, for it coincides with the spatial intuition of the corresponding figure.

(3) The syntax is rich, for it describes all the respective spatial positions of the figures and their displacements. (Nevertheless it is expressed verbally by a small number of concepts, such as incidence, the combinations of which are unlimited.)

Formal or algebraic language

(1) The equivalence class is defined by identifying a written symbol with itself: it is therefore formalisable.

(2) The 'meaning' of an algebraic symbol is established with difficulty or is non-existent.

(3) The syntax, which is the way in which possible operations can be combined, is rich, for, in principle, it is limitless.

One sees from this comparison how Euclidean geometry is a natural (and perhaps irreplaceable) intermediate stage between common language and algebraic language. Geometry allows a psychological widening of the syntax, whilst still retaining the meaning always given by spatial intuition. At the same time, the meaning of an element can already be given by a formal definition. The move – in line with modernist dogma – to eliminate elementary geometry to make room for calculus and linear algebra, has little to recommend it psychologically, because the algebraic objects (the symbols) are too poor semantically to permit themselves to be understood directly as is the case with a spatial figure.

I shall add that the language of elementary geometry offers a solution to the following problem: to express in a one-dimensional combination – that of language – a morphology, a multi-dimensional structure. Now this problem recurs in a form 'everywhere dense' in mathematics, where the mathematician has to communicate his intuitions to others. In this sense, the spirit of geometry circulates almost everywhere in the immense body of mathematics, and it is a major pedagogical error to seek to eliminate it. To this argument one may add the heuristic poverty of algebra, where each new difficulty presents itself like a wall which necessitates entirely new methods if it is to be surmounted. There is nothing of this in geometry, where the combination of figures allows a host of exercises which are well-graded according to difficulty.

The balance sheet

If I have been hard on the modernists, this does not mean in the least that everything which has been contributed by this movement must be set on one side; a return to the *status quo* is doubtless impossible. There is, in particular, one positive point which one should retain in any case. Formerly, there existed between secondary and higher education in mathematics a kind of gulf that young students who had just left the secondary school had much difficulty in bridging. By the introduction of set notation (presented without any theory, as simple abbreviations) and the rudiments of linear algebra, one can help make this gap disappear. In my opinion, a pupil leaving secondary education (16–17 years) and intending to take up a scientific career should be at about the same mathematical level as a Leibniz with, in addition, some notions of more modern linear algebra. It seems possible to achieve this result without sacrificing the teaching of elementary geometry. In doing this one need not try to obtain an impossible rigour; one will keep the substance of Euclid's *Elements* (in a more supple and less axiomatic presentation) while relinquishing the method of procedure which, in any case, has long been out of date.

Perhaps such a moderate conclusion will be disappointing. But the mathematical community has in these last years allowed itself to be led astray by declarations and ill-considered promises. There has been talk of a 'revolution in mathematics' and assertions that, thanks to new syllabuses and new methods, the most average pupil would be able to complete his secondary studies in mathematics. It is time to put a stop to these utterances which border on deception. No miracle is possible and one can only hope to ameliorate the existing situation step by step, and by small local improvements. Then what was responsible for the birth of this modernist movement? One has not explained everything, happily, when one has drawn attention to the commercial interests involved in alterations to curricula and textbooks. I should venture to suggest the following hypothesis – with certain obvious reservations: there was without any doubt a feeling of relative frustration in the mathematics community during the years 1950–60: jealousy with regard to Physicists, favoured financially by the development of nuclear energy (and devices); jealousy with regard to Biologists, made famous by the discovery of DNA and the genetic code. During these same years, mathematics was making very great advances, notably in algebraic geometry and algebraic topology, but these advances did not arouse the interest of the general public.

The launching of satellites (1957–60) drew public attention anew to mathematical techniques (and notably to the computer). It was in order to revive this declining interest that recourse was made to 'modern mathematics'. If this hypothesis has the ring of truth, it would be well to remind our colleagues that it is a law of our society that the important things in it are never those of which one speaks; in our time, even more than in the time of Nietzsche, new ideas arrive on the feet of doves.

References

[1] Thom, R., Les Mathématiques 'Modernes': Une erreur pédagogique et philosophique? *L'Age de la Science*, **3**, 1970, 225–36. (Translated into English: Modern Mathematics: an educational and philosophical error? *The American Scientist*, **59**, 6, 1971, 695–9.)

[2] Ladrière, J., Objectivité et réalité en mathématiques, *Revue philosophique de Louvain*, **64**, 1966, 550–81.

I.H.E.S.,
91 Bures-sur-Yvette,
France.

III

A SELECTION OF CONGRESS PAPERS

Investigation and problem-solving in mathematical education

Edith Biggs

Investigation can play a vital part in the learning of mathematical concepts and in problem-solving. At all stages the teacher has an essential part to play. He sets the scene, providing real materials or a challenging problem when necessary. He observes what his pupils do with these and asks questions which will help their learning.

There are different stages in learning by investigation. All are important for sound and lasting learning.

(1) Free exploration. A problem arises, or the teacher asks a question. The children use materials which they find for themselves or which are provided by their teacher. When materials are not necessary pupils explore the problem for themselves. Very often they will discover relations which the teacher has not thought of. These should not be rejected but postponed if the teacher wants to pursue a particular concept.

(2) Directed discovery. Here the teacher wants the pupils to investigate a particular idea which has developed during the first stage. This is probably the idea which the teacher originally planned to develop. His questions are now focused on the concept he has in mind. Since pupils vary in background, in ability and in attitude, it is useful to group them so that questions can be appropriate to the needs of each group.

(3) Once pupils have had experience of a concept or have solved the problem in hand they will require further varied experience or practice to fix the concept. This stage should not be omitted since a pupil's confidence often depends on both knowledge and skills.

Group work (often friendship groups) is very valuable in work of this kind, especially in stages 1 and 2. Pupils discuss, interchange and develop ideas and achieve far more than they would when working individually. Such group activity normally increases the pace but teachers need to keep a careful eye on slower pupils to see that they have adequate experience to ensure understanding and adequate practice to ensure learning.

Most teachers are more confident in their classroom when they have a plan of action, either in mathematics or in the development of topics which include mathematics. In the United Kingdom such planning is normally done by the headteacher, in consultation with his staff, or by a group of teachers at a teachers' centre. As far as mathematics is concerned there are certain topics which we should probably agree are essential (up to the age of thirteen). These would include number in various aspects; measurement of all kinds (including volume, angles etc.); statistics and probability; the properties of shapes (three-dimensional as well as two-dimensional, scale, congruence, symmetry and tessellations). Pupils should have first-hand experience of certain mathematical concepts in all these topics; sorting, matching and classification; inequalities, arranging in order of magnitude, conservation; the operations of addition, subtraction, multiplication and division; estimation, approximation and averages; patterns such as direct and inverse proportion, squares, cubes, growth patterns; variables, generalisation leading to algebra and limits; representation of many different types. Of course there would also be a wide range of topics which would be regarded as optional.

In general, teachers would plan the starting points for the important and essential topics. However, many of the mathematical topics which have engaged pupils' interest over a period of time have been sparked off in other aspects of the curriculum than mathematics. One useful outcome is that whereas pupils are sometimes less interested in purely mathematical problems they become completely absorbed in problems which arise in other fields and normally persist until they have obtained a satisfactory solution as the following examples illustrate.

A seven-year-old boy needed to draw a circle for the model he was making. His teacher found him sitting with his finger in the middle of a square turning this around. He told her, excitedly, that the corners traced a circle as he turned the square. The teacher asked him to find the middle of the square, which he did using string, so that she could nail the square to a sheet of paper on a board. This activity attracted many children not concerned with the original problem. They used a variety of shapes nailed at the centre or at corners and rotated these slowly, drawing round each successive position. The final picture was painted in very attractive colours. Later the boy improved his method of drawing circles, first by using a strip of wood nailed to a board and later by using a long loop of string knotted at various points.

A year later the teacher experimented with another group of children. She suggested that they should choose a plastic shape and rotate this to see what happened. To her surprise this group of children used templates in an entirely different way. For example Helen started drawing 4 squares, then continued drawing round her square template until she had surrounded the 4 squares. She numbered each square she used. She continued adding layer upon layer and wrote down the number of squares added each time. She recorded 'I drew round the square and then numbered the squares and the number was 4. The second time I went round the number was 12 and the third time the number was 20, and the fourth time the number was 28. The number went up in 8 each time. I think the numbers would go on like this: 36, 44, 52, 60, 68, 76, 84, 92, 100.' When the teacher asked if she could do this in another way, Helen started with one square and built round it.

1	2	3	4
12	1	2	5
11	4	3	6
10	9	8	7

Other children used equilateral triangles and rhombuses, each time recording the number of units added. It is interesting that these children who tackled this problem without the inducement of discovering a method of drawing a circle used an entirely different strategy.

This problem could, of course, be used to develop the idea of scale – for example, what happens to the perimeter and area of a square when it doubles (trebles, etc.) its edge? The pattern of linear scale often arises when children are comparing their own vital statistics. For example, after asking a group of six- to seven-year-olds to arrange themselves in order of height a teacher asked them to represent this in some way. After some discussion they drew round the tallest of the group, then marked the height of each group on this cut-out. The teacher then asked them to cut off their 'string height'. She gave them a large sheet of paper and asked them to arrange their string heights on that in order of height. After considerable discussion (and asking in vain for another sheet of paper) the members of the group decided to halve their string height. (But in their efforts they forgot to arrange them in order!)

An interesting problem on scale arose with a class of ten-year-olds. This time the children did not discover the answer to this question because the teacher did not, at that time, know enough mathematics to develop the topic.

After a radio programme the children had become interested in the blue whale. They found all the statistics they could and measured their classroom to see how many classrooms they would need in a row to accommodate one blue whale. They then measured the playground and found that five blue whales could be fitted into the space. Next day, on the way home from school, a girl from the class saw a model blue whale in a cleaner's shop. She asked the manager if she could borrow this, since she was working on the blue whale at school, to see if it was a true scale model. The manager agreed, if the girl could find someone to transport the 3-metre model. This was eventually accomplished in a van and the children discovered that the model was a reasonably accurate scale model of an adult whale. This created an interest in baby blue whales. The children found that the ratio of the lengths of adult and baby whales was 4 to 1. They were therefore surprised to find that the ratio of the corresponding weights was 15 to 1. They then switched their interest to humans. They worked out, from an example they knew, that the ratio of the heights of adult to baby was 3.6 to 1, whereas the ratio of their weights was 14 to 1. Now the children (and their teacher) had expected the weights to be in the same ratio as the heights (whereas I was surprised because there was not a *greater* difference in these two ratios). But here, for the time being, the investigation had to stop because the teacher did not know how to develop the topic further. How would you have followed up this problem?

The next example also concerns animals. Some ten- and eleven-year-old children had been asked to find the average pressure on their feet (when standing on both feet). To do this each divided his weight in pounds by the total foot area in square inches. The results (to 2 places of decimals!) were then arranged in order from largest to smallest. The children then turned their attention to animals. One child wrote: 'Our class wondered what the pressure on an elephant's foot would be. So before Christmas I wrote to Bellevue Zoo asking them to draw round an elephant's foot. In about a week I received the elephant's foot below.' The zoo had also supplied the elephant's weight (3 tons 5 cwt). The pressure per square inch on the elephant's foot turned out to be over 13 pounds, very different from that on the children's feet (maximum 2.6 pounds). After receiving the answer from the zoo, the children collected results from their own animals: cats and dogs, rats and hamsters. A scientific enquiry had begun; Professor David Hawkins of Colorado University also became interested in this problem. Could this be developed with other types of animal, e.g. birds? Insects?

A problem on scale which concerned eight- and nine-year-olds (in the USA) arose when they were studying rocks. After making their collection of rocks some began by comparing textures (by feeling with eyes shut, and trying to find suitable words to describe what they felt). Others began to compare the size of their rocks. They weighed them, found the perimeter and cut a string model and finally made a paper covering to fit each rock. They were still not satisfied that they had compared their rocks in every way. One boy suggested filing the rocks, collecting the filings in identical jam jars so that the contents could be compared. They started, but since the rocks were made of granite, little headway was made. At this point I offered the boys a clear plastic container holding some water and asked if this would help. 'No', they replied, 'because all rocks float.' When I pressed them to find a stone which floated they produced a piece of pumice! I hoped they would now try to float their rocks but 'No', they said, 'Rocks disappear in water – like salt and sugar'. At this moment the calls were made for the buses (at this voluntarily integrated school most children travelled in buses) and the children disappeared. Next morning I was prepared to give the children the opportunity to study solution – but there was no need. Every member of the group had tried a rock in water for himself and assured me that rocks did not, after all, disappear in water.

And now the children were eager to put their rocks in water. As the first went in, I asked what had happened. 'The water's risen', they said, 'we knew it would.' 'Can you tell me anything about it?' I asked. Slowly a boy said 'That risen water is what my rock would be if it were made of water.' He paused. 'If we could weigh it, it would weigh the same as the rock.' 'Do you all agree?' I asked. Most of the group said yes. The others were unsure. They tried to pour off the risen water with the rock still in the container. The rock became uncovered so they abandoned this, removed the rock and marked the water level. Then they replaced the rock and marked the second level. One boy decided to remove the rock and measure the volume of water he had to put in to fill the container to the second mark. While he was deciding what units to use another suggestion was made. 'Let's fill a container to the top and collect the risen water when the rock is put in, in a polythene bag and weigh it.' This was done and the water was weighed. Now the rock weighed $4\frac{3}{4}$ lb and the risen water only $1\frac{1}{2}$ lb. The children decided that they must have spilt some water so they repeated the experiment – with the same result. Still they did not believe the result so they tried a third time. 'The water weighs much less than the rock' they said. One boy added, 'The rock is about three times as heavy as the water.'

At that moment a boy began to shape the water in the bag (firmly closed with an elastic band). I enquired what he was doing. 'If this is what my rock would be if it were made of water I must be able to make the water into the shape of the stone,' he said. This made me realise that this boy really understood volume.

The following day the children decided that they would make rock books. They searched for paper the colour of their rocks and wanted to make the covers of the same shape as their rock. For most of them this meant drawing round their rocks and then making an enlargement. One boy cut a piece of string the length of the perimeter and doubled this, because he wanted a rock 'twice the size'. He indicated that he meant twice as long, twice as wide and twice as high. He had great difficulty in trying to arrange the double perimeter round the rock so that the two shapes were the same. I could not think how to help him without telling him 'the trick' so he completed this 'by eye'.

Some time later I related this story to some teachers of children of ages five to eleven. I asked them if they could find a way of enlarging shapes. After some false starts I suggested that they should start with a square, put in the diagonals and then see what they had to do to obtain a square with edges half the length of those of the original square. It was some time before they discovered that their second square could be obtained by joining the mid-points of the half diagonals. They then tried doubling the original square – and found the perimeters to be doubled. 'What about areas?' I asked. The 4 to 1 relationship was discovered and other enlargements were tried.

Suppose you took the point for enlarging or reducing anywhere else in the square, would the same method work? Suppose the point is on the perimeter of the square or outside, will the same method work? There was much experiment and argument. Other geometrical shapes and finally some very irregular shapes were enlarged and reduced in various ratios. Would it work for a circle, I asked. What would be the ratio of the perimeters and areas? (I produced some logiblocs in a 2 to 1 linear ratio of squares, rectangles, equilateral triangles and of circular discs of the same thickness.) The ratio of the perimeters caused some trouble, despite the previous work. All were convinced about the 4 to 1 ratio of areas except for the circular discs. Eventually a teacher of younger children (five to seven) suggested we might use balance scales to see if 4 small discs balanced 1 large one of the same thickness. We completed this investigation the next day by developing different strategies for building the largest cube we could, using an uncounted pile of identical cubes. We then repeated this, building the largest square using thin identical squares. We also built a consecutive sequence of cubes and a consecutive sequence of squares and found all possible number patterns – which we subsequently investigated and grouped.

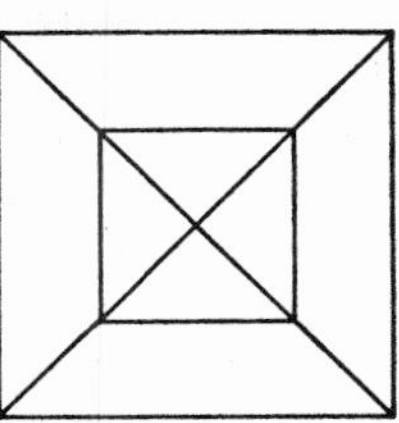

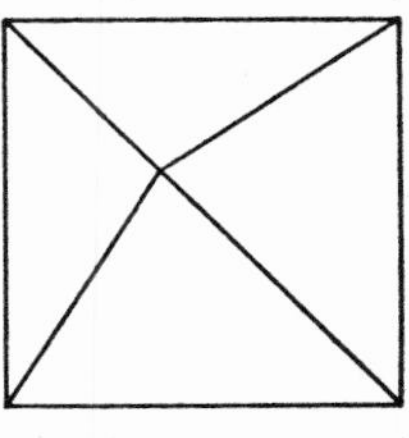

I should now like to return to the problem of growth of humans (and of whales). Recently, two secondary teachers worked on this problem and came to the following conclusion. The ratio of the lengths of a new born baby to an adult is approximately *1 to 4* (50 cm to 200 cm).

The ratio of their girths is approximately *1 to 2* (50 cm to 100 cm).

Therefore we would expect ratio of areas of cross-sections to be 1 to 4 (and not 1 to 16).

Therefore the ratio of volumes will be approximately 1 to 16 (and not 1 to 64).

This also seems to be true for whales!

Another example occurred with twenty-four graduate mathematics students in a school of education in the USA. I was asked to talk to them about the teaching of mathematics with young children. As in this article, I posed the problems undertaken by pupils of the age range five to sixteen – but gave no answers. The final problem was one set in a public examination taken by sixteen-year-olds. 'Investigate triangles of fixed perimeter.' I made string and squared paper available. Twelve students used the string and, within half an hour, had investigated every aspect of this problem. The others, using paper and pencil only, solved one aspect but were still floundering at the end of an hour. I discovered later that the former group had not been given normal lectures but investigations (both individually and as groups). The other group had been given the usual diet of lectures. In consequence of this experiment it was recommended that all students should be given investigations as part of their training.

A final example illustrates the need for more background knowledge on the part of teachers and for careful planning by teachers to ensure progression on the part of the pupils they teach. Two nearby schools in England covering the age range five to eleven years, were asked to concentrate on the topic symmetry for a few weeks. It was interesting to notice that every teacher began with mirror symmetry, partly because this was the first experience their children had had of symmetry and partly because this was the type of symmetry which was familiar to every teacher. The five-year-olds used paint prints of their two hands and of their two feet to illustrate this type of symmetry. At the other extreme a ten-year-old made a paint blot pattern of great delicacy and intricacy which she called 'The Universe'. Little was done to develop the equivalences which could arise from such work because the teachers were not aware of the possibilities. Children of eight and nine made cut-out patterns with two axes of mirror symmetry by paper folding. The nine-year-olds included the axes of mirror symmetry of common two-dimensional shapes. They also explored symmetries of a variety of number patterns and of coloured rods.

The ten-year-olds studied for the first time, planes of mirror symmetry of the regular three-dimensional solids they made. (This might have been tried with far younger children if their teachers had thought of this.) Furthermore, it was not until the age of ten that children were given experience of rotational symmetry. The teacher responsible gave her children a variety of experiences which led them to discover the angles of rotation of regular two-dimensional shapes. This did not include the rotational symmetry of geometrical shapes such as the parallelogram and rectangle. It was evident from this work that teachers in Britain require a far more extensive first-hand experience of symmetry if they are to explore this topic to the full with their pupils. For example, no experience was given of symmetry in graphs or of algebraic expressions. We have found that when pupils (and teachers) are given experience of examples of such symmetry they are quick to notice equivalences.

So investigations and problem-solving have a very important place in the learning of mathematics. Children and students learning through investigations are accustomed to problem situations (real or imaginary) and do not find problems difficult. Sometimes the solution of the problem requires the use of materials and sometimes of paper and pencil only. As pupils grow older, if they are accustomed to learning by this means they will require far less first-hand experience and should be expected to use far more imagination. So we shall be encouraging pupils to use their creative powers to the full in mathematics.

Because mathematics is an abstract subject, results of all investigations should be communicated in forms becoming progressively more abstract: by a picture or diagram, in words, by a table, by a graph or by an algebraic relation.

I cannot do better than finish by quoting Professor Pólya, who has experimented extensively with the teaching of mathematics to university students.

'Abstractions are important; use all means to make them more tangible. Nothing is too good or too bad, too poetical or too trivial to clarify your abstractions.'

2 Carlton Gardens,
London, W5 2AN.

Intuition, structure and heuristic methods in the teaching of mathematics

E. Fischbein

1 Intuition and comprehension in mathematical education

When the pupil is presented with a logical proof, is it necessary for him to have to add to this his own means of direct comprehension, that is to say, what is known as his intuition?

This is not a new problem. However, it has recently attracted much attention due to the increase in rigour of the mathematical proofs given in teaching situations. In my opinion, in order that these more axiomatised demonstrations do not stifle the mathematical reasoning process, it is absolutely essential to encourage the use of such intuitive support. This is the first problem that I should like to examine.

First, I consider that there are a number of distinctions that should be made: it is necessary to distinguish between what I call intuitions of adhesion and intuitions of anticipation. The intuition of adhesion expresses itself in the feeling of evidence about a certain fact. It is intuitively evident that the relation of equality is transitive, that from any point not on a straight line there can be only one perpendicular to that line, that there is always a natural number greater than a given number, etc. When I say that something is 'intuitively evident' I refer to the fact that the need for a mathematical proof is not felt in these cases (though, from the mathematical point of view, such a proof may be necessary). By 'anticipatory intuition' I mean the global vision of the solution to a problem. This vision precedes the rigorous and explicit construction of the solution. These two types of intuition, though interdependent, play two different roles in understanding and in the psycho-pedagogical aspect of science in general and of mathematics in particular.

I should like, for the moment, to dwell on the problem of the intuition of adhesion. What is its source? In this paper I cannot enter into all the details, but I support the opinion that intuitions base themselves on mental habits. It is possible, in certain cases, that at the origin there are hereditary elements but usually these express, to a certain degree, the experience of the individual which, in turn, may well have been influenced by society.

Let us consider a current intuition, for example, space is not isotropic. The notions of vertical and horizontal, 'above' and 'below', seem to be absolute properties of space. It is evident that this particular vision of the world cannot be seen as a pure conceptualisation of space; this vision, in fact, expresses a mental structure that is deeply rooted in human behaviour as a consequence of a terrestrial life.

The essential fact to be borne in mind when considering the didactical process is that intuition cannot be created, eliminated, or modified by either explanations or short learning exercises. There are at least three situations which must be taken into consideration:

(*a*) In the learning situation the information given to the pupil about a certain notion can be similar to the intuitive knowledge the pupil has of this notion; this type of agreement can be extremely useful in education (for example, the shortest distance between two points is a straight line).

(*b*) In certain learning situations the intuition the child has about a certain notion can be very different from the notion itself, thus there will be a contradiction between the intuition and the objective truth or the 'truth' that can be arrived at through proof (for example, the set of natural numbers has the same cardinality as the set of rational numbers).

(*c*) In some situations there will be no established intuitive attitude (for example, the altitudes of a triangle are concurrent).

In fact, things are not quite as simple as they would seem from the above classification, even in the case of the first category which we would call favourable intuitions. In the deductive organisation of various branches of mathematics, certain of these favourable intuitions are considered as axioms, whereas others are considered as theorems whose proof is necessary and possible. Such a distinction is not made on intuitive grounds and is therefore not intuitively evident. For this reason theorems are often not understood to be theorems (that is to say a proposition that needs a proof). The fact that it is intuitively evident (from the psychological point of view) that from a point not on a straight line there is only one perpendicular to the line, makes the necessity for a proof not intuitively evident.

As I have already mentioned, intuition can also be contradicted by a mathematical truth. The whole field of the transfinite would enter into this category. There are several levels of intuition about this idea. The very fundamental idea of the 'absence of obstacles' (boundlessness) which is the basis of this concept is very clear even to a child of nine or ten years. A straight line can be continued indefinitely; the sequence of natural numbers goes on forever; these truths are intuitively evident. However, the statement that the set of real numbers cannot be put into a one-to-one correspondence with the set, also infinite, of natural numbers seems to be intuitively surprising.

How many permutations of five objects are there? A research project carried out by our team showed that there was a natural tendency to underestimate the number. (The subjects, children and adolescents, estimated on the average that sixteen permutations could be obtained; that there are 120 seemed to them extremely surprising.) It is also surprising to discover that when throwing a pair of dice the probability of obtaining a double, for example 5 and 5, is half that of obtaining a mixed pair, for example 5 and 6. The hypothesis could be formulated that, in order to be efficient, the teaching of a subject must be preceded by an exploration of the intuitive knowledge of the pupil, just as, for example, the construction of a building is preceded by an investigation of the nature of the site.

Some colleagues and I have tried to explore the child's intuitive level of certain elementary concepts in the theory of probability by using a method we call 'teaching by programmed discovery'. This method consists of a series of questions related to a certain concept. The questions begin at the most general and formal level to which the subjects have access, and, in case these cannot be successfully answered, they continue until they reach the most rudimentary, global and intuitive level of the subjects. We have been able to establish that within the subjects there is a favourable intuitive basis for the concept of probability [1], and for the calculation of probability [2] in the case where the probability of a compound event is equal to the sum of those of the elementary events which constitute it. The law concerning the multiplication of probabilities is based on the intuition that one reduces the chances when one imposes additional conditions (intersection of events), but the operation of multiplication, as such, does not appear to have an intuitive basis. In the case of the law of addition, there seems to be an almost complete lack of understanding of the compound character of certain events and consequently no idea of the necessity to make an inventory of the different situations which will give rise to a particular event. In this case it is not only a question of the absence of intuition, but also an intuition that has been contradicted [3].

The different types of intuition quoted above are natural intuitions. They are constructed during the ontogenesis of the subject, before and outside of any sort of systematic intuition. These types of intuitions we shall call 'primary intuitions'. Can the intuitive factor of understanding be reduced to primary intuitions?

In fact, the situation is more complex. New intuitions can be built up which have the same character of adhesion to a certain fact and to a certain interpretation, these we will call 'secondary intuitions'. In this manner it can be accepted as evident the fact that Euclid's postulate is only pseudo-evidence; that the set of real numbers cannot be put into one-to-one correspondence with the set of natural numbers; that without the intervention of a force, a body in motion will continue its rectilinear and uniform movement.

However, these secondary intuitions cannot be constructed, as we have already said, simply by explanations or short learning exercises. These intuitions need to be based on mental habits and the creation of these habits requires an extremely long training which can extend over the whole period of the growth of intelligence (above all the period of concrete operations).

If the hypothesis of secondary intuitions is accepted, then one must reject the Bergson point of view according to which intelligence and intuition are opposing and irreducible modalities of knowledge. According to Bergson, intuition is a direct knowledge of vital phenomena and this is an extension of the instinct, whereas intelligence founded on the spatial characteristics of matter is basically an instrument of action.

According to our hypothesis, the rational modality of knowledge, through intelligence, can, by a long familiarisation with a certain field, transform itself into an immediate form of synthetic, global knowledge having the specific characteristics of intuition. In our opinion the pupil should learn consciously to compare his intuitive interpretation of certain terms and procedures with those that are used in their rigorous mathematical interpretation. He should learn to rethink the elements that come from his primitive experience in such a way that they agree with his new conceptual framework.

Our hypothesis, therefore, is that this process of refining and correcting the intuitive basis should not be allowed to go on in a haphazard manner (or not to happen at all) but should be an integral part of the teaching process. If an intuitive basis is lacking, as can frequently happen, for example, in the field of probability, it is vital that these intuitions should be constructed with the help of well-programmed exercises spread out over a long period whilst intelligence is developing.

2 Structures in mathematics and psychology

The second problem that I should like to discuss is that of structure in mathematics and psychology.

Piaget has defined structure in the broadest sense as a system and this system is a totality that has laws and properties that are characteristic of it as a totality [4].

A structure is constituted of a set of elements between which there are certain relations. It is well known that for Bourbaki there are three types of structures: (*a*) algebraic, (*b*) order, and (*c*) topological. With the help of these structures the diverse branches of mathematics can be brought together to form an architectural unity.

The problem which faces mathematical educators is the following.

On the one hand, should one leave the general schemes of thought to form themselves gradually, by a sort of natural generalisation, after the pupil has assimilated a fairly considerable amount of mathematical knowledge?

Or, on the other hand, is it better that the child should be given the opportunity to function with these schemes, these structures, very early on in his development, so that they can be used as true matrices for the formation of his mathematical thought?

Arguments can be found for and against these two alternatives.

For the first point of view, that is, that acquaintance with these structures should be left until such time as a good preparation in mathematics provides opportunities for them to disengage themselves naturally:

(*a*) The natural course in the development of knowledge is from the particular to the general, from the concrete to the abstract.

(*b*) Mathematical structures, by their nature, are concepts that require an extremely high degree of abstraction. They could not, therefore, be understood, assimilated and used until such time as intelligence has reached the stage of formal operations and above all the stage of final equilibrium (from about the age of fifteen or sixteen years).

(*c*) Mathematical structures arose out of the confrontation of diverse mathematical domains. The pupil must also be capable of understanding on a fairly broad mathematical basis (in arithmetic, algebra, geometry).

For the second point of view, that is, that the teaching of mathematical structures should start at a very early age, even before seven years old, or at least during the period of concrete operational thinking (from the age of seven years):

(*a*) These structures express the fundamental structures and general schemes of intelligence and are not just a means of giving information or a manner of proceeding in a particular instance. Consequently their assimilation must be structured in such a way as to allow them to be integrated into the total architecture of intelligence. Short learning exercises will not help this objective. A gradual and carefully constructed elaboration is necessary. It is easy to memorise the axioms of a group, but, if the group concept is to become an efficient and productive instrument in thought, it must be assimilated within the dynamic architecture of the intellect.

(*b*) Mathematical structures must be allowed to function during the period of the growth of intelligence if they are to be integrated in a really organic way into the mathematical thought of the child.

(*c*) Contemporary developmental psychology has shown the characteristics of the evolution of intelligence. The most important work in this field is, undoubtedly, that of Piaget. His work shows very clearly that intelligence develops through a series of stages [5]. The essential idea for our discussion is that each fundamental system of knowledge must be anticipated and prepared for in earlier stages by means specific to these stages. According to this law, the learning of mathematical structures during the period of the final equilibrium of formal operations must already be prepared for during the period of concrete operations by means appropriate to this period. This will permit the structures to become efficient instruments in mathematical thought.

To sum up then, the essential psycho-pedagogical problem is the following: mathematical structures, like all other fundamental mathematical concepts (relation, function, equivalence, continuity, etc.) and the fundamental logical operations, are, by their nature, abstractions of extreme generality. The child should start to learn these structures in a very empirical manner during the period of concrete operations in order to integrate them into his scheme of intellectual activity.

The problem appears to be without solution. Two important discoveries in developmental psychology would, however, seem to suggest possible approaches. The first is due to Piaget, who has shown the close relationship between the important mathematical structures and the organisation of human intelligence. According to him, mathematical structures are closely related to the main operational structures of intelligence gradually built up during the subject's ontogenesis, and group structure is at the core of this relationship. At the concrete operational level, intelligence has already acquired, although only partially, characteristics that are analogous to those of a group [6].

The second discovery is linked to the name of Jerome S. Bruner: an abstract structure can be transmitted and assimilated as such, that is remaining unaltered, by means of various embodiments [7]. Enactive, iconic and symbolic representations can all serve as vehicles for an embodiment and transmit the same mathematical structure, although several embodiments may be necessary for the structure to be understood. By this means a pupil will slowly grasp a fundamental idea common to all the embodiments. Dienes has called this procedure 'the principle of perceptual variability' or in its most general form 'the principle of multiple embodiments' [8]. He and his colleagues have invented a tremendous variety of embodiments for mathematical and logical structures. The principal element of these is that of play and thus they appeal directly to the interest of the pupil.

Dienes' activity has inspired other research workers, for example Tamas Varga (Hungary), Mrs Marguerite Robert (France), Mrs F. Morine and her team in Italy, Professor B. Zörgö (Roumania), and many others. This approach has shown itself to be extremely productive and accumulating observations have revealed the interest and 'receptivity' of children when they have been asked to carry out such activities. For the moment, however, the results of this work can only be considered as hypothetical. Only rigorous longitudinal studies can establish the effectiveness of this development in mathematical education.

According to Professor Freudenthal (see pp. 101–14), with whose opinions I agree, the child, when being introduced to mathematical structures, should start with structures more primitive and simpler than that of the group. He puts forward a number of examples which are both simpler and at the same time more suggestive in showing how the idea of a group can be developed. These same examples prove extremely useful in the study of regularities in nature and in mathematics.

Richard Skemp has, on the other hand, pointed out: 'An appropriate scheme means one which takes into account the long-term learning task and not just the immediate one' [9].

The correspondence between the model used and the mathematical structure must be as complete and as natural as possible so that the models themselves can suggest new problems, new directions in finding solutions and even new models for the same mathematical structure. In [10], models having these qualities are called 'generative models'. It is a fact, though, that many of the models suggested by educators, teachers, etc. have an extremely limited range and consequently very little educational value.

3 Heuristic methods

The third problem I should like to touch on is that of improving our techniques in problem-solving by systematically learning heuristic procedures and strategies. A large variety of studies have already been published dealing with this subject.

It is generally recognised that heuristic procedures are elastic schemes which allow a certain degree of variability and adaptability to given conditions and which guide our investigatory activity.

George Pólya has described a certain number of heuristic procedures used in mathematics, for example, the use of analogies and models, the reduction of a problem to a simpler one, etc. In a recent piece of research, Max Jerman of Stanford University [11] studied strategies in problem solving. (His paper, incidentally, contains an extremely good bibliography of the whole problem.) Jerman's results show that those subjects who followed a programmed learning sequence in problem-solving strategies did no better than the control group. In reality, the subjects of the experiment made better use of the correct procedures but their results were no better because of the difficulties they had with computation.

In general, the results of research on the learning of heuristic procedures in problem-solving do not provide any convincing practical conclusion. The results are, in fact, far less spectacular than might have been expected from the expounded theory.

I feel that the following might be an explanation of the situation.

The solving of a problem is certainly a conscious activity. It is conscious because a goal is set, there is an understanding of the meaning of the problem, and a specific direction in the respective field is chosen, but the 'solving' process as such is not conscious in its detail. The subject does not control, nor is he aware of, the mechanisms involved in the resolution of the problem. This situation is not specific to the art of invention, it can be found in all human activity no matter how simple. When I pick up a glass of water, I am conscious of the action because I am conscious of its finality. However, the details of the movements, the successive muscular contractions are not the result of a conscious order.

For this reason, there are a certain number of behavioural rules that exist when a subject is trying to solve a problem but they are not used in the same manner as, for example, a cook might use his methods in the preparation of a special dish.

In problem-solving, therefore, such procedures operate in an implicit manner. If the subject becomes conscious of the process and tries to think about these procedures in an explicit manner, he can no longer think of the problem that has been raised. When the creative process of finding a solution is interrupted a useful result can no longer be found.

Nevertheless an awareness of heuristic procedures can be useful for the following reasons. First, these procedures can be integrated into our activity, into the hierarchical structure of our intellectual habits as a result of systematic and persistent practice. I would mention, for example: practice in the comprehension of the text of a problem; appraisal of facts; determination of unknown variables; appraisal of images, should such images exist; the construction of auxiliary figures, schemata and diagrams; changing of point-of-view; the use of analogies; the provisional consideration of simpler problems, etc.

There are times during the solution of a problem when certain heuristic procedures could be used consciously. At the beginning, when the variables involved in the problem must be sorted out before the actual problem-solving process can be started, certain rules could be of help. For example, 'Look carefully at the wording'. 'Have you understood completely the meaning of each of the terms used?' 'Try and find out exactly what is being asked and, as far as possible, the steps you think will be necessary to obtain the answer', etc.

During the process of problem-solving there are times when creative ideas no longer seem to flow, there is the feeling that the wrong direction is being taken, and that things need to be reconsidered. In such moments, heuristic procedures could be of great help.

Clearly, the most important recommendation is that the capacity to solve problems can be practised by exercises in problem-solving. However, I feel that the idea of programming ought to be better appreciated and applied. Often, in collections of problems to be solved, the problems themselves are so diverse, that there is insufficient opportunity for the subject to construct those supple, harmonious and polyvalent systems of mental habits essential to problem-solving.

Conclusions

In this paper I have discussed three apparently independent subjects: the problem of intuition, the role of structures and the learning of heuristic procedures. In fact, all the fields are closely related in problems of creativity and the pedagogy of mathematics.

I feel that if this relationship were to be better appreciated it would contribute greatly to an improvement in mathematics teaching. Creative mathematical thinking, which becomes apparent in problem-solving, reveals a whole variety of heuristic procedures which are inspired and guided by intuition. These intuitions, both the intuition of adhesion as well as the anticipatory intuition, express the stabilized organisation of mental structures in a certain field.

References

[1] Fischbein, E., Pampu, I. and Mînzat, J., L'intuition probabiliste chez l'enfant, *Enfance* **2**, 1967, 193–208.

[2] Fischbein, E., Pampu, I. and Mînzat, J., Comparison of ratios and the chance concept in children, *Child Development* **41**, 2, 1970, 377–89.

[3] Fischbein, E., Pampu, I. and Mînzat, J., Intuitions primaires et intuitions secondaires dans l'initiation aux probabilités, *Educational Studies in Mathematics* **4**, 1971, 264–80.

[4] Piaget, J., *Six Psychological Studies*, University of London Press, 1968. (Editions Gauthier, Paris, 1964.)

[5] Piaget, J., Les stades de développement intellectuel de l'enfant et de l'adolescent, in P. Osterrieth *et al. Le problème des stades en psychologies de l'enfant*, P.U.F. Paris, 1956, pp. 33–41.

[6] Piaget, J., *The Psychology of Intelligence*, Routledge & Kegan Paul, London, 1950.

[7] Bruner, J. S., *Toward a theory of instruction*, W. W. Norton & Co., New York, 1968.

[8] Dienes, Z. R., *An Experimental Study of Mathematics-Learning*, Hutchinson, London, 1963.

[9] Skemp, R., *The Psychology of Learning Mathematics*, Penguin Books, Harmondsworth, 1971.

[10] Fischbein, E., Pampu, I. and Mînzat, J., Effects of age and instruction on combinatory ability in children, *British Journal of Educational Psychology*, *November 1970* **40**, 3, 261–70.

[11] Jerman, M., Instruction in problem solving and an analysis of structural variables that contribute to problem solving difficulty, Technical report No. 180, 1971, Psychology & Education Series, Institute for Mathematical Studies in the Social Sciences, Stanford University.

Institute of Psychology,
Bucarest,
Roumania.

Mathematics and science in the secondary school

Anthony J. Malpas

Three questions which the work described in this paper seeks to answer are the following:

(1) What mathematical skills are required in the new secondary school science courses?

(2) To what extent do courses in modern mathematics provide for the development of these skills?

(3) In what ways can the work of science and mathematics departments in schools be more closely linked to promote more effective learning of these skills?

With the end of the nineteen sixties and the coming to fruition in Britain and the USA of the first generation curriculum projects in science and mathematics, the mood of teachers in the schools in these countries has changed. With increasing confidence in their own new materials and methods of teaching, they are beginning to have the time and energy to look across subject boundaries and to consider the possibility of inter-subject cooperation. Phrases like 'Integrated Studies' and 'Interdisciplinary Enquiry' are appearing increasingly as 'subjects' on school timetables. The new emphasis on children's cooperative, rather than competitive, activities (project work, small group activities of all kinds) is being matched in some places by first attempts at cooperative ventures among teachers (team teaching and 'integrated' approaches to the curriculum). This new spirit also finds expression in many of the second generation curriculum projects (exemplified in Britain in the sciences by Nuffield Secondary Science, Nuffield Advanced Physical Science, and the Schools Council Integrated Science Project, and in mathematics by the Mathematics for the Majority Continuation Project) which all share the marked characteristic of an approach to the curriculum on a thematic rather than a traditional 'subject' basis. Appointments are already being made in some schools of 'Head of Mathematics and Science'. This is therefore the right time to pose questions such as the above and to try to obtain some good answers to them.

1 What are the mathematical requirements of modern science courses?

This question as posed above, although the right one to ask, is too general to admit of a full answer for all countries at the present time, and this paper is a report only of some work which has recently been done in Britain.[1] Here efforts have been made to study the links between the new mathematics and science programmes, and a joint working party composed of members of the Association for Science Education, the Mathematical Association, and the Association of Teachers of Mathematics has been set up and has produced reports.[2] To limit the scale of the work reported in this paper, attention was confined to the published materials of the Nuffield Science Teaching Project's Biology, Chemistry and Physics Ordinary Level (eleven to sixteen years) schemes. A comprehensive analysis of these schemes was carried out and the mathematical skills and abilities implicit in the activities of the courses were briefly described.[3] These mathematical assessments of the courses were then carefully considered and it was concluded that the mathematical skills required could be classified into three broad groupings. The biggest and most important of these groupings is that cluster of ideas concerned with ratios, rates, proportion, straight line graphs, and formulae. The first three rows of table 1 show the extent to which use of this cluster of ideas is called upon in Nuffield science courses. Every science teacher knows that these skills are central to the organisation and interpretation of scientific data, so it is perhaps not so surprising after all to find them widely required at every level in all subjects of Nuffield science (and, one would add as a good guess, in other new science schemes and in 'traditional' science subjects as well).

[1] For similar work in USA see James F. Thorpe (Del Valle High School, Walnut Creek, California) and James G. Lindblad (Lowell High School, Whittier, California), *Resource materials for the teaching of the new mathematics programs in application to the sciences*. Max S. Bell, The University of Chicago, is also working in this field in conjunction with the School Mathematics Study Group, Stanford University.

[2] See, for example, 'Do the new maths and science schemes have much in common?' by B. R. Harris, Association for Science Education/Mathematical Association/Association of Teachers of Mathematics Science Mathematics Links Working Party *Education in Science* **9**, 47, April 1972, 17.

[3] The primary data resulting from the analysis are not included in this paper for lack of space. Readers who wish to examine these data are invited to do so by writing to the author.

TABLE 1. *Ratio, proportion, linear relations, and related concepts in mathematics needed in Nuffield science and treated in SMP mathematics*

	Year of the secondary school course				
	1 (11–12 years)	2 (12–13 years)	3 (13–14 years)	4 (14–15 years)	5 (15–16 years)
Nuffield Biology	Sc Sc R	Sc V R G R Ra R C R V	% % G G G R R R Ra % R % R R R	G G R G	G % G G R % % P C
Nuffield Chemistry	R (density)		Ra R Ra R	C R R Ra Ra Ra R Ra Ra G C R G	R G R G G G G Ra % Ra R F S % R C
Nuffield Physics	R (density) P G P R (pressure) Ra Ra R % P	R G R R R Ra P R	R R R E Ra Sc G G G V S G R reciprocals A A	G P G F F G F F F F G F R V A F S Ra R R R R G % F R R F F	F V F F F F S F F S F F S G C V F F
SMP 'O' level mathematics	Coordinates; linear relations (graphical ready reckoner); algebraic relations; graphing algebraic relations.	Similarity; areas of similar figures; enlargement; graphing functions; law of natural growth; (slide rule); volumes of similar solids; solving equations; ratio and proportion; %.	Rates of change; gradient; rate of change at an instant; graphing equations and orderings; equations; F, S.	Solution of equations graphically and algebraically; gradients and tangents; searching for functions; P R Ra F G (logs, growth functions and reciprocals).	Areas and graphs; areas of irregular figures; functions and graphs. Review, summary and occasionally extension of previous work.

Key
- A area under graph
- C curvilinear relations
- E enlargement
- F manipulation of formulae
- G straight line graphs and gradients
- P proportion
- R rates of change
- Ra ratios
- S substitution of values in equations
- Sc scale and scale factors (including similar figures)
- V variation (including inverse variation and inverse square law)

Note The number of entries of a concept or skill in any one cell of these tables (R R R Ra G etc.) is intended to give a rough idea of the number of separate occasions in science lessons when these concepts are required. The descriptions of the SMP mathematics are chapter and section titles.

The second grouping of mathematical skills, distinguishable from but merging into the first group, is those concerned with measurement and the statistical treatment of data, including descriptive statistics and probability, calculation of averages, approximations and the use of standard form in handling very large and very small numbers. As may be seen in the first three rows of table 2, these too are widely required, particularly in Nuffield Biology and Physics.

A third, somewhat smaller grouping concerns some aspects of geometry and trigonometry. As the first three rows of table 3 show, these arise mainly in Nuffield Physics, although in Chemistry symmetry and tessellations are important concepts.

Any attempt at classification of ideas in this way is bound to seem somewhat arbitrary and to leave some items as difficult to classify. By using the broad groupings just described however, very little of the mathematics required for Nuffield Science has been omitted.

2 To what extent do modern mathematics courses meet these needs?

Having made, as described, an assessment of the mathematics needed for Nuffield science, the question naturally arises to what extent do the modern mathematics projects meet these needs? As is well known, the various mathematics projects in Britain introduce mathematical topics in a variety of different orders[1] so that a general answer to this question cannot easily be given. Instead of trying to do that, we have selected the 'O' level course of the School Mathematics Project (SMP) as a project comparable, in the scale of its operations in England, with that of the Nuffield projects in the sciences.

Tables 1, 2, and 3 in their fourth rows show, in outline for each year, the extent to which the SMP course covers the topics required by the sciences. As can be seen in each of the tables, the agreement between demand and supply is very close. In some cases (e.g. vector geometry) supply even exceeds demand. In very few instances can it be said that demand exceeds supply. Moreover, with one or two notable exceptions, the timing of the introduction of the various concepts and skills seems to keep remarkably well in step; in most cases they are introduced in the same year in mathematics and in science and sometimes a year earlier in mathematics. Exceptions

[1] The Mathematical Association's pamphlet, *Mathematics Projects in British Secondary Schools*, G. Bell and Sons, London, 1968, in its 11 to 16 Syllabus Analysis shows the extent to which projects vary in their order of treatment of mathematical topics.

TABLE 2. *Measurement and the statistical treatment of data*

	Year of the secondary school course				
	1 (11–12 years)	2 (12–13 years)	3 (13–14 years)	4 (14–15 years)	5 (15–16 years)
Nuffield Biology	DS DS DS Av M	DS DS M Av Av	DS D DS DS SF SF DS DS Av	DS DS SF	P P DS Av Range, std. devn. R D P P DS Binomial distribution
Nuffield Chemistry	DS DS	DS	SF A DS	DS DS	DS DS DS Av
Nuffield Physics	SF SF A A Av D P Av		A Av	A A A A A A A SF SF SF SF P (random walk) Av (RMS value)	A SF SF Av P SF
SMP 'O' level mathematics	A (bread and butter arithmetic).	Estimation and accuracy (A), DS D Av, Large and small numbers: SF	P DS D Av, cumulative frequency.	Thinking statistically; Av P D limits of accuracy; P (tree diagrams).	SF DS significance. Review, summary, and occasional extension of previous work.

Key
- A approximate calculation
- Av averages
- D distributions
- DS descriptive statistics
- M measurement
- P probability
- SF standard form (also known as scientific notation)

(For interpretation of the table please see note on table 1.)

TABLE 3. *Geometry and trigonometry – some aspects used in science*

	Year of the secondary school course				
	1 (11–12 years)	2 (12–13 years)	3 (13–14 years)	4 (14–15 years)	5 (15–16 years)
Nuffield Biology	(areas of similar figures – see table 1)		Parallelogram area $b \times h$	Topology: feed-back loops and control systems (implicit).	
Nuffield Chemistry	Electrical circuit diagrams		Tessellations in 2- and 3-D (close-packing of spheres).		
Nuffield Physics	Regular solids; 3-D arrays; angle, plane, face; volume of cuboid; sphere.	Intuitive ideas of geometrical transformations of a square; angle; rotation; circuit diagrams.	Waves; reflection, symmetry; equal angles; circles, parabolas, ellipses; (enlargement, similar triangles) properties of circle; reflection; symmetry; angles; parallel lines; $\sin i/\sin r$.	Area of triangle; vectors (momentum).	Motion in an orbit; ellipses; crossed chords method of showing centripetal force is mv^2/r; similar triangles; waves; sine, cosine; vectors (velocities).
SMP 'O' level mathematics	Angle, polygons, and polyhedra; area and area measurement; symmetry; parallelograms and triangles.	Topology; reflections and rotations; translations and vectors; volume (including calculation of volumes); filling space with polyhedra; trigonometry; sine and cosine; Pythagoras' Theorem.	Transformations including reflection; the circle; π; circumference and area; cylinders; 3-D geometry: points, lines, planes, and angles; waves, sine and cosine functions; areas of parallelogram and triangle.	Trigonometry; tangents and gradients; relation between sin, cos, and tan; parabola; hyperbola; ellipse; co-ordinates and vectors in 3-D; vector geometry.	Vectors and trigonometry; displacement and velocity vectors; sphere: volume and surface area. Review, summary and occasional extension of previous work.

include the early use of the rate concept in the form of *density* in the Nuffield Chemistry and Physics courses in Year 1, and early use of standard form in Year 1 of Nuffield Physics (though in neither case is the need for these regarded by the scientists as crucial). As a general conclusion, agreement seems close and the situation, on paper, appears remarkably satisfactory. Yet three comments need to be made.

(1) One is struck, in undertaking the above analysis, how little use is made in the science courses of the many other mathematical ideas which go to make up a modern course like the School Mathematics Project. All of the work on structure in mathematics, most of the transformation geometry (including networks and topology), and much of the approach to algebra and the mathematics of functional relations stand alone in SMP mathematics and find little or no echo in Nuffield science. It would seem to be time to examine ways in which these powerful ideas can be brought to bear and usefully exercised in modern school science.

(2) The analysis above shows that provision is made in the structure of the courses for the *possibility of cooperation* between teachers in school mathematics and science departments over the topics listed in tables 1, 2, and 3. We have to ask how far that possibility becomes a reality in the average school. I believe that one reason why cooperation is so little of a reality in some schools is the lack of materials which could be used in a joint approach to the teaching of the topics in the overlap areas. We have made a beginning, in the Shell Mathematics Unit at the Centre for Science Education, with remedying this situation, with the preparation, in a trial edition, of modules of work[1] designed to be used jointly by science and mathematics departments in schools. Other similar mathematics/science modules are in preparation[2] and will be tried out in schools during the coming academic year. This we think is at least part of the answer to the third question raised at the beginning of this paper.

(3) There are some mathematical topics about which, notwithstanding the fact that they are treated consonantly in both mathematics and science courses, there are persistent reports from teachers

[1] *Indices and Molecules*, Nuffield Foundation, 1971. Trial version not for publication. Nuffield Mathematics Teaching Project. A second module also completed is entitled *Symmetry and Crystal Structure*.

[2] Other modules in preparation include ones on shape, size, and growth in biology, combining ratios in chemistry, density, rates of change, and measurement.

of students' difficulties.[1] One such topic is proportionality, linear relationships and variation, which, as table 1 shows, is widely needed in science courses and quite fully treated in SMP mathematics. Such persistent reports of difficulty suggest that, as Inhelder and Piaget[2] and others, e.g. Lovell,[3] have pointed out, there may be an important psychological component to which more attention should be given, in the development of students' mathematical skills and their ability to handle concepts like ratios and proportion. This is a point on which we are doing further work.

Acknowledgements

The work described in this paper was supported in part by Shell Grant 35/2851. The author wishes to thank Mrs Margaret Brown, Shell Mathematics Unit, Centre for Science Education, for undertaking some of the analysis of the Nuffield Physics course, and Professor Geoffrey Matthews for his constant encouragement and support.

Centre for Science Education,
Bridges Place,
London, SW6 4HR.

[1] E.g. an unpublished report *Mathematical difficulties of pupils studying Nuffield 'O' Level Chemistry* by Dr R. B. Ingle, Centre for Science Education, Chelsea College, University of London.

[2] Inhelder, B. and Piaget, J., *The growth of logical thinking from childhood to adolescence*, Routledge and Kegan Paul, London, 1958.

[3] See for example *Intellectual growth and understanding mathematics*, a paper given by Professor K. Lovell, University of Leeds, at the Psychology of Mathematics Education Workshop, Centre for Science Education, Chelsea College, University of London, January 1972, which contains many other references.

Geometry as a gateway to mathematics

Bruce E. Meserve

Introduction

The role of geometry in the study of mathematics has been a special interest of mine for several years. During the past year I have enjoyed a sabbatical from my university teaching and made a special effort to discover what is happening to the role of geometry. I have found two papers particularly enlightening and would like to quote from them as background for our considerations of geometry as a gateway to mathematics. I believe that geometry serves this role at all levels – in elementary schools, in secondary schools, and in colleges and universities.

Professor E. Spanier wrote in 1970, in an article entitled 'The Undergraduate Program in Mathematics', that:

> Broadly speaking, the goal of undergraduate mathematics education should be to help the student to understand something about mathematics both in its internal structure and in its relations with other disciplines. He should get a feeling of the vitality of the subject and enough history to appreciate current trends and progress. He should have studied some areas of mathematics, possibly only small parts, in depth, but he should also obtain some sort of global view of mathematics by the time he graduates. These objectives are important for all mathematics majors.

Relative to geometry, Professor Spanier writes:

> The classical geometry courses have been dwindling because they are not needed for graduate work. Today's teachers have been taught to distrust the practice of drawing a figure and using intuition as an aid in understanding a result. They insist on presenting a subject in the 'right' way, which usually means in the most abstract setting available to the teacher in question... Even the most elementary properties of curves and surfaces in 3-space can't be discussed without a machinery appropriate for general manifolds of n-space.
>
> When so much abstract machinery is presented before the student's intuition has developed, he may learn how a result can be proved, but he is unlikely to get a true understanding of the result. The most important

things about a theorem do not necessarily include its proof. On the contrary, to understand a theorem one should know what it says, what motivates it, or why it is stated, as well as instances where it applies or does not apply, and some of its consequences as well as its proof. These things are not necessarily easy; indeed, patient step-by-step verification of a proof may be considerably easier. We should not be afraid to omit proofs. It is good pedagogy, especially in undergraduate courses, to state a theorem (such as Stokes' theorem) and discuss its consequences without giving a proof of it.

In his conclusion Professor Spanier says:

It is certain that there is much room for improvement in what we are teaching undergraduates, and that this need lies deeper than mere rearrangement of the curriculum. It is not clear what should be done to effect improvement, but unless we define our goals and recognise the defects of current practices, we can't even begin.

The second paper that I found particularly interesting is Professor T. J. Willmore's report of his address 'Whither Geometry?' at the April 1970 Annual Congress of the Mathematical Association in England. To establish a concept of geometry Professor Willmore uses the following quote from the opening pages of Semple and Kneebone's *Algebraic Curves*:

Geometry is the study of spatial relations, and in its most elementary form it is conceived as a systematic investigation into the properties of figures subsisting in the space familiar to common sense. As mathematical insight grows, however, the 'space' that constitutes the geometer's ultimate object of study is seen to be an ideal object – an intellectual construction that reveals itself to be essentially different from any possible object of naïve intuition. Nevertheless, even the most abstract geometrical thinking must retain some link, however attenuated, with spatial intuition, for otherwise it would be misleading to call it geometrical; and it is an historical fact that, throughout the long development of mathematics, geometers have again and again arisen who have given a fresh impulse to formal mathematics by going back once more for inspiration to the primitive geometrical sense.

I shall not repeat Professor Willmore's presentation of developments in Euclidean geometry, affine geometry, projective geometry, algebraic geometry, and differential geometry – his own speciality. However, his four conjectured lessons that can be learned from the past development of geometry seem particularly pertinent. I quote:

I suppose that the first lesson is that mathematics no longer consists of separate water-tight compartments, and that geometry as such is no longer a subject. What is important is a geometrical way of looking at a mathematical situation – *geometry is essentially a way of life.* We have geometric topology, geometrical dynamics, differential and algebraic geometry, but not just 'geometry'. The geometry of a manifold is described by the Lie algebra of the group of transformations which preserves the structure, and it is also described by global analysis of the manifold. The geometric, algebraic and analytic structures are all inter-related.

The second lesson to be learned is the power of invariant methods of describing a geometrical situation – real progress is made when one concentrates on geometric (invariant) properties. An analytical approach is purely formal and can easily degenerate into a morass of symbols whose significance is obscure.

The third lesson to be learned is the advantage of familiarity with axiomatic methods, especially with structures where the axioms do not form a categorical system.

The fourth lesson...is that much is to be gained by detailed study of particular cases of mathematical situations. The theoretical edifices of various structures are a very important part of mathematics. But the life blood which guarantees a continuing and vigorous development of the subject is to be found in trying to solve problems which present themselves naturally. When the problem solvers are no more, mathematics will be moribund.

Professor Willmore then stated his view of the future of geometry. With reference to university level geometry he conjectured that:

geometry as a self-contained body of knowledge will become less important, while the geometrical attitude towards mathematics will become increasingly important.

With reference to the teaching of geometry in the schools he said:

We should certainly try to achieve the following:

1. To give our students some idea of the nature of euclidean geometry, and the nature of the axioms on which it is based.
2. To let them see that there are several different geometries of which euclidean geometry is only one example.
3. To emphasize the influence of Descartes on geometry.
4. To use set language to describe geometrical configurations, following the ideas of Papy.
5. To encourage the student to make his own conjectures of results which might well be true.
6. Above all, we should try to impart to our students the intellectual excitement associated with geometrical discovery, and the shared enjoyment of understanding the discoveries of others.

As a further basis for our discussions I shall

(1) describe my interpretation of the causes of the present status of geometry,

(2) recommend a specific concept of the role of geometry, and

(3) suggest one possible approach to the reestablishment of geometry as a major area of mathematical study and exploration.

My remarks reflect primarily the situation in the United States and are not intended to be definitive but rather to serve as a stimulant to discussion. Thus I shall try to provide a framework for the consideration of geometry as a gateway to mathematics, an approach to numerous topics throughout all branches of mathematics. Those sharing my concern for the present role of geometry should be able to extend this framework readily into their own areas of special interest and to reinforce the framework with a substantial number of significant illustrative examples.

What happened to reduce geometry to its present status?

It seems to me that the present down-graded role of geometry has arisen from increasing specialisation and narrowing of our areas of concern. Rather than evolving with our ever-changing intellectual environment, we have again and again walled ourselves off into smaller and smaller areas of interest relative to the scope of mathematics with our students 'learning more and more about less and less'. Accordingly, we are in increasing danger of stagnation and suffocation. Incidentally, I feel that the entire discipline of mathematics is showing definite signs of following this same unfortunate path toward immobilisation by failing to be actively alert and sympathetic to the concerns of logicians, statisticians, teachers, and most recently, information scientists.

However, let us restrict our detailed considerations to geometry. 'A society of gentlemen' emphasised the changing nature of geometry in 1751 in a London publication printed for John Wilcox and entitled

THE MATHEMATICIAN containing many curious dissertations on the rise, progress, and improvement of geometry.

I quote from the footnote on page 2:

Geometry, like many other sciences, has outgrown its name; it originally meant no more than measuring Earth, or surveying the land, as is plain from both its etymology and the principal use that was made of it; whereas now, it means the whole science of extension and magnitude, and contemplates the nature and properties of all kinds of figures abstractly considered without any regard to matter.

Thus the abstractions of geometry have been in progress for over two hundred years; they should not be blamed for the increasing lack of interest in geometry during the last fifty years.

During the last fifty years topology has attained substantial recognition independent of geometry. The study of linear transformations has become linear algebra, which in turn has become algebra. Currently graph theory and combinatorics may be attaining independence. You can undoubtedly cite other examples. The point is that over the ages, and today, geometric concepts provided the bases for advances that have become separate branches of mathematics and geometric concepts provided the insight for explorations in practically all branches of mathematics. I feel that the present status of geometry has arisen primarily from two trends:

(1) the spin-off of new branches of mathematics, and

(2) the increasing recognition of the interrelations among the various branches of mathematics.

I recognise that geometry is not the sole approach to the new branches of mathematics under consideration and geometry should not expect an exclusive claim to them. Assuming that geometry and other branches of mathematics are mutually interrelated, two questions remain:

What should be our present concept of the role of geometry?

How can students be prepared to make effective use of geometric concepts in their chosen careers?

A concept of the role of geometry

Historically a large part of mathematics was based upon geometric concepts and even geometric representations. The influence of algebra is now seen in analytic geometry, linear algebra, algebraic geometry, and the somewhat restricting concept of a geometry as a study of invariants under a group of transformations. The influence of analysis is seen in differential geometry. It seems to me that there can be no serious question either of the value of other branches of mathematics in the study of geometry or of the value of geometry in the study of other branches of mathematics. One question to discuss is whether geometry inherently retains its identity as a fundamental, recognisable area of mathematics or should be absorbed into other mathematical areas.

Professor Pedoe, in his book *A Course of Geometry for Colleges and Universities* takes as his 'main thread' 'the algebraic methods available for a study of elementary geometry'. I am sidestepping my concern for how we approach geometry and looking at the aspects of geometry that we would like to convey to our pupils. Indeed, I view the problem of the present status of geometry as in part a public relations problem of obtaining recognition of the advantages and respectability of a geometric approach.

What is, or should be, the role of geometry today in the overall study and uses of mathematics? The point of view that I am suggesting is based upon the following three premises:

(1) Geometry provides one or more points of view, or ways of looking at, nearly all areas of mathematics.

(2) Geometric interpretations continue to provide insights leading to both the intuitive understanding of, and advances in, most areas of mathematics.

(3) Geometric techniques provide effective tools for solving problems in most areas of mathematics.

From these premises it seems to me that:

> geometry is an essential part of the study of mathematics at any level and a vital catalyst for effective use or study of any branch of mathematics.

This concept of the role of geometry seems to have many implications for both our classroom practices and our public relations. I would emphasise two general implications:

(1) The widely publicised 'Down with Euclid' statements must be accepted not as synonymous with 'down with geometry' but rather as strong indications that geometry must be taught as a living and growing subject instead of a collection of ancient rules.

(2) Geometry should be presented in such a way as to prepare the students to use geometry.

This second implication could have been taken from Oswald Veblen's article 'The modern approach to elementary geometry' published in 1934. Veblen said:

> It seems to me that elementary geometry should be presented in such a way as to prepare the student for other sciences which he is to study later, and in which this very geometry is going to be used. This means that the methods of geometry should not be singular ones, peculiar to the subject itself, but should as far as possible be methods which can be used over and over again in other branches of science.

Veblen was arguing for the inclusion of coordinate methods as well as synthetic methods. Now – nearly forty years later – we are concerned with both of these approaches (synthetic and coordinate). We are concerned with an informal intuitive approach to geometry (especially for ages five to thirteen). We are concerned with transformations and with vectors. We may still add other approaches in our discussions. We need to find a balance in our selections from the various approaches to geometry. The use of a variety of methods is an essential part of our desire to prepare our students to make effective use of geometric concepts.

But just what are we trying to accomplish? It would be very helpful if we could prepare educational objectives for our students in specific behavioural terms. However, such considerations would require much more time than we have available. As we look at the teaching of geometry at all levels, one major role of geometry seems to stand out above all others – the use of geometric representations. These geometric representations may be simple sketches or pictorial representations. Geometric representations may be at an informal intuitive level or part of a formal axiomatic system. Geometric representations may be interpretations using abstract geometric figures and their properties. At all levels geometric representations appear to provide the basis for the use of geometry as an approach to the study of mathematics.

Think of our uses of number scales, number lines, complex planes, and all sorts of graphical representations. Operations with fractional numbers may be represented by rectangular regions. Operations with complex numbers may be represented on a complex plane. Hyperbolic geometry may be represented on a Poincaré model. At all levels the use of geometric representations provides the basis for using intuitive geometric concepts, applying known geometric relations, and using geometric transformations in the solution of problems.

The role of geometric representations as mathematical models of a wide variety of problems provides a primary basis for our selection of topics and methods for a geometry course. However, we need to consider not only the theorems that we would like our students to know but also the techniques that we would like them to be able to use.

We would like our students to be able to explore relations among geometric figures using continuity and using symmetry. We would like our students to be able to use algebra as in analytic (coordinate) geometry, finite geometries, and algebraic geometry. We would like our students to be able to use calculus as in differential geometry, to be able to use vectors, and to be able to use transformations that leave invariant the essential aspects of a problem while converting the geometric representation to one in which known results provide useful information for solving the problem.

These objectives are mentioned to emphasise the need for a broad concept of geometry. This breadth is needed if students are to use their knowledge of geometry effectively as one approach to their study of mathematics.

My own special interest in geometry is at the undergraduate level of the university, especially in its relation to the preparation of teachers for elementary and secondary schools.

In the United States the most commonly used course for prospective elementary school teachers (with students of ages five to thirteen) seems to be a very weak secondary school course in Euclidean geometry. I feel very strongly that prospective elementary school teachers have a serious need for experiences involving explorations in geometry in the pedagogical spirit that they should use in their own teaching. This pedagogical need is much greater than their need for a review of the theorems of secondary school geometry. I have taught a course based upon explorations in geometry and I strongly recommend such an approach. If you are interested, you will find excellent suggestions among the current supplementary materials for elementary school teachers and the materials used in experimental programmes.

Prospective secondary school teachers need a broad preparation in geometry since they will themselves be expected to provide a broad preparation for their own students. In addition to the approaches that have already been mentioned these students need an overall view of the place of Euclidean geometry among a wide variety of other geometries. For example, they might consider the hierarchy of geometries shown in the diagram on p. 249. The discussions of some of the geometries, such as the spherical and non-Euclidean geometries, could be quite informal.

Carl B. Allendoerfer, in an article published in 1969 and entitled 'The dilemma in geometry', suggests the following major objectives for geometry in our elementary and secondary schools:

1. An understanding of the basic facts about geometric figures in the plane and solids in space.

2. An understanding of the basic facts about geometric transformations such as reflections, rotations, and translations.
3. An appreciation of the deductive method.
4. An introduction to imaginative thinking.
5. Integration of geometric ideas with other parts of mathematics.

I share his desire for the consideration of plane and solid geometry at all levels. The emphasis in the role of geometry that I have suggested is upon his last objective – the integration of geometric ideas with other parts of mathematics – but with the added objective of maintaining an awareness that geometry is involved.

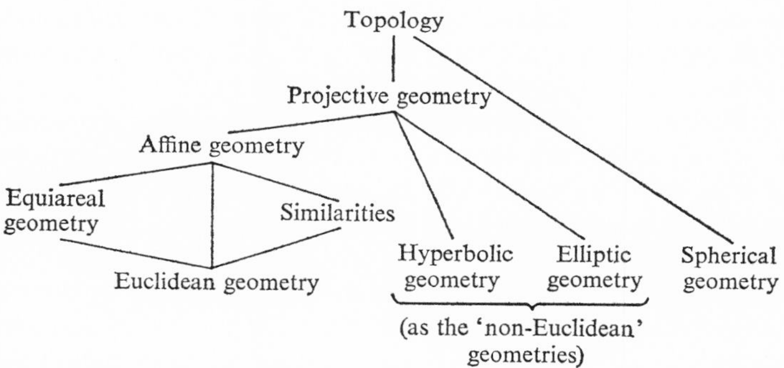

Professor Hans Freudenthal in the introduction of his book *Mathematics Observed* notes that

> The trained mathematician uses the modes of thought of mathematics at every turn, usually without knowing that he is doing so, or in what way.

Our concern might be expressed as a paraphrase of that quotation:

> The trained mathematician, and each person who makes extensive use of mathematics, uses the modes of thought of geometry at nearly every turn, often without knowing that he is doing so, or in what way.

The reestablishment of geometry through the recognition of the uses of its modes of thought should be consistent with a contemporary view of mathematics as a unified subject. Again quoting Professor Freudenthal

> Formerly, it was possible to distinguish (with some difficulty) between pure and applied mathematics or between geometry, algebra, and analysis; today it is impossible to say where one begins and the other ends.

My concept of geometry as one approach to mathematics is closely related to my concept of a really good mathematician as an inherently lazy person who seeks the easiest way of accomplishing fully the task that he wants to do. He should be able to use geometry as one approach to his task.

A suggested approach

My suggested approach to the reestablishment of geometry as a major area of mathematical study and exploration is a university course in geometry that would provide students with a geometric point of view and competencies for using geometry throughout their study and use of mathematics. I have *not* written a textbook for such a course and do not have an existence proof that such a course is possible. However, an emphasis upon the modes of thought of geometry, and the prerequisites for applications of geometry, could be the key to the reestablishment of geometry as a major mathematical discipline. Accordingly, I propose such a course as one approach to the revitalisation of geometry.

Without trying to assign priorities or to structure a course, I shall comment briefly upon three essential ingredients of a university geometry course to help students prepare themselves for using geometry as an approach to their study of mathematics. These same three ingredients seem to me to underly the teaching of geometry at all levels.

1 Basic facts

Discussions of basic facts about plane and solid figures have dominated many of our geometry courses. Obviously facts are essential. However, relative to the student's future use of facts, the manner in which they are presented is of critical importance. Student conjectures and testing of their conjectures, relations among facts, and recognition of a variety of situations in which specified facts are applicable are very important. Also it should suffice to introduce many facts informally, to develop some facts deductively, and to explore many facts with coordinates, vectors, transformations, continuity, symmetry, algebra, or calculus. Throughout our emphasis upon geometry as an approach to mathematics, a variety of geometric techniques and their applications must be considered. Accordingly, a restriction to the style of an elegant deductive system is unacceptably narrow.

2 *The deductive method*

As indicated in Professor Allendoerfer's list of major objectives for school mathematics, the deductive method needs to be considered enough to be appreciated. At the university undergraduate level I feel that we tend to overemphasise the deductive method. Our students need to recognise the ultimate authority of the deductive method but they also desperately need experience in formulating problems, trying a variety of geometric approaches and representations, and formulating conjectures that they will then test deductively. The deductive method is a mode of thought that has carried over from geometry to other branches of mathematics and other sciences. However, our emphasis in geometry should be not only on the use and appreciation of the deductive method but also on several other aspects of geometry.

Poincaré emphasised the insufficiency of the deductive method in his 'The Value of Science':

> What you gain in rigor...you lose in objectivity. You can rise toward your logical ideal only by cutting off the bonds which attach you to reality. Your science is infallible; but it can only remain so by imprisoning itself in an ivory tower and removing all relation with the external world. From this seclusion it must go out when it would attempt the slightest application.

From this point of view I have been suggesting that we must go outside our ivory tower to revitalise the teaching of geometry. Later Poincaré said:

> in becoming rigorous, mathematical science takes a character so artificial as to strike everyone; it forgets its historical origins; we see how questions can be answered, we no longer see how and why they are put.

3 *Geometric intuition*

The third basic ingredient on which I wish to comment is geometric intuition. In his 'Science and Method' Poincaré said:

> The principal aim of mathematical teaching is to develop certain faculties of the mind, and among these intuition is not the least precious. It is through it that the mathematical world remains in contact with the real world, and if pure mathematicians could do without it, it would always be necessary to have recourse to it to fill up the chasm which separates the symbol from reality. The practician will always have need of it, and for one pure geometer, there should be a hundred practicians.

and later:

For the pure geometer himself, this faculty is necessary; it is by logic one demonstrates, by intuition one invents. To know how to criticize is good, to know how to create is better. You know how to recognize if a combination is correct; what a predicament if you have not the art of choosing among all the possible combinations. Logic tells us that on such and such a way we may be sure not to meet any obstacle; it does not say which way leads to the end. For that it is necessary to see from afar, and the faculty that teaches us to see is intuition.

Geometric intuition provides the basis for much of Allendoerfer's imaginative thinking. It is one of Freudenthal's modes of thought that we need to find ways of developing in our students. I feel that our own pedagogical approach is fully as significant as the mathematical content within which we endeavour to develop geometric intuition.

Numerous topics could be suggested for a university course to help students use a geometric approach to their study of mathematics. From my own experience one topic, the topology of the real line, stands out as essential. The completeness of the line, continuity, the separation of the line by a point of it, and the order relations among the points of a real line are used extensively in elementary mathematics. In general, a broad selection of topics commensurate with the mathematical maturity of the student is needed. Probably different selections of topics are needed for different groups of students. Throughout the treatment of these topics an emphasis upon intuitive concepts and upon applications of geometry should provide the basis for a sound geometric point of view, even though numerous formal details of graduate level rigour are postponed until later courses.

Conclusion

I have tried to define some of our goals while recognising that it is not completely clear what should be done to implement them. It may be that I have been wasting your time commenting upon the obvious. However, I hope that my presentation will have served to emphasise a contemporary point of view of geometry and to focus our attention on ways of teaching geometry to develop facility in the use of geometry as a gateway to mathematics.

References

Allendoerfer, C. B., The dilemma in geometry, *The Mathematics Teacher* **62**, March 1969, 165–70.

Freudenthal, H., *Mathematics Observed*, World University Library, McGraw-Hill, New York, 1967, pp. 7 and 9.

Gentlemen, a society of, *The Mathematician*, John Wilcox, London, 1751.

Pedoe, D., *A Course of Geometry for Colleges and Universities*, Cambridge University Press, 1970.

Poincaré, H., The Value of Science (trans. G. B. Halsted), in *The Foundations of Science*, The Science Press, New York, 1913, pp. 210–22 (pp. 216 and 217).

Poincaré, H., Science and Method (trans. G. B. Halsted), in *The Foundations of Science*, The Science Press, New York, 1913, pp. 430–47 (pp. 437 and 438).

Semple, J. G. and Kneebone, G. T., *Algebraic Curves*, Clarendon Press, Oxford, 1960.

Spanier, E., The Undergraduate Program in Mathematics, *The American Mathematical Monthly* **77**, August–September 1970, 752–5.

Veblen, O., The modern approach to elementary geometry, *The Rice Institute Pamphlet* **21**, 4, October 1934, 209–21; reprinted in *The Mathematics Teacher* **60**, February 1967, 98–104.

Willmore, T. J., Whither Geometry? *The Mathematical Gazette* **54**, October 1970, 216–24.

University of Vermont,
Burlington,
Vermont,
USA.

The International Baccalaureate

J. B. Morgan

PART I – GENERAL

1 International schools

The need for international schools was first publicly recognised in 1924 with the foundation of the International School of Geneva, largely to cater for the families of officials working in the headquarters of the League of Nations. Since then the steady growth of the great international companies and the world-wide operations of the United Nations has caused this pattern to be followed in many cities all over the world. Dozens of international schools have sprung up to cater for the children of a largely mobile population of families from overseas. Children who attend these schools come from a multitude of backgrounds, stay in one area for varying periods of time and have an enormous number of different plans for further education in colleges, universities and training schemes.

International schools can now be broadly divided into two types of foundation:

(i) schools whose main purpose is to serve the foreign families living in the area (for example, the International School of Geneva and the International College of Beirut);

(ii) schools whose main purpose is to serve the cause of international understanding, cooperation and peace (for example, Atlantic College in Wales, UK, the first of a developing chain of United World Colleges).

Both types of school (and they are steadily growing closer together) have two main problems to solve: the design of a common syllabus to cater for the needs of a highly mobile population, and the provision of a common leaving qualification which will be acceptable to universities and colleges in all countries where their students wish to continue their studies or begin professional training.

2 The International Baccalaureate

Following a plan initially launched in 1962 by the International School of Geneva, in conjunction with the International Schools Association, various committees were formed to work out syllabuses and design trial examinations. In 1965 Atlantic College joined the experiment, followed in 1967 by the United Nations International School in New York. Meanwhile, in 1966, Mr A. D. C. Peterson of Oxford University (UK) had been appointed Director General of the experiment, and a conference at Sèvres, near Paris, attended by experts from eleven countries, led to the foundation of the International Baccalaureate Office (IBO) in Geneva. During 1968–70 there were many trial examinations in the separate subjects, and a Pilot Project was worked out for the six years 1971–6, covering a two-year terminal course.

The first stage of the Pilot Project, 1971–3, is nearing completion, and a detailed revision of the regulations and syllabuses has been prepared for the second stage, 1974–6. It is intended that a complete (but flexible) scheme will be ready shortly after the conclusion of the 1976 examinations for adoption by some form of inter-governmental agency, possibly under the guidance of UNESCO, and that the IB will then expand its field to take in many other schools and many other countries beyond the necessarily limited number who have taken part in the Pilot Project.

3 The IB Diploma Programme

To qualify for the Diploma a candidate must satisfy the examiner in one subject from each of the following six sections; three subjects must be passed at Higher Level and three at Subsidiary Level.

(1) *Language A* (the working language) including a syllabus of world literature in translation.

(2) *Language B* (or second language *A*), which must be different from the language chosen under section 1.

(3) *Study of man*; one of the following: history, geography, economics, philosophy, psychology, social anthropology.

(4) *Experimental sciences*; one of the following: biology, physics, chemistry, physical science, scientific studies.

(5) *Mathematics.*

(6) *Other studies*; one of the following: arts (plastic arts or music), a third language (classical or modern), a second subject from sec-

tion 3, a second subject from section 4, further mathematics, or a syllabus designed by the school and approved by the IBO.

In addition all candidates for the Diploma must have followed a common course in Theory of Knowledge (including logic), and have engaged satisfactorily in an artistic or creative activity. The course in *Theory of Knowledge* is aimed at making the student familiar with the various processes of thought, and capable of understanding their relationships, whether the reasoning is applied to mathematics, the humanities, the experimental sciences, morals, the arts, or any other field. The freedom allowed in section 6, and in the design of certain optional topics (see §10) provides each school with the opportunity of making the fullest possible use of local interests, resources and teaching talent.

The plan is based on the principle that 'learning how to learn' has now become the prime function of school education, and, in particular, pays special regard to:

(i) the need for a broad general education, firmly establishing the student in the use of 'tools' he will need whatever the career he chooses to follow;

(ii) as flexible as possible a choice among the subjects to be studied, so that, subject to (i), the student's options correspond as far as possible to his particular interests and capacities.

Students who do not need to follow the full Diploma course may offer single subjects, and there is then no restriction upon their choice except feasibility within their school programme. The IBO awards certificates for such subjects, showing the grade in each case.

4 Assessment

Each subject is individually assessed by the Chief Examiner on a scale rising from Grade 1 (very poor) to Grade 7 (excellent). To gain a Diploma, a candidate must have been awarded a mark of at least 4 in each of the six subjects examined. A system of cross-compensation allows lower marks in one or two subjects to be counterbalanced by higher marks in others, while a mark of 6 or 7 in the Theory of Knowledge course adds one point to the candidate's total.

Different methods of assessment are used by the examiners in the various subjects. At present six types of assessment are used, but experiments are carried out each year and the present position is very fluid; the six types are:

(1) Independent research (higher level only); an extended essay

in language *A* and history, and field work in geography, followed by an oral examination; in other subjects independent work is optional.

(2) Written examinations; these are held towards the end of May and include essays, short answer questions and multiple choice objective tests.

(3) Oral examinations; in language *A* these are traditional face-to-face orals, but in most other subjects tape recordings are used.

(4) Practical assessment; assessment of practical work in sciences is based on a combination of teachers' continuous assessment, school inspections and evaluation of experiments presented by film; in art, dossiers and slides are submitted to a panel of examiners.

(5) Listening comprehension test; taped conversations and prose extracts upon which short written replies are based (mostly language *B*).

(6) School assessment of the student during the 2-year IB course is taken into consideration by the Chief Examiner in each subject; it is also used for the Theory of Knowledge and Aesthetic Activities courses, and for special school syllabuses under *Other Studies* (with moderation by a visiting examiner).

5 Research unit

A special research unit, located at Oxford University, prepares detailed statistical reports for the information of participating schools, the IBO, examiners and members of the Council of Foundation (which is responsible for the general direction and administration of the IB). Details analysed include the correlation between school assessment and IB grades, the distribution of IB grades (rising from 1 to 7) by subjects and by schools, and the progress of IB candidates in their subsequent studies.

6 University recognition

In the past international schools have, in broad terms, adopted one of the two methods described below in order to provide their students with the qualifications necessary for admission to the university and faculty of their choice:

(i) Upper forms were divided into separate groups, each group working towards the objective laid down by a particular country; this method defeats the aims of truly international schools and leads to an expensive duplication of teaching staff.

(ii) All students were prepared for the leaving qualification of the host country and admission requirements were negotiated with individual countries or universities; this method defeated the aim of mobility and led to an impossible burden of secretarial work.

The IBO has therefore made approaches to many countries and universities, and in May 1972 there were already twenty-nine countries in which universities recognised the IB Diploma within the framework of their own regulations for admission. Two examples are given: in the UK all universities recognise the IB for all applicants, although a particular faculty may make special requirements in relation to subjects chosen and grades awarded; in France the universities recognise the IB for all foreigners and for all French students whose parents have been living abroad for at least two years.

The list of countries and universities is growing steadily, but the arrangements will have to be re-negotiated in many cases at the end of the Pilot Project in 1976. Details are given in the General Guide (see §13).

PART II – MATHEMATICS

7 Special problems relating to mathematics

(i) The background and technical skills of students vary greatly both in quality and nature; this variation is due not only to the personal interests and experience of the students but also to the differing speeds and directions of development of mathematical courses in different countries.

(ii) The aims and destinations of students, whether they relate to further education or to careers, are far more varied than in national schools; so are the views of their parents.

(iii) The qualifications required by colleges and universities in different countries vary considerably both in level of attainment and in the type of thinking required.

8 Aims of the syllabuses

(*a*) The teacher is required:

(i) to develop the student's understanding of mathematics as an academic discipline;

(ii) to develop an attitude to mathematics in the student favourable to subsequent learning and application of the subject;

(iii) to develop the student's ability to learn mathematics on his own;

(iv) to encourage those students who lack confidence in their own knowledge of mathematics and experience in the subject.

(*b*) The examiner is required to assess the student's

(i) knowledge of mathematical concepts and essential terminology;

(ii) ability to formulate proofs of some of the theorems about these concepts;

(iii) ability to represent situations in mathematical terms (mathematical models), to examine their implications and possibilities, and to arrive at definite conclusions by the application of mathematics as a tool.

9 General considerations

Mathematics is a compulsory subject in the IB. It may be offered at Higher Level, Subsidiary Level *A* or Subsidiary Level *B*. There is also a subsidiary subject, Further Mathematics, intended mainly for those students who intend to read mathematics at the university.

Higher Level is intended for students who have good mathematical ability and especially for those who will need the subject in their future studies.

Subsidiary Level A is designed to provide a background of mathematical thought sufficient for students planning to pursue university studies in science, economics, and so on.

Subsidiary Level B is designed for students who, for the purpose of admission to colleges and universities, offer a combination of subjects which may not include mathematics, and for those not intending immediately to continue their formal academic studies; it is part of IB policy that all diploma candidates should continue to study mathematics while at school as part of their general education.

Further Mathematics may be offered under *Other Studies* of the general programme as a separate subsidiary subject, but only by candidates who enter for the Higher Level.

10 Design of the Higher and Subsidiary Levels

At each level, except Further Mathematics, the syllabus is divided into two sections: section 1 is the core of the respective syllabus and is compulsory; section 2 contains optional topics from which a selection must be made. In addition to the options in section 2 schools may submit topics of their own design for approval by the Chief Examiner in Mathematics.

Logic has been excluded from the *core* section in each case because it is included in the Theory of Knowledge course which is compulsory for all students who enter for the IB Diploma, but it occurs as an option at Subsidiary Level, mainly for the benefit of those students who are taking only a Certificate course.

Both Subsidiary Levels, *A* and *B*, have a list of items of preliminary knowledge required, as a guide to teachers in drawing up their individual schemes of preparation in mathematics for the years preceding the IB course.

At all levels the syllabus includes a few topics, marked with an asterisk, which it is hoped teachers will include in their courses, but which will not be examined. It is also possible for teachers to allow their quicker students to work on additional topics in section 2, and it is felt that this provides a good opportunity for individual work.

To illustrate the range of topics included, the main headings occurring in the Higher Level and Subsidiary Level *A* syllabuses are reproduced below.

Higher Level

All candidates must have studied section 1 of Subsidiary Level *A*. Candidates are expected to choose at least three options in section 2.

Section 1 1. Mathematical induction. 2. Sets, relations, mappings and algebraic structure. 3. Particular functions. 4. Polynomials. 5. Analytical geometry. 6. Differential calculus. 7. Integral calculus. 8. Vectors. 9. Matrices. 10. Complex numbers.

Section 2 1. Statistics and Probability. 2. Linear algebra and geometry. 3. Analysis and differential equations. 4. Mechanics. 5. Numerical calculations. 6. Theory of numbers. 7. Geometry. 8. Further calculus. (OR an individual topic.)

Subsidiary Level A

Candidates are expected to choose at least two options in section 2.

Section 1 1. Sets. 2. Relations. 3. Number. 4. Numerical calculations. 5. Algebra. 6. Trigonometry. 7. Vectors. 8. Matrices. 9. Functions. 10. Calculus. 11. Probability. 12. Statistics.

Section 2 1. Algebraic concepts. 2. Geometry. 3. Calculus. 4. Business mathematics. 5. Probability and statistics. 6. Logic. 7. Vectors. (OR an individual topic.)

11 Syllabus revision

The IB policy is one of continuous consultation with schools and revision of details of syllabus and examination, with a major revision between stages 1 and 2 of the Pilot Project. This major revision began with a conference in Oxford (October 1971) attended by teachers, examiners and advisers. Between November 1971 and February 1972 the draft syllabuses were circulated, and there was considerable correspondence with schools. In February and March 1972 several schools which had not attended the Oxford conference were visited, and in March 1972 a final drafting panel (Chief Examiner and two assistant examiners, one English and one French) met in Geneva, with help from the IBO staff. Altogether four new syllabuses, each in two languages, were drafted, aimed at meeting the wishes of twenty-two schools in eleven countries. The new syllabuses will be examined in 1974.

12 Annual Consultative Conference

This is convened (usually once a year) to advise on all educational matters. Its members are representatives of the teaching staff and students of participating schools, members of the Executive Committee and Research Unit, examiners, interested observers and specialists. Working groups discuss individual subjects and special problems.

13 Information

Further details can be obtained from the following sources:

(i) The Director General: Mr A. D. C. Peterson, Department of Educational Studies, Oxford University, 15 Norham Gardens, Oxford, UK.

(ii) The Director of the International Baccalaureate Office: M. Gérard Renaud, 1 rue Albert-Gos, 1206 Geneva, Switzerland. Chief Examiners can be contacted through M. Renaud.

(iii) The Research Director is Dr W. D. Halls, IBO Research Unit, 15 Norham Gardens, Oxford, UK.

(iv) The official *General Guide to the International Baccalaureate*, which contains full details of all syllabuses, can be obtained from M. Renaud, at IBO Geneva.

(v) The book, *International Baccalaureate*, by Mr A. D. C. Peterson, deals more fully with the philosophy, aims and future of the IB; it is published by G. G. Harrap & Co. Ltd.

The Gate House,
Lower Ufford,
Woodbridge, Suffolk.

The role of axioms in contemporary mathematics and in mathematical education

Toshio Shibata

1 What do we mean by 'Axiomatics'?

Modern mathematics, as it has developed during the last century and is still progressing, is characterised both by the axiomatic method and a tendency to abstractness. There are two types of mathematics constructed axiomatically, namely, categorical and non-categorical[1] theories. Examples of the former are Euclidean geometry and the theory of the natural numbers, and of the latter, group, ring, field, vector space and metric space. Roughly speaking, the former is an axiomatisation of a substance – an entity – and the latter is an abstraction of a structure.

A categorical theory can be constructed in two different ways. One way is to discover the essential basis, look for the foundation of a theory, and axiomatise the theory. This is in the spirit of Euclid and Hilbert and may be called the *historical development*. Historical Euclidean geometry, Hilbert's rigorous theory and Peano's theory of the naturals are examples of this historical development.

The other way is as follows. First, we break down a theory into essential pieces, observe some similarity in different theories, and abstract a common structure. Thus we obtain a non-categorical theory. Next, we organise several non-categorical theories to characterise a categorical theory. This is in the spirit of modern mathematics and may be called the *modern development*. Thus, an approach in which the Euclidean plane is characterised as a two-dimensional linear space with an inner product typifies this development.

Though it is very difficult to visualise this feature of mathematics, or the process of mathematisation just mentioned, we may summarise it as in diagram 1. (See also appendix §1.)

One of the purposes of mathematics education is to give students

[1] An axiom system is said to be categorical if every two models of the system are isomorphic.

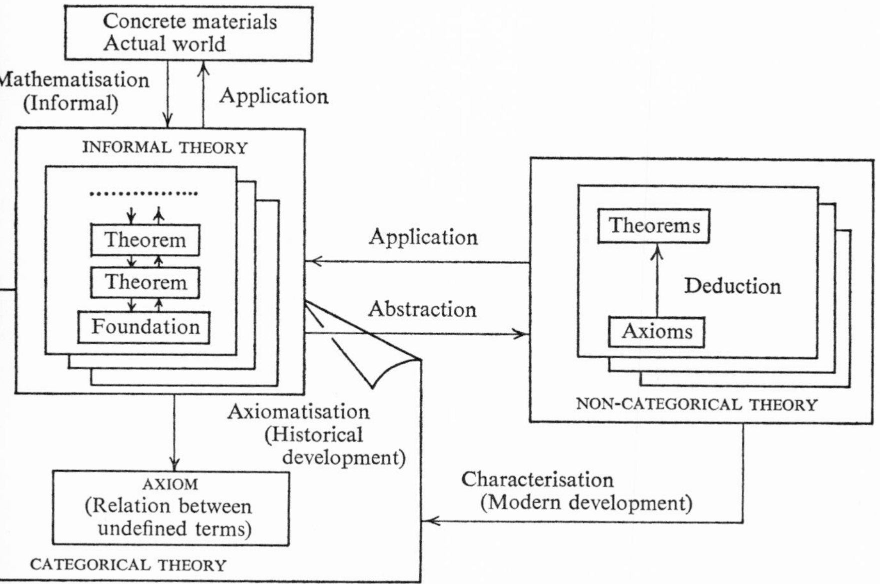

Diagram 1

an answer to the question 'What is mathematics?'. School mathematics should not be an account of already-completed mathematics and, in my opinion, school mathematics should not be developed axiomatically from the beginning. It is more important for students to understand the processes of constructing mathematics, that is, the processes of axiomatisation and abstraction, including the progression from concrete materials to informal theories. In particular, there will be many differences between the way in which one approaches the historical development of a categorical theory and that in which one introduces the modern development through non-categorical theories. I discuss these differences and point out some problems which arise in teaching axiomatics in the following sections.

2 How should we approach non-categorical theory in school mathematics?

The development of a non-categorical theory goes as follows. First, we observe several concrete theories occurring in different branches from one viewpoint, attempt to discover some similarity and abstract a structure by axiomatising. Secondly, we deduce some

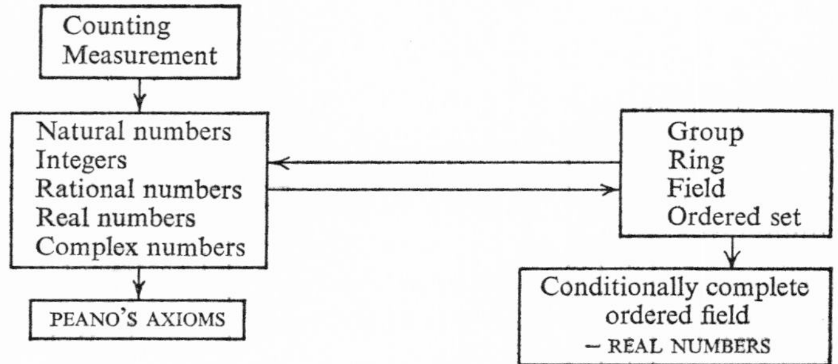

Diagram 1 applied to the *world of numbers*

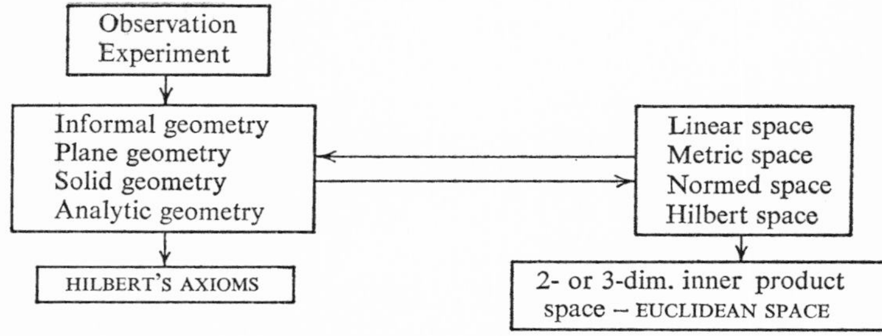

Diagram 1 applied to the *world of figures*

useful theorems from the axioms obtained. Thirdly and finally, we apply these theorems to a concrete theory. Briefly speaking, there are three stages, abstraction, deduction and application. The simpler a system of axioms is, the more concrete theories are included in it and the wider the applications will be. An axiom system ought to be meaningful so that we are able to obtain rich consequences from it. Moreover, the significance of teaching non-categorical theory will be lost unless the circuit of the above three stages: abstraction, deduction and application, is completed. Considerable background experience is necessary if the abstraction stage is to be understood and sufficient training in deductive thinking is essential at the deduction stage. If knowledge of concrete theory is lacking, then it is impossible to develop the application stage.

For example, after careful observation of the properties of operations such as addition, multiplication, permutation and transformation, we abstract the concept of a group. We then deduce, for example, Lagrange's theorem on the order of a subgroup which is applied to the classification of symmetries. In this application stage we need some correct knowledge about figures.

One more example (at the university level): after obtaining considerable knowledge about real numbers and elementary geometry, we abstract the concept of a metric space and define the concept of completeness. Then we may easily deduce the Contraction Mapping Theorem in a complete metric space. The theorem has remarkable applications such as the existence theorem of the solution of a differential equation. In this application stage, we need much knowledge about continuous functions.

Although many materials have been devised so as to permit the abstraction stage for several structures to be considered at a school level, such an introduction must be accompanied with other rich experiences in order to avoid, say, the too hasty abstraction of the group concept before the students have met examples of non-commutative cases. Furthermore, even when the above condition is fulfilled, we still need more new materials which can stimulate meaningful deduction, resulting in significant applications which are new to our students. It is obvious that the deduction stage is important, but, for instance, a mere examination of a set of equivalent axioms for a group, is, I think, meaningless to our students.

The activity of thinking mathematically may be regarded as starting with observations and experiments on concrete materials followed by classifications and arrangements. All of these processes are repeated gradually in a developmental way as students become more mature. This may be regarded as building the foundations for the abstraction stage.

It seems to be a recent tendency to introduce an abstract concept such as that of a group into the early stages. Certainly, it is desirable to observe concrete materials from an abstract viewpoint such as those of the set and group concepts if by so doing we help students to understand essential properties of the materials; and the group concept will be the most suitable one through which to approach non-categorical theory.

However, the introduction of an abstract concept is only the first of my three stages, and if there are not the materials available to allow one to complete all three of these, it would be better to replace a hasty abstraction by the collection of other materials, further experiences and more varied viewpoints.[1]

[1] Cf. appendix §2.

3 What significance does categorical theory have in school mathematics?

As I have mentioned already, a categorical theory is developed in two different ways, that is, the historical development and the modern development. The latter is a product of this century and it is especially attractive for mathematicians. It might be a royal road leading to a theoretical construction of mathematics, but before entering upon it, suitable analysis of its characteristics is essential and we should be aware that we shall not be able to drive on it without a thorough understanding of non-categorical theories. There might be some significance in characterising an object, but, in my opinion, the contents of a theory are more important for our students than is its framework. The modern development of a categorical theory is a matter to be handled at the university level.

The method of the historical development of a categorical theory is a suitable way in which to obtain a good understanding of the contents of the theory. In a definite world, for example, in the world of numbers or that of figures, we observe many properties and deduce some properties from those previously known. We examine the process of deduction and do some reverse thinking, step by step. After these considerations we attempt to seek foundations for the theory. Lastly, we fix the essential basis, *axioms*. Though it is difficult to demonstrate rigorously a historical development of a categorical theory, it is desirable that the method of the historical construction of mathematics be known. An understanding of this method enables students not only to gain accurate knowledge of a subject but also to learn meaningful deductive thinking. Such activities may be needed to understand non-categorical theory and the modern development of a categorical theory.

There are two outstanding examples of the historical development of a categorical theory, namely, Peano's theory and that of Euclid and Hilbert. Numbers and figures have been matters of great concern for human beings from ancient times until the present, and these two subjects are axiomatised and completed by these two famous theories.

It would be wonderful for students to know that the world of numbers can be constructed using only the five axioms of Peano. However, the road of construction is so long. The frequent recourse to mathematical induction is too dull and the classification according to an equivalence relation at too high a level of abstraction for students. If we are to treat Peano's theory in school mathematics, it will be as an example of inductive definition or as a story of the axiomatic development of the world of numbers.

On the other hand, it may be strange for students to know that *point* and *straight line* are undefined terms. It will also be more difficult for them to understand Hilbert's axiom system and, in particular, the role of the axiom of continuity, even at the university level. However, if we recognise the importance of illustrating the historical development of a categorical theory in order that our students should understand how to organise a theory systematically, then I think geometry is a better medium than algebra.

Comparing the world of numbers and that of figures in school mathematics, the development of the former is rather simple and straightforward starting from counting, or natural numbers, while that of the latter is complicated, starting from the observation of several figures, other than a point or a straight line. Students have been familiar with certain properties of numbers since their pre-school stage and there will be no necessity to analyse these properties for them. On the other hand, there are many viewpoints on how to analyse figures, for example, size, shape and position, and many properties of figures which depend on different foundations are obtained by intuitive consideration and experimental activities. There will naturally be a need to analyse these properties. It is important to know how to find a simple approach in such complicated situations.

Moreover, it is very important to know the meaning of proof. In geometry, we can consider some deductive relationship of several properties by first observing drawn figures. Geometry is thus a suitable medium in which to foster meaningful, deductive thinking and an understanding of the essence of proof.[1]

To summarise, therefore:

Axiomatics can be classified into three types:

non-categorical theory, categorical theory developed in a 'modern' way and categorical theory developed in a 'historical' way.

For teaching non-categorical theory, which has three stages, abstraction, deduction and application, we have to develop suitable materials which will allow the student to complete all three stages. It is better to approach the historical development of a categorical theory through geometry than through algebra.

[1] Cf. appendix §3.

Appendix Some supplementary thoughts[1]

1 Some additional notes on diagram 1 (p. 263)

The various blocks of the diagram are built up in a particular order which I explain below. To facilitate the explanation, in the accompanying figures each block is represented only in outline.

First: figure 1 shows the world of so-called school mathematics. Here there are three stages:

(1) Mathematisation from the actual world to a more theoretical world.

(2) Development of informal mathematics.

(3) Application to concrete materials.

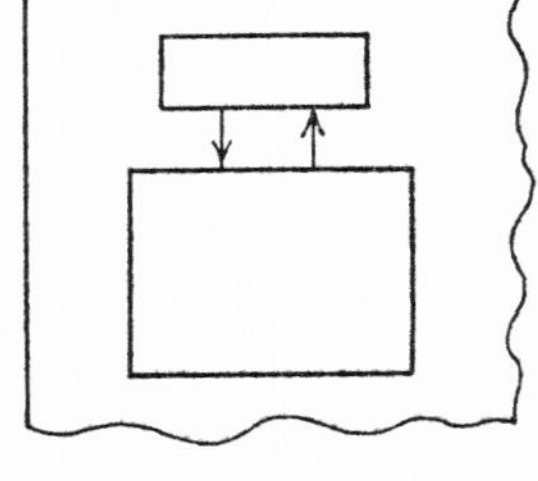

Fig. 1

At stages 1 and 3, activities such as abstraction or formalisation are repeated. Experience and intuition will play important parts here.

Stage 2 provides repeated opportunities for deductive and inductive thinking, in an informal sense.

This three-stage circuit is developed gradually. Thus school mathematics will be constructed step by step.

Next (see figure 2): About 2000 years ago, Euclid produced his axiom system. At the end of the nineteenth century, Hilbert reorganised Euclidean geometry from a more rigorous standpoint and opened the door of axiomatics, the characteristic of modern mathematics.

In the world of numbers, Peano completed his axiom system for the natural numbers.

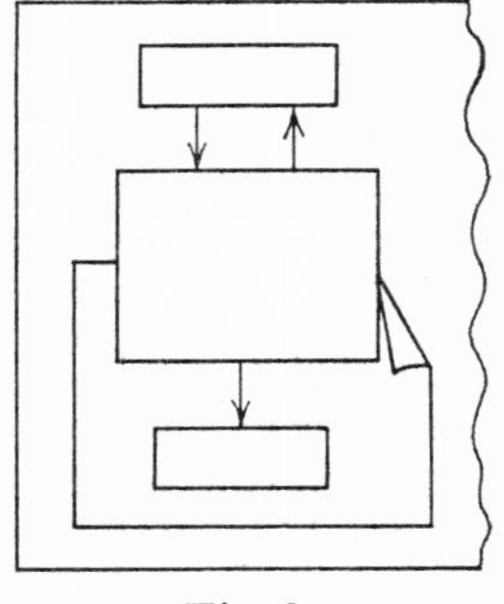

Fig. 2

These theories were constructed by seeking for foundations in a definite world, those of figures or numbers. Each of them is an example of the historical development of a categorical theory and can be said to be an axiomatisation of a 'substance'.

[1] The material in this appendix was discussed by Professor Shibata at a meeting of the working group on Contemporary Presentations of Geometry at School and University Level.

Thirdly (see figure 3): 'Modern mathematics' has approached mathematics in a completely different way. It breaks down various objects into their essential parts and abstracts a common structure. Different abstract theories such as group theory or metric space theory are constructed and applied to many concrete theories.

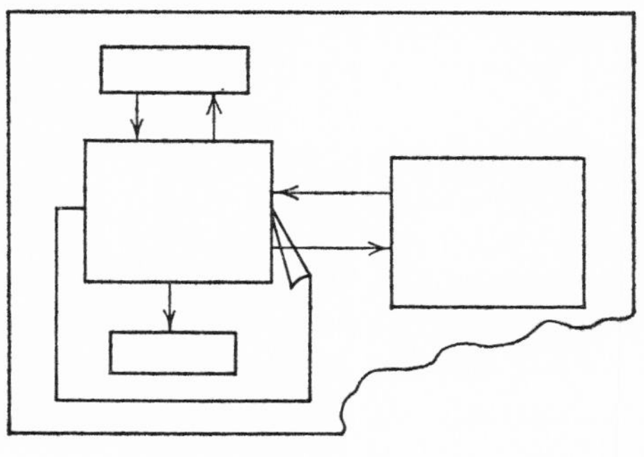

Fig. 3

The circuit of the three stages, abstraction, deduction and application, is similar to that of the school mathematics construction, mentioned above, although more rigorous.

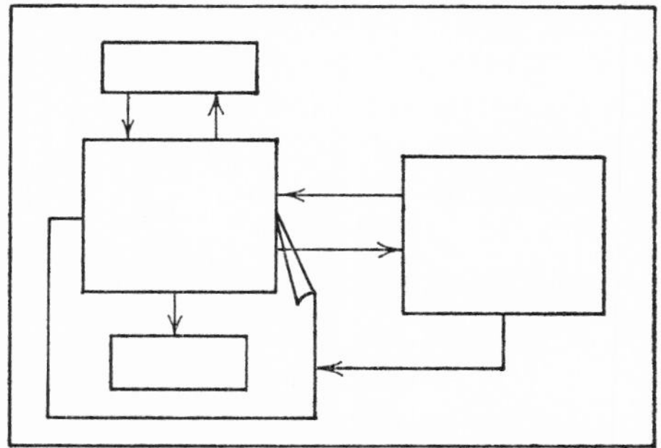

Fig. 4

Last (see figure 4): A definite world is characterised by organising several non-categorical theories. This is a modern development of mathematics.

The historical development of mathematics and the modern abstraction of structure are the warp and woof, the latitude and longitude of the theoretical construction of mathematics.

The diagrams on p. 264 show how these ideas can be applied to the world of numbers and that of figures.

Which should we stress, historical development or modern development, axiomatisation of a substance or abstraction of a structure?

These two aspects have different natures; we can neglect neither of them.

2 *Some subjects related to non-categorical theory in school mathematics*

As I mentioned in section 2, there is much in school mathematics from which we can abstract some structure. The outstanding problem, though, is whether we shall then be able to treat some meaningful theorems or not.

I shall list some of the material in the following table. It is regrettable that there are so few items in the column labelled 'Theorem'.

Basic material	Abstract concept	Theorem
Various operations on numbers, figures	Group	On the order of a subgroup
Integers, polynomials	Integral domain	LCM, GCD
Large and small in numbers	Ordered set, lattice	—
Set inclusion	Boolean algebra	—
Rational numbers Real numbers Complex numbers	Field	—
Various operations on numbers, vectors, functions	Linear space	—
Distance in 2- or 3-D space Convergence	Metric space	—
Uncertain events Dice experiments	Probability	—

3 *An example of a development of plane geometry*

Here, I give an example of how we can handle and analyse properties of figures using a well-known theorem. I shall illustrate this diagrammatically and add a few words of explanation.

In elementary school, students are able to obtain property (1) in the following diagram, by cutting a triangular piece of paper, and they may then solve problem (2) easily.

In secondary school, after obtaining a knowledge of parallel lines,

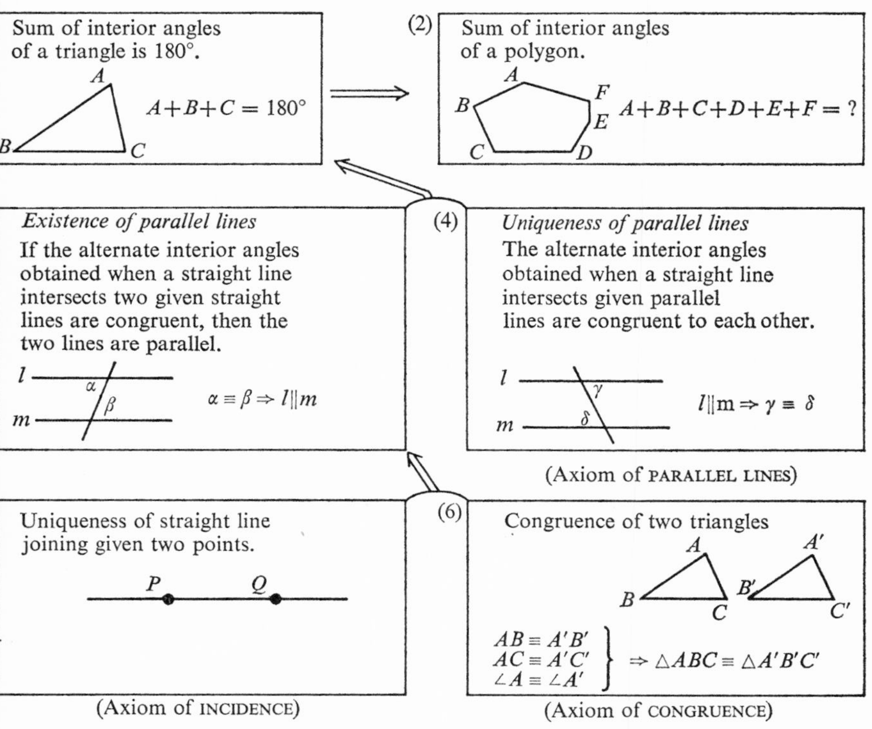

the student will prove property (1) by drawing a straight line through point A which is parallel to the line BC. Careful examination of the proof will reveal that its foundations lie in facts (3) and (4). These two propositions are mutually converse and proposition (4) is nothing other than the so-called axiom of parallel lines.

At a more advanced level, perhaps in upper secondary school, property (3) may be proved by *reductio ad absurdum*. The basis of the proof is facts (5) and (6); fact (5) being one of the axioms of incidence and (6) being one of the axioms of congruence.

In this way, starting with a familiar property, we are able to go back and search for an essential basis step by step.

This work was supported by a grant from the Japanese Ministry of Education.

Science University of Tokyo,
1–3 Kagurazaka Shinjuku-ku,
Tokyo.

Implications of the work of Piaget in the training of students to teach primary mathematics

Mary Sime

Introductory remarks

Many mathematicians, whatever their feelings about 'New Mathematics' still love to start with axioms. Therefore I hope to capture your attention by offering you three axioms as a starting point to this paper. While to me the following statements are self evident, it may well be that to some of you they are not. Nevertheless, I give them to you as axioms.

The first is that mathematics should be enjoyed. I would consider that many teachers in the last few decades have tried to make it so by enriching primary school children's lives with plentiful, enjoyable experiences in true 'pre-mathematics',[1] as contrasted to a drilling in 'sums', thus laying a foundation for both emotional and intellectual appreciation of the subject.

I also take as an axiom that there are five 'cornerstones' of learning of which mathematics is one. The others would be language, movement, some form of scientific exploration and some work that is normally considered creative. (This statement is difficult to word unambiguously since, to some of us, mathematics is creative.) These five cornerstones are vitally important in early education since, as well as being of maximum value in their own right, they are the essential tools of all future learning. Hence, in the integrated work that goes on in many of our primary schools their contribution is of double worth.

My third axiom would be that trainee teachers need to be given an understanding both of mathematics and of how children form mathematical concepts and mathematical habits of thought. From this axiom I wish, later in the paper, to develop the line of thought

[1] I am being a purist and playing safe in this conference of very real mathematicians by calling the concrete explorations of children towards mathematics, before the age of hypothetical thinking, 'pre-mathematics' as mathematics itself is abstract.

that the Piagetian theory of developmental psychology sees mathematical form (coming to a climax in group and lattice form) in the intellectual activity of the adult brain. Consequently it seems that the concurrent and even integrated study of mathematics and of Piagetian theory can enrich and clarify, for any student, both the mathematics and the developmental psychology.

If I may invent the word 'sub-axiom' I would slip one in here. Psychology has not been truly studied unless it can be applied. Far too many students divorce their study lamentably from classroom work. Therefore, just as the primary school child needs plentiful experience in pre-mathematics, so a student needs experience in diagnostic testing (*à la* Piaget) and of attempting, under tutorial guidance, to relate his teaching to the results of the testing. To this one must add a 'caveat'. In the schools teachers will not have clinical conditions in which to do Piagetian testing. Unless, in the colleges, students are given experience in adapting the testing to non-clinical conditions most will cease to do such diagnostic work once they qualify. This is also a theme I shall develop later.

After these few introductory remarks may I turn now to enlarging on them by examining the challenges to be found in first infant[1] and then junior[2] schools.

The challenges in the infants' classroom

Piaget calls infancy the 'intuitive period'. It is a period during which, above all else, the child needs to be precipitated into a wealth of experiences with carefully chosen materials so as to enable him to abstract from those experiences properties that are themselves abstract. So he will form concepts and also develop the logic skills of classification and seriation.

Amongst the earliest preconcepts to develop into concepts are those of number (Piaget [1]), of area (Piaget [2]), of sequence (Piaget [2]), of the horizontality of the surface of liquids (Piaget [2]), and so forth. I stress that they develop through experiences and not through the materials themselves. Materials that are not manipulated are 'dead materials': those that motivate to activity bring seething life into an infants' classroom. A good student will foresee and plan for them to bring the maximum benefit.

[1] UK equivalent of USA grade KG and grade 1.

[2] UK equivalent of USA grades 2, 3, 4, 5 and possibly 6. 'Primary' is UK equivalent of USA KG to grade 5 or 6.

So, in providing materials that have properties relevant to the concepts that children should be forming I would suggest students need to consider, too, the play-element that such materials can be expected to provide. Hence my words 'carefully chosen materials'. To satisfy those who prefer all work to be offered open-ended, I would modify my words only to this extent. Certainly an infant will learn from all experiences, whether foreseen or not. The occasional lazy student will try to escape preparation on these grounds. But we are asking for optimum learning with a strong element of the 'cornerstones' in it and in this paper we are pin-pointing the mathematics 'cornerstone'. For this *either* the experiences need to be foreseen and the materials carefully chosen *or* the student needs to be very well grounded in mathematics and very astute at recognising and exploiting the mathematical elements in any situation. Most students are not secure enough in their mathematics to take the second of these two courses, so they need to plan ahead, taking into consideration Piaget's theories. Careful initial planning does not inhibit a later development into open-endedness if the students or the children see further tempting fields of investigation opening out.

Many of us know of the materials encouraged in the UK by Edith Biggs and by the Nuffield Project, and it is not hard to imagine the enjoyment which they give to children. The teacher is hard put to it to supply sufficient of such wisely chosen materials from which mathematical experiences can grow, and – this is my next crucial point – from which results of the experiences can be recorded mathematically by some such method as block graphs or Papygrams or any other early form of the written language of mathematics.

Together with this pre-applied-mathematics the infant needs, too, experience with the beauty of the symmetry and rhythm in geometrical plane and solid shapes. Manipulating them will plant in the child an intuitive appreciation of geometrical form. Is an infant too young for preconceptual learning of transformation geometry through tiling patterns? I think not. Similarly one can encourage one's students to introduce into the infants' classroom toys that prepare the ground for mappings, for sets, for equations and so forth. As preconcepts of these gradually develop into concepts one may encourage children to talk in mathematical terms.

Parallel with all this is the mathematics that can be absorbed through structured apparatus. Cuisenaire rods, in their imperceptible way, help a child forward to the abstractions of length, relationships and number and also, concurrently, to the logic skills of classification and seriation (see Piaget [3]). Logic blocks, seen as fun, promote the skill of classification, sometimes to the pitch of classification by negation.

What of the student? At the infant stage many a child can absorb happily more pre-mathematics than many a student has on entering college. And it is such a student who, more often than not, chooses primary teaching as a career. Untutored he could do irreparable harm. And he cannot be allowed to avoid mathematics for he would impoverish the intellectual lives of generations of children. So he needs careful tutoring in mathematics. Even more, I think, he can benefit from a good tutoring on Piagetian theories, for much of the mathematics that he needs will be absorbed, incidentally, as he practises Piagetian testing. Many a student has come to me after carrying out the well-known, very simple tests, such as any of those on sequence (the linen line) (Piaget [2]), area (the cows and the fields and houses) (Piaget [2]) or any of those on number (Piaget [1]) or classification (Piaget [3]) and has remarked that he was just becoming conscious of forming the appropriate concept himself. I have often suspected that, as well as having diagnostic value, Piagetian tests have a teaching value for the child though, so far as I know, Piaget himself does not claim it. Certainly the non-mathematical student seems to learn mathematics as well as developmental psychology from them.

I think this is for two reasons. The very indirectness of the mathematics learning is a help. For one thing, as he focuses his attention primarily on the developmental psychology of the child and only obliquely on the mathematics involved, the student loses the inhibitions and the fears set up in him by poor teaching in his own school days. The first few examples of success are sufficient for him to break through his anxiety barrier. Also, he sees the child's struggles at the middle Piagetian stages and perhaps identifies himself with the child. So he learns with the child, loses his fears, takes an interest in exploring more mathematics which inspires him to more Piaget and so on to more mathematics. An ever widening spiral of learning has been set up.

A mathematics and an education tutor, cooperating, can now lead such a student to explore further afield in both areas and help him to become an excellent primary teacher. A colleague and I have now enjoyed such close cooperation and integration of our work for six years. Our students, conscious of our happy cooperation, have also gained in the sense of security it has given them.

I have mentioned this point as I speak of work in the infant school. It applies equally well in the junior school situation and I turn to that now.

The challenge in the junior classroom

Juniors, most of whom are at the 'concrete operational' stage, need a teacher to provide them with constant experiences that will satisfy their natural urge to exercise their early concepts, now securely formed, in reasoning out problems as they manipulate materials. Similarly they need to exercise their now fast maturing skills in classification and seriation but this, too, with the help of concrete materials. They cannot yet work from the abstract to the particular. As they find answers to problems they can demonstrate these answers but they cannot prove them. To ask it of them would muddle their thinking. They are still forming the late developing concepts such as those of weight and of volume. Above all, through the activities and concrete reasoning that I have just described, they are beginning to tread out the paths of intellectual patterns of thought that should be abstracted into formal concepts in their adolescence.

Let us add to this the simple fact that junior children are at an age at which they most enjoy working in small groups and sharing problems, responsibilities, decisions and successes (Piaget [4]). Consequently, if the teacher harnesses this trait in their psychology by inviting them to work in such groups, their learning will be cumulative as they discuss and argue about their efforts and discoveries.

These facts led me to encourage my students to create learning situations in junior schools in which the student could foresee specific potential developments that have distinct mathematical value. Much of the learning is oblique. Very simply I will mention two such projects carried out by first year students in my presence. Incidentally, the students were also working in teams of about six. I find that such small teams, if well knit, benefit as junior children would do from the cumulative effect of discussion during preparation and from a later pooling of their observations and classroom experiences.

One of the projects[1] was the building of a two-roomed Wendy House out of an enormous crate. It had viable hot water and elec-

[1] Both projects are described in full in Sime [1], as is the testing on 'horizontality' described briefly on p. 281.

tricity systems, geometrically accurate doors, windows, eaves and so forth and a floor rich in transformation geometry. The other project was a carefully prepared measuring up and scale modelling of Stonehenge by a class of nine-year-old children. In this the students were aiming at the oblique teaching of scale, of angles, of triangulation and at the formation of the late developing concepts of weight and volume. This project became open-ended and the children moved on to a study of leverages and tensions.

Learning situations that are shallow in content, but yet might give the casual impression of being of the same value as the two just mentioned could have been planned empirically by students and have had little learning value in them. In students' classes one meets innumerable jerry-built Wendy Houses and many approximate models of Stonehenge, copied merely from pictures in books and with no measuring or reasoning or calculation and no oblique learning having been brought into play. I think it is obvious where and how an understanding of the Piagetian stage can influence the bringing of oblique, sound learning into the more carefully planned project work.

One could go on indefinitely suggesting similar projects both closed- and open-ended, all rich in mathematical content and in concrete reasoning. These would all be examples of what I called in my introduction 'mathematics for enjoyment in its own right'. Now may I turn to junior school pre-mathematics as a root of future learning, coupling this with a mention of the formal concepts that I promised to enlarge upon.

In *The Growth of Logical Thinking from Childhood to Adolescence* Piaget [5] (together with Inhelder) has pointed out to us that the mental skills and patterns of thought that are used by adults as they reason logically and abstractly, are developing gradually as a result of concrete experiences throughout childhood and are then abstracted from those experiences. On reaching perfection they become what Piaget calls formal concepts. Examples of these intellectual skills and formal concepts are:

(*a*) The skill of recognising one's own contradictory statements (investigated by experiments with flotation).

(*b*) The skill of recognising and reacting to reciprocal implication (investigated by exercises on a billiard table).

(*c*) The skill of eliminating negative factors in a problem (investigated with a pendulum).

(*d*) The skill of holding constant all factors in a problem except the one to be tested (investigated with flexible rods).

(*e*) The skill of forming a mental lattice of all the possible combinations of factors to be tested (investigated with colourless, odourless chemicals).

(*f*) The skill of counterbalancing the value of factors within a problem (investigated with a balance or with a moving snail on a moving board).

It is in this last skill that Piaget brings me to the climax of my appreciation of his work by illustrating that the fully alert adolescent mind brings into action a consequent formal concept in the pattern of a mental Klein 4-group activity (see p. 84).

Any teacher of secondary mathematics would agree it is necessary to give exercise to these formal concepts through work on mathematical problems, subsequently building more mathematics upon them. I go beyond this. I would claim that in the junior school the teacher should be nurturing the middle stages of their development and that he therefore needs to be fully conversant with the diagnostic testing for that development and, of course, necessarily, conversant with the mathematical patterns themselves.

At this point I think we can move on to look more closely at the students.

A. The student who offers mathematics as one of his academic subjects

I would simply make four isolated points about him.

One is that, unfortunately for the primary schools, very few of the mathematically able students opt for primary school teaching. Equally, not all mathematically able students enjoy mathematics and they would need to enjoy it to 'get it across' creatively to primary children. This idea of personal enrichment through mathematics is as important to the student as it is to the children. Such enjoyment is more likely to be achieved if the psychology supporting the mathematics is always taken into consideration.

My next point is that many a good mathematics student sees the subject purely in its isolation and abstraction. He therefore needs an enormous amount of tutorial help if he is to see how to present it to children through integrated work in the primary schools.

Similarly, many a good mathematics student finds it difficult to envisage modern mathematics as a primary school subject since he, himself, probably did not touch it until his last few years at school. So he needs help with the psychology of a practical approach to it to prevent him from trying to present it formally to children who are at a concrete operational stage.

Nevertheless, this same student is the one who can most easily be guided into appreciating the Piagetian theories. He does, at least, know the mathematics of such forms as groups and lattices: he will therefore find it easier than most students to learn about the corresponding patterns of mental activity. His strength in mathematics becomes a doubly valuable attribute. This opens up a particularly pleasant chance of integrated work to the mathematics and education tutors. So, in spite of three drawbacks, I would say that it is probably easier for an education tutor to train a mathematics (or science) student in developmental psychology than to train any other student. It is, consequently, correspondingly easier for such a student to plan really rich integrated learning in a primary school. Such learning will have plentiful creative content. Some other students, in contrast, can be too often satisfied with drawing half the potential out of children, particularly out of bright children.

B. The non-mathematical student

This student is, of course, the one who is the greatest challenge to the training colleges. And training colleges are evading their duty if they ignore the problem.

Concomitants of the problem are:

Such students generally have a fear or a dislike of mathematics.

Probably they are the victims of attempted formal teaching in their own primary school days and this has given them an inbuilt muddled thinking in mathematics and therefore a confused state of hypothetical thinking generally.

They rarely perceive the mathematical content in a general situation.

They have probably never met modern mathematics.

They always record facts in words, never mathematically. They would, for example, never record statistics directly on to a graph nor would they take note of a graph included in the middle of a text; they would just ignore it.

Of the above problems the 'phobia' is probably at the root of it all. Therefore the indirect approach that I have mentioned is probably the most valuable.

Closing thoughts

I would add to this that, as well as giving direct value to the student in enabling him to become a teacher of mathematics, an understanding and appreciation of mathematics is also of much more general value:

(*a*) He needs to understand mathematical forms in order to understand the intellectual patterns by which a child learns *any* subject.

(*b*) He needs a sense of proportion, given by mathematics, in other activities, as for example in planning curricula or in dealing with discipline problems, as well as in other subjects.

(*c*) I would emphasise that the mathematical patterns of thinking that Piaget describes also influence the way in which a child's moral judgement develops [4]. Certainly facing truth of the success or failure of a mathematical exercise seems to me a better moral training than any preaching could be: I can remember, as a child, having it impressed on me how intellectually (and morally) wrong it would be to put QED unless I was sure that a problem was solved and proved. I should very much like to enlarge on this if only there were time.

Lastly, we should remember that Piagetian testing, which I claim will help a student in the ways I have just mentioned, is not nearly as simple and straightforward as books would suggest it is. What are the pitfalls? How do we train students to avoid them?

I consider a student should have continuous experience of testing, throughout his training. At first experience should be in clinical conditions, until he has acquired the skill of framing the follow-up questions to the child's early responses in such a way that he discovers what the child really means. No answer is right unless given for a right reason nor if given as a result of a leading question. Similarly, no answer is wrong unless the child's reasoning is wrong. Responses need not be verbal. Many responses, incidentally, are highly amusing.

I am convinced that after a short period of clinical conditions a student needs to go on to diagnostic testing in normal classroom situations and, at the climax, to diagnosing by merely watching children's normal behaviour and listening to their conversations. Let me quote three examples.

The first is an example of non-clinical testing which brought forth a right answer for wrong reasons. A trainee teacher watched six infants who obviously enjoyed their milk and suggested, one day, that they should pour it from their bottles (which they had all agreed contained equal quantities) into various shapes of cups, mugs and glasses. From previous observation she had expected them to be at stage 2 in the test. Not suspecting that they had done the test several times with their teacher she was surprised when, on being questioned, the children all persisted in stating that there were still equal quantities in all containers. So she said,

'All right! Now you can drink it.'

Then came the truth, without words, as they all stretched out their hands to the tallest glass.

My second example is of a wrong answer for an unexpected right reason. It was given in clinical conditions but could well have happened in a classroom. A farmer's son, a bright little boy, having helped a student place equal numbers of 'houses' on 'fields' of agreed equal area persisted in his answer that the cow on one field had more grass to eat than the horse on the other field. 'Why?' asked the student. ''cos you know that a cow needs more grass than a horse' said the farmer's son.

As an example of diagnosing by merely watching children's behaviour, you will probably be fascinated to hear of the antics of a class of five-year-old children when they were suddenly faced with the problem of drinking milk (through straws) from opaque cartons instead of from the glass bottles to which they were accustomed. I will describe four children in particular, though they only illustrate four stages of solving the problem that were shown by fairly equal numbers of children throughout the class.

Caroline, having drunk about half her milk was quite unable to find the rest. She held her inverted carton high above her head, with the straw pushed right through the milk to the air pocket above its surface. The milk trickled down the outside of the straw and down her chin and neck. She twisted the carton about, but it was obvious that all her explorations were random.

Philip held the carton in front of him and poked the straw forwards to what had been the bottom of the carton before tilting. He expected the milk still to be at the bottom. After a time, he failed to find any there, so he squeezed the carton to get some out that way.

Beverley found the milk by bending the straw. By this means, she emptied the carton.

Mark found the milk with confidence.

As we watched these children, we realised that they were all at different Piagetian stages of appreciating how liquid finds its own level. So we applied the well-known Piagetian tests (Piaget [2])

and found that most of the class of thirty-six drew the milk in the Piagetian 'bottles' just about where they were hunting for it in the cartons. In particular, Caroline (Piaget stage 1) scribbled vaguely in the middle of the drawn bottles. Philip (stage 2*a*) drew the milk in its original position in the bottle at whatever angle the bottle was tilted (thus, sometimes, giving it a vertical surface). Beverley (stage 2*b*) drew the milk in various interesting positions, but, at least, did not have a vertical surface. Mark (stage 3*a*) always put the milk approximately in the right position, but very rarely gave it a level surface.

It was a student who first spotted this situation and telephoned me to go out and help her with the tests and take photographs. This is the sort of Piagetian testing by observation that I consider most valuable of all since the average alert teacher will be able to react to it throughout his or her teaching career.

I have tried to make these examples light-hearted as well as illustrative for, to me, it is essential that the developmental psychology that supports the mathematics should be as enjoyable as mathematics itself should be.

To close, may I quote from Lunzer in the *Times Educational Supplement* of February 1972.

> 'If a teacher has absorbed the true essence of Piaget's approach he will not be prepared to let Nature take its course.'

I apply this particularly to the teacher of mathematics.

References

Piaget, J., [1] *The Child's Conception of Number*, Routledge and Kegan Paul, London, 1952.

Piaget, J., [2] with Inhelder, B., *The Child's Conception of Space*, Routledge and Kegan Paul, London, 1956.

Piaget, J., [3] with Inhelder, B., *The Early Growth of Logic in the Child*, Routledge and Kegan Paul, London, 1964.

Piaget, J., [4] *The Moral Judgement of the Child*, Routledge and Kegan Paul, London, 1932.

Piaget, J., [5] with Inhelder, B., *The Growth of Logical Thinking from Childhood to Adolescence*, Routledge and Kegan Paul, London, 1958.

Sime, M., *A Child's Eye View*, Thames and Hudson, London, 1973.

College of Education,
Chorley,
Lancs.

Are we off the track in teaching mathematical concepts?[1]

Hassler Whitney

1 The whole child

After centuries with little change in the mathematics curriculum in schools, we find ourselves in an era of 'New Math', typified by the teaching of concepts. At the same time, though many children find they can go much further and faster ahead, the great majority are confused, turned off, and fearful of the subject. What are the real causes of this failure? Research studies, with control groups and statistics, do not go deep enough. We must study individual children, work with them in the classroom, to discover bit by bit what the basic problems besetting them are, and how to overcome them. In brief, our focus has been too much on the subject matter, not enough on the child himself. Through various examples, we will see the manifold ways in which good ideas, put into practice, go wrong, and will look for roads to improvement. We must keep coming back to the whole child as the main focus. When we think of concepts, they must be end results, expressed first in the child's terms. But more than anything else, we discover what an extraordinary being a young person is, capable of learning, in his own ways, with eagerness and speed; we must promote this, not suppress it.

My own view of the problem, after a life's work as a mathematician with basic interests in education and children, has evolved greatly through five years of working with children and teachers in schools at all levels. The forces at work on the children are extremely varied and complex. Only with great patience and understanding, with real respect towards all in the school and the community concerned, can true progress be made. We can then let the poorer methods gradually drop away of themselves.

[1] This is a shortened version of the paper presented at Exeter. The full text is reprinted in *Pre-School and Primary Mathematics* (Ward Lock, 1973), a collection of papers submitted to the working group with that title.

2 The coming of the New Math

It will help the picture to see how the New Math arose. Since the last world war there has been a greatly growing penetration of mathematics into science, engineering, and other fields of application. This has required an ever increasing understanding of mathematical method by more and more people. It is not enough for them to know mathematical facts; it is the basic comprehension that is important, so that new problems or old problems in new guises can be attacked successfully. Seeing how children in school normally learn mathematics by rote, with consequent inability to apply it to new situations, a number of mathematicians undertook to improve the situation. From this came two general sorts of study:

(1) Find what the basic mathematics is. This led to a formulation of elementary mathematics, starting from a set-theoretic foundation and building it up in a more or less logical sequence.

(2) Enlist the help of psychologists and educators to find the best ways of teaching the material to children.

In different countries, the story took on varying forms; the essential features were similar. In the USA, through a number of projects, large and small, experiments in teaching were carried out, and preliminary texts were written; this work is continuing. Out of this developed series of texts by the different publishing firms, competing for attractiveness to school systems. In these texts, supposedly to make it easier for the children, concepts were broken into tiny bits, and teachers' manuals give explicit directions on how to teach, mark answers, and so on. Gone is the child who thinks for himself; he is supposed to catch on to exactly what he is to do. He is to learn fancy language first, then concepts which do not relate to his experience. Where the children are encouraged to explore first, a good start is being made; the problem is then how to continue so that understanding takes place, first in the child's terms, later in more adult language.

3 The cycle: student to teacher

A generation ago, the vast majority of elementary school children learned mathematics under teachers who were insecure in the subject, or obtained security through rote learning. The children's questions about why and wherefore were evaded; their own creative ideas were squelched, and answers not given in precisely the expected form were marked wrong. The children soon learned to look towards the authority, book or teacher, for what was right; never mind possible hidden meanings. In higher grades, they started bogging down in fractions; the subject was confusing, and the complexities tended to be overwhelming. By the time they were in high school, algebra was fearful; they learned formulae by rote, and that was essentially all that was asked. In college, after a couple of years without math, the thought of taking another math course was frightening. In fact, they were mostly no better in arithmetic than six years before. Their point of view was now: 'Tell me what I should know; don't ask me to think.' If they do not expect to deal further with math, they happily join those who say 'I never could do math!' What percentage of adults claim not to be in this group?

With some liking for children, or thoughts that they can handle them, they now become teachers. In math, they are quite insecure; fortunately there are teachers' manuals, which they can follow to the letter if desired. Their students soon learn not to ask questions but to look to the authority, and we are back full circle.

4 Pushing theory

In the latter part of first grade, children are learning to 'go over ten'. In the New Math, in the USA for instance, a teacher may follow a manual, and teach:

$$\begin{aligned} 8+4 &= 8+(2+2) \\ &= (8+2)+2, \qquad \text{by the associative law,} \\ &= 10+2 = 12. \end{aligned}$$

Here is the effect on the children:

(*a*) The expression $8+(2+2)$ is confusing. Why put in the curly signs? Writing $8+2+2$ is simpler. Perhaps $2+2 = 4$ is recognised; but why choose $2+2$?

(*b*) Now the curly signs are moved around. What is a 'law'? Does this mean that I am told to do something, and therefore do it? I have really stopped trying to see what this is about, anyway.

(*c*) I feel uncomfortable, especially since the teacher does too. If she is expressing what school is supposed to be like, I do not want to go to school.

(*d*) There is 12 at the end. Why not just count four more than eight, and get twelve?

(*e*) I am told that the 1 in 12 means ten. But I know that you write 10 for ten, not 1. I hope this will stop soon.

This is, of course, a horrible example of the New Math in action. But it is, alas, quite common. Most ways of pushing New Math are more subtle; but this makes it only harder for the children to object, and leaves them with greater insecurity if they cannot see through it.

Let us look for a better way. We can straighten a coat hanger, let the children put ten beads of one colour and ten of another on it, and bend over the ends. How fast can the children show three beads, by sliding them to one side? Show ten! Show eight! They quickly learn that they find eight fastest by taking two less than ten. Now show eleven; fifteen; twenty-one (silly, there are not that many!). Another game: first show eight; now four more. How many is this? Twelve, of course! And this is the children's answer; if the teacher said thirteen, they would wonder what went wrong.

Another game: make spacers out of cards with slots; show $8+4$.

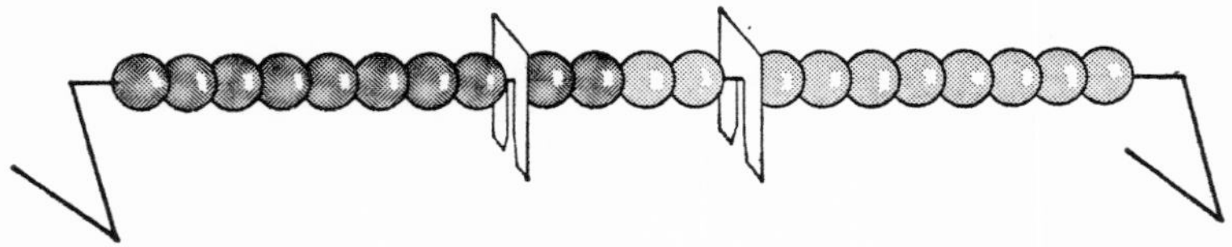

Another game: show twelve; now show four fewer. With the spacers, we have the same picture as before. Some children will notice this; here is a chance for the teacher to promote a good discussion. The children learn from each other, and the teacher sees new things herself.

In this way the children can have lots of experience in a short time, with immediate mathematical meanings. Moreover, it is easy for them to give each other problems, and find quick solutions.

If the teachers are in a setting where they can do a little of this at a time, they will learn to be more of an adviser and helper; gradually their insecurity and need to be the authority will lessen. The spontaneity of the children will reflect on the teacher, the class, and the school.

5 Language versus reality

The numbers 3, 4, 7 are related through both addition and subtraction; for a given relation, two of the numbers determine the other. Hence the New Math texts give pages of problems of the sort shown opposite:

Let us watch the child doing his assignment. He has a number of problems to do. If they are all of the same pattern, some clues may well show him this; after putting in a few numbers, the others are inserted quickly. Thus his powers of detective work, if not of mathematical comprehension, are encouraged. If clues fail, he thinks, should a larger or smaller number go in? This may suggest a number; he puts this in. Now he goes to the next, and the next, till impatience and boredom make him stop or put in almost anything. How about the pictures? Just as he does not read the text, he does not try to fathom them; they are not *his* pictures.

$7-\square=4$

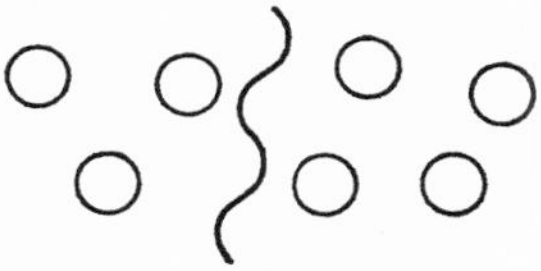

The root of the difficulty should be clear. A good reasoning process is devised for the child to go through, which will lead him to put down the right answer. But a child's mind follows its own channels; they are seldom those we devise for him. We hide from ourselves the fact that he is presented with a language he does not understand, and he is asked to get answers that make the language take on more meaning. This is exactly the reverse of what makes sense. The child must grasp the relationships in his own way first, then find some way in which to express it. Later the expression can take the form we have chosen.

The real goal is not for the child to learn particular answers; it is for him to grow in powers of finding answers, or rather, of exploration into processes. We therefore replace *teaching* by *learning*, or better, by *investigation*. We think up a game. One child puts a small group of counters (or buttons, etc.) on the table; each child can count them. They are now hidden by a sheet of paper. Another child pulls some out, and keeps them hidden under his hand. The paper is removed, showing how many are left. How many are under the hand?

For children who find this too hard, we change the manner of playing. A child can count out his own pile, the same number as under the paper. He may now try removing some, to leave the number shown later; thus he finds the answer by experiment. And there are many other things the child is experiencing. For instance, he may be noting that $7 = 6+1 = 5+2 = 4+3$ in an intuitive way.

Because he needs to use it, he notes that when his pile corresponds to the hidden pile, and what is left after pulling away corresponds similarly, there is a third correspondence. The texts would not dare teach something like this, for the children, when tested on it, would practically all fail. (Please do not teach this! But it might appear in a discussion.)

This kind of game is real to the child, and the answers are his own; he becomes steadily more secure with the answers. When the children are first asked to make records of the games, in any way they find, they may at first write simply 7 4 3. Later they can start with 7 − , continue to 7 − , 4, and end with 7 − 3, 4. They may then put in the equal sign, though without much understanding of its significance.

Here is another sample of the game. There are five counters; some are slid out; all are left. There are none under the hand! It is exciting to verify this. To be taught that $5-0 = 5$ as a 'property of zero' is pretty deadly. Five under the paper; none left. Hand is lifted: six. You cheated! Compare this with 'You cannot subtract a larger number from a smaller one'.

6 Concepts through activities

In recent times, mathematicians have seen how to base the theory of natural numbers on set theory, through the notion of cardinality. Hence it is natural to teach young children set theory first, to reinforce their understanding of number. In the Math Lab approach, the child is given an assignment. A card or sheet shows two circles, with pictures of dolls in one and caps in the other. He is asked if there are enough caps for the dolls. The child counts first, finding that there are six dolls and only five caps; he knows the answer. Now he copies the pictures. It is difficult to draw the dolls, and he may lose count. Next he draws lines from the dolls to the caps. A line may go through two dolls; a cap may be left out. The work is shown to the teacher, who points out the mistakes; they are corrected, and he has now finished the job.

Is this a useful experience for the child? Certainly, provided that it is not pressed too hard and the child works with willingness; he is clearly gaining skills of various sorts. But it has little to do with the original reason for setting up the problem, and is very slow at that.

If we put the child's growth first, we think up somewhat different activities. We may, for instance, put red counters and white counters in a bag. A child draws out a small handful. Are there more red or more white counters? Counting tells the answer. Can you do this without counting? A child will think of matching; this is easy and fast, moving the counters around. Play the game a number of times; he finds that there are usually more white counters. Why so? Children may guess that there are more whites than reds in the bag. They may even get a preliminary concept of ratios. Verifying by emptying the bag is exciting. How do we match all these? A child may think of making piles of four before matching; how educational! He is getting notions of numbers in other bases (of course not expressed in this language).

7 Keeping in touch

In the third or fourth grade there are a number of children who cannot do a subtraction problem such as $41-15$. Let us consider some ways of helping such a child.

(*a*) The teacher or an aide gives direct help. 'You cannot take five from 1. Hence you look at the 4. What does the "4" mean?' The child has been through this many times, and feels quite uncomfortable. He vaguely thinks he is supposed to say 'forty'. The helper senses the child's withdrawal, tries to close her mind to it, and attempts to keep the mental connection, to go through the process. Some right words are elicited or placed in the child's mouth, and the answer is obtained. Another problem is done; then the child does one or two by himself. Why is it, then, that a month later the child can still not do such problems? The answer is really perfectly clear: the problems were done by the aide, not the child; on his own, the child's insecurity comes back, and he does not dare begin.

(*b*) An aide brings materials for the child to use. Exchanging a ten length stick for ten small blocks, the problem is solved, and the answer found. Now the aide helps the child write down the answer in the right way. The child looks up at the aide to see if this is the right place to write the '2'; with an affirmative nod, it is written down. This is certainly far better. Yet the child may later again have qualms: what he finally wrote down was with the aide's assent, and he has not the aide now to give the assent. The aide led the child to find his own way (it would have been better for the child to have chosen the materials); but at the end, the aide took over in writing the answer.

(*c*) It is a big school system, and everything is well organised. Each year, a group of slow children from each class is given special attention. With written tests, it is determined which concepts the children do not understand; they are now given training in these concepts. The next year, the same group is given more special work. The children and the teachers know that the record will be of further and further failure. This is the extreme of keeping carefully out of touch with the individual.

(*d*) Children who have fallen behind have lost confidence and some of their inner security; this needs to be built up. You cannot really help here unless you gain their respect by showing that you are truly interested in them as humans and understand their difficulties. Talking with them to get in touch is the natural way to start. Then you can carry out some activity with them that contains elements of challenge, and they will be ready to accept this and use their own thinking powers. A simple activity that can be carried out with little challenge is a buying game. You give them some money, say plain popsicle sticks or coffee stirrers for dollars and red ones for tens. A storekeeper offers things for sale. The store can only accept exact amounts; change can be made at the bank. For instance, a child has four red sticks and one plain, which he records. Wishing to buy a painting for $15, he exchanges a red for ten plains, and records: 3 red, 11 plain. He now records the cost of the painting, pays for it, and records the amount left (2 red, 6 plain). Later, only amounts of money will be recorded (41, 15, 26). This kind of work leads to real understanding, and soon to an algorithm.

red	plain	
4	1	
3	11	
1	5	painting
2	6	

8 Math and the real world

So far we have shown how an exaggerated focus on concepts has hurt the growth of the children. We now point out a distortion of concepts that has given rise to enormous confusion in schools and great problems for scientists in mathematical phases of their work.

It is asserted that mathematics deals with numbers, not quantities. Hence in school, equations shall contain numbers only. If materials are used, their purpose is only to get concepts about pure numbers;

we must then banish the materials from our minds. But in real life, the reverse is the case. Mathematics grew up because of its enormous power in applications. It is very important for children to experience this from the outset. Let us go directly to the positive side, and show how this may be done.

As an early experience, two blocks, with three blocks near them, give five blocks. This may be verbalised; or we might write it as

(1) Two blocks and three blocks makes five blocks.

Later this could be changed to

(2) $2B$ and $3B$ is $5B$.

We get abstract ideas of numbers from experiences of this sort; the symbols 2, 3, 5 evolve, we form $2+3$, and finally we write

(3) $2+3 = 5$.

We can now go back, and interpret B, $2B$, $3B$, and so on, as abstract symbols for numbers of blocks. (The child, trying the experiment, is learning to think of numbers of blocks, neglecting their individuality.) Just as we invented the sign $+$ for numbers, we now invent it for our quantities, and write $2B+3B$. We can now use mathematical notation to tell us what we see:

(4) $2B+3B = 5B$.

There are six children at a party; each is to have three cookies and four gum drops. What should we get? Figure it out (and draw a picture also):

$$6(3C+4G) = 6(3C)+6(4G) = (6\times 3)\,C+(6\times 4)\,G$$
$$= 18C+24G.$$

How easily we get the answer! We are now told all sorts of things: You cannot add two different kinds of things, you cannot use cookies in an equation, and so on. Who cares? We have found powerful methods, so let us use them. Anyway, we can define addition here and make good sense.

Suppose a child is sent to the store for loaves of bread and cans of soup, and is then sent back for more. He might think (or even write)

$$4L+5C = \$2.43, \qquad 2L+3C = \$1.31.$$

From the second equation, he finds $4L+6C = \$2.62$. Using the first now shows that $C = 19$ cents and hence $L = 37$ cents. How can we help him give meaning to these equations? If L means the price of one loaf and C means the price of one can, the equations are true, and the operations on them are clear.

In school we are told how to change units. In later professional work, in chemistry or engineering for instance, one may get terribly mixed up with various units, and feel quite insecure. Let us allow ourselves to write equations with quantities and see how we fare. Suppose you are going at 40 miles per hour; how long does it take to go 100 feet? First,

$$\frac{40 \text{ miles}}{\text{hr}} = \frac{40 \times 5280 \text{ ft}}{60 \times 60 \text{ sec}} = \frac{2112 \text{ ft}}{36 \text{ sec}}.$$

If we do not know what to do with this, we can try. Multiplying by 100 ft comes out in an unwanted kind of quantity. Dividing by 100 ft gives

$$\frac{2112 \text{ ft}}{36 \text{ sec}} \times \frac{1}{100 \text{ ft}} = \frac{2112}{3600 \text{ sec}}.$$

Evidently we must turn this upside down; the answer is 1.7 seconds approximately.

For more details on these methods, see my paper, 'The Mathematics of Physical Quantities', *Am. Math. Monthly* 75, 1968, 115–38, 227–56.

9 Fractions

The first major breakdown in school math is apt to occur when fractions are studied intensively. Moreover, under stress, children are likely to associate 'fractions' with fractures, fracturing, and hospitals. The stress is caused particularly by the tremendous confusion of ideas. The root of this is the mathematician's insistence that you do not work with quantities. You show half a pie, but are supposed to call it 'half', not 'half a pie'. A third of a pie has neither the same shape nor size as a third of a rectangle, yet they are both supposed to be $\frac{1}{3}$.

In a child's early experience, fractions were parts of things; expressed in mathematical language, fractions operate on quantities. Twice three balls is six balls; also half of six balls is three balls. Of course the child's view of fractions is coloured. If his piece of bread is cut in half by Mother (worse, by big brother), the two halves do not equal a whole. Certainly two halves of a doll are not one whole doll. On the other hand, two big halves of two cookies may be better than one cookie.

In school, the child is asked, what is $4 \div \frac{1}{2}$? Suddenly $\frac{1}{2}$ is an abstract object, perhaps called a number, that he has no idea of the meaning of. We may draw pictures of rectangles and halves of rectangles to help him. They are our pictures, and he does not know why we came to draw them. He is supposed to reason in terms of quantities and then translate into numbers; at the same time, he is not supposed to represent quantities by equations. No wonder he tends to feel helpless.

We teach fractions like this because we always have, not because it makes good sense. Now consider what the children's problem is, psychologically. With such a question, they are supposed to give an answer; perhaps make a first attempt to give an answer, and if it is wrong, a better attempt. In other words, the *answer* is put first, and the attempt to find one, second. Perhaps we give them enough time to think of the answer. This is still wrong: the looking for an *answer* is put first, the *exploration* towards the answer, second. And even this is wrong: What is desired on the part of the students is the exploration *towards* answers; much better, exploration of the *general subject*.

Hence a better question is: What are halves like? What can you do with them? This is an open-ended question. Different students may explore in different ways, then compare what they are doing and finding. How might halves appear in everyday life? Can you think up some problems with them?

One student might think: there are four pieces of bread on the table. More people come; Mother cuts each piece in half. How many half pieces are there? Eight of course. Whether this has much to do with the first posed problem is not too clear; but let us look into that later. The student is finding out about fractions, in a real life and honest fashion, with an answer in his terms that he understands and is sure of. This is a major step in the right direction. With more such problems, one looks for general methods, then perhaps relations with operations such as addition and multiplication. Gradually abstract operations on fractions appear. For instance: With *br* for a piece of bread,

$$4br = 8 \times (\tfrac{1}{2}br), \quad \frac{4br}{\frac{1}{2}br} = 8.$$

This may suggest writing $4 \div \frac{1}{2} = 8$. This step is similar to that from (2) or (4) to (3) above; it may be slow in coming. The important thing is that the student is finding out about fractions, *and* their use in life situations.

A wonderful tool for exploring multiplication and division is the rubber band stretcher. One person holds a stretched rubber band over lined paper; another makes marks on it with a felt pen, say every fourth line. One can now use it to show where to cut a candy bar in half (or a picture of a candy bar). Next, cut another into thirds; it is interesting that four marks are used, one at each end and two in between. For a long bar cut in half, the students find they can best use five marks; they see quarters at the same time. Now one may ask, what is two-thirds of five inches? It looks like nearly $3\frac{1}{2}$ inches. One looks at one-third of five inches at the same time; also another mark, $1\frac{1}{3}$, or $\frac{4}{3}$, of five inches. Thinking things over, the student is likely to find that the answer comes out in thirds of an inch.

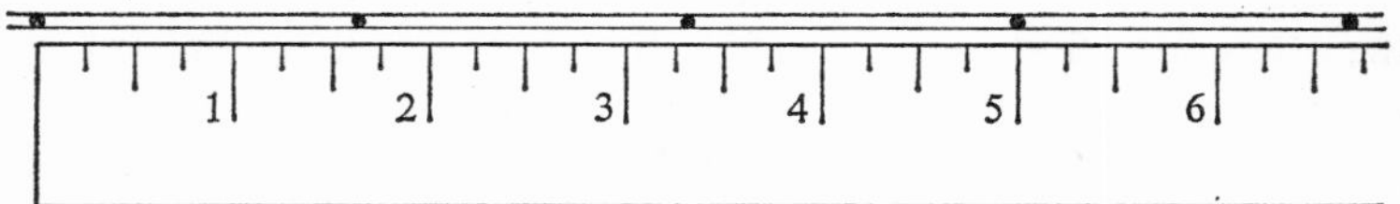

It will also become apparent that the stretcher is not perfect. This is an introduction to practical science: there are experimental errors; moreover, the causes of errors will interest the student, and he is learning about how math is used in science.

10 Escape from reality

We return to our basic problem. For the great mass of students passing through high school, math still means mystery and anxiety. We may have accomplished many things, but not what is most important. It is clear that our attempts at improvement have not been sufficiently deep and determined. The real determination should be not to get our way in making changes, but seeing that the full facts are faced squarely. We show here how some things that are going on in schools are an escape from reality, rather than facing the facts. In each case, there is some 'authority' behind which one hides. In large measure, we find behind the authority a higher authority, commanding that the important concepts be learned, and that this should be proved through tests.

Some teachers take out their emotional difficulties on their children; many of these children will do the same later with theirs. In this case, we see the teacher herself or himself as the authority, and we are blocked. Other teachers hear the exhortation 'Stress this concept!' (Stress: to subject to the action of external forces; to overstrain.)

They pass it on: 'Tom, say the *set of* boys in the room; Alice, say *numeral*, not *number*.' The children learn to shut up, as the safest way. These teachers feel the higher authority too strongly. If we tell her not to do this, she is left in still more of a vacuum; we would better help her find more positive methods to replace this.

Failure may be sensed in a larger way. With the difficulty not only of finding success, but of convincing the school of it, an educational consultant is called in. Behavioural objectives are set up. (What an escape! We drop the child, and only measure what he does.) New teaching methods are brought in, with packaged materials. These materials have been statistically proved, and the children will be pre-tested and post-tested. By the end of the year, the children may be making better scores. But there will be a growing sense that most children are losing their creative identity; this will show up especially in later years.

A group of parents and teachers may feel the degradation of the children, and set up a 'free school', or even turn the whole school into an 'open space' school. In the latter case, to satisfy the other parents, evaluation may be brought in early, and the tone, academically, is likely to be more restrictive than before. In either case, in spite of the preliminary months of constant meetings, the jump into the new system was too sudden; the escape is from the many realities of a whole school and its relation to the community. The school is likely to disappear, or revert to its former status, with great anger at those who caused the change.

Some school systems, with great pressure from tax payers and vocal minorities, take refuge in firms that will run things for them, with programmed materials and computer-assisted instruction. 'Each child works individually, at his own pace.' This has a wonderful sound (and is praised in education journals). One does not notice that the 'individual' applies merely to what page the child is on, due to what he put down on a pre-test; the individuality of the child himself is lost. The children may be content; they prefer to be told to go back to item so and so by the machine rather than be marked wrong by the teacher, and the game is rather fun, at least for a while. Score sheets with innumerable 'concepts learned' checked off satisfy the parents. The direction one is going in is shown by a quote from a particular program, which claims it develops 'the correct motor response to given visual and auditory stimuli'. How can a whole community be so complacent?

Behind most of this we see the ogre of testing. Our pleas to see what is happening to the child are brushed aside, or drowned by the scientific findings of the multiple choice tests. The testers have grown to such power that those fighting them are just laughed at, or slyly put aside. It hurts when those in the humanities hear that their subject is vague (cannot be monitored continuously by machine) and hence not true education. When we think of evaluation, and still more of accountability, we turn to the testers as the final judges of the revered concepts, thus putting the testing procedure on a plane so far above us that we cannot touch it.

11 A new lease of life

We are too used to thinking of subject matter, and how children can learn it. We must start with the children, to see what they really are. In a kindergarten class, we see them running around, and busy at activities. We take many pictures, analyse them, and make statistics. Have we found the children?

Follow an individual child, for half an hour (if you can concentrate this long), trying to be keenly aware of him. You will only begin to sense the incredibly quick and varied experiences the child is undergoing. He climbs on to a couch after a cat, while readjusting a toy in his hand and turning to hear a remark by the teacher and swinging his leg around for better balance, in the space of a few seconds. A year later we teach him the commutative law (for abstract numbers, or cardinal numbers of sets where the child sees no order, or what?). How utterly barren for him, in terms of what he can experience! In many places, in the past and the present, opportunities have been given children, both 'bright' and 'disadvantaged', to show their enthusiasm and powers; their achievements have been spectacular. This can be done more generally if we find ways for it.

The title of this paper represents one way in which we must change our point of view. The most fundamental problem is to spread a better point of view to all concerned with school children; this necessarily includes parents, and essentially, all adults. If we can achieve a new lease of life for a good body of children in a school or a community, we may hope it can spread to wider regions. This has been the case in the past, and can be so in the future.

Institute for Advanced Study,
Princeton, NJ 08540.

APPENDICES

Appendix 1 The Congress Committees and Officers

Chairman: Sir James Lighthill, F.R.S.
Hon. Secretary: Mr D. G. Crawforth
Hon. Treasurer: Mr M. Goldsmith

Organising Committee

Sir James Lighthill, F.R.S. (Chairman), the Congress Secretary, the Congress Treasurer, Professor J. V. Armitage, Professor H. Freudenthal, Mr R. C. Lyness, H.M.I., Professor G. Matthews, Dr E. A. Maxwell, Professor D. Rees, F.R.S., Mrs J. Stephens, Dr B. Thwaites, Mrs E. M. Williams, C.B.E.

Programme Committee

Mrs E. M. Williams, C.B.E. (Chairman), Mr J. B. Hoare (Secretary), the Congress Secretary, the Congress Treasurer, Dr T. J. Fletcher, H.M.I., Dr A. G. Howson, Professor G. Matthews, Dr E. A. Maxwell, Mrs J. Stephens, Mr B. J. Wilson, Professor H. Freudenthal (Netherlands), Professor J. Novak (Czechoslovakia), Professor A. Pescarini (Italy), Dr H. O. Pollak (USA), Professor A. Revuz (France), Professor S. L. Sobolev (USSR), Professor H. G. Steiner (German Federal Republic), Professor J. Suranyi (Hungary), Professor I. Wirszup (USA).

Local Committee

Mr G. Duller (Chairman, until 27 April 1972), Dr D. Hammond Smith (Chairman, from 27 April 1972), Miss C. M. Cornelius, Mr A. E. B. Duval, Mr J. Fox, Mr D. Hughes, Mr R. Jady, Dr T. E. R. Jones, Mr P. Kaner, Mr D. Lee, Mr W. J. A. Mann, H.M.I., Mr H. Pratt, Mr J. V. Wild, C.M.G., O.B.E., Mr D. A. Wort.

Organiser of Working Groups Mrs M. Brown
Organiser of National Presentations Mrs J. Stephens
Editor of Congress Proceedings Dr A. G. Howson
Publicity Officer Miss I. Fekete

Appendix 2 The working groups

Logic at school level

Chairman: Professor W. Servais, 60 rue des Desportes, Morlanwelz, Belgium. *Secretary:* Mr R. D. Nelson, Ampleforth College, York, YO6 4HE.

Algebra at school level

Chairman: Professor S. Iyanaga, 12–4 Otsuka 6-chome, Bunkyo-ku, Tokyo, Japan. *Secretary:* Mr G. Wain, School of Education, University of Leeds, Leeds, LS2 9JT.

Contemporary presentations of geometry at school and university level

Chairman: Mme Dr A. Z. Krygovska, Oleandry 6/6, Krakow, Poland. *Secretary:* Mr R. L. Lindsay, The University of Nottingham, University Park, Nottingham, NG7 2RD.

Calculus and analysis at school level

Chairman: Professor T. M. Apostol, California Institute of Technology, Pasadena, California 91109, USA. *Secretary:* Mr H. Neill, The University, Durham.

The teaching of probability and statistics at school level

Chairman: Professor Lennart Råde, O Fogelbergsgaten 3, 41128 Goteburg, Sweden. *Secretary:* Mr D. Kaye, University of Manchester, Department of Extra Mural Studies, Manchester, M13 9PL.

Links with other subjects at secondary level

Chairman: Professor M. S. Bell, University of Chicago, USA. *Secretary:* Professor G. Matthews, Centre for Science Education, Bridges Place, London, SW6 4HR.

Application of mathematics

Chairman: Dr H. O. Pollak, Bell Telephone Laboratories Ltd., Murray Hill, New Jersey, USA. *Secretary:* Dr Margaret Rayner, St Hilda's College, Oxford.

WORKING GROUPS

Mathematics for specialists at university and college level

Chairman: Professor B. H. Neumann, F.R.S., Australia National University, P.O. Box 4, Canberra, A.C.T., Australia 2600. *Secretary:* Dr R. R. McLone, Department of Mathematics, University of Southampton, Southampton, SO9 5NH.

Mathematics for social scientists/biologists at university and college level

Chairman: Professor D. Sida, Carleton University, Ottawa, Canada. *Secretary:* Dr E. D. Tagg, University of Lancaster, Cartmel College, Bailrigg, Lancaster.

Mathematics for scientists/engineers at university and college level

Chairman: Professor W. Martin, Massachusetts Institute of Technology, Cambridge, Mass. 02139, USA. *Secretary:* Professor A. C. Bajpai, C.A.M.E.T., University of Technology, Loughborough, Leics.

Relations between the history and pedagogy of mathematics

Chairman: Professor P. S. Jones, University of Michigan, Ann Arbor, Michigan 48104, USA. *Secretary:* Mr L. F. Rogers, 17 Windsor Road, Teddington, Middlesex.

The psychology of learning mathematics

Chairman: Dr E. Fischbein, Institut de Psychologie, Bucharest, Roumania. *Secretary:* Miss Joan Bliss, Centre for Science Education, Bridges Place, London, SW6 4HR.

Mathematics as a language

Chairman: O. Professor dr F. Schweiger, Mathematisches Institut der Universität Salzburg, A-5020 Salzburg, Austria, Porchestr, 1/1. *Secretary:* Mrs A. Cormack, 16 Kelross Road, London, N.5.

Research in the teaching of mathematics

Chairman: Professor Bent Christiansen, Royal Danish School of Educational Studies, Copenhagen, Denmark. *Secretary:* Dr A. J. Bishop, University of Cambridge, Department of Education, 17 Brookside, Cambridge.

Individual learning methods

Chairman: Professor L. R. B. Elton, Institute of Educational Technology, University of Surrey, Guildford. *Secretary:* Mr K. Gray, France Hill School, Camberley, Surrey.

Creativity, investigation and problem-solving

Chairman: Professor G. Glaeser, IREM Strasbourg, Department of Mathematics, University of Strasbourg, rue René Descartes, Strasbourg,

France. *Secretary:* Mr C. Edwards, 16 Fairfields, Great Kingshill, High Wycombe, Bucks.

Extra-curricular mathematics

Chairman: Professor W. W. Sawyer, University of Toronto, Canada. *Secretary:* Mr A. Sherlock, Millfield School, Street, Somerset.

Teaching methods at university and college level

Chairman: Professor K. O. May, Department of Mathematics, University of Toronto, Toronto, 181, Canada. *Secretary:* Dr K. E. Hirst, Department of Mathematics, The University, Southampton, SO9 5NH.

Pre-school and primary mathematics

Chairman: Professor Mary Folsom, University of Miami, Coral Gables, Fla 33124, USA. *Secretary:* Mr E. G. Choat, Rachel McMillan College, Creek Road, Deptford, London, S.E. 8.

Structure and activity in mathematics: teacher's choice of curriculum materials and tasks for 9–13 age group

Chairman: Dr Daniel Duclos, University of Lyons, France. *Secretary:* Mr A. W. Bell, Shell Centre for Mathematics Education, University of Nottingham, University Park, Nottingham, NG7 2RD.

Mathematics and the slow/reluctant learner

Chairman: S. Mellin-Olsen, Pedagogisk Seminar, University of Bergen, 5000 Bergen, Norway. *Secretary:* Mr P. A. Kaner, 3 The Cloisters, Cathedral Close, Exeter.

Curriculum design and evaluation

Chairman: Professor Howard Fehr, Teachers College, Columbia University, New York 10027, USA. *Secretary:* Miss H. D. Shuard, Homerton College of Education, Cambridge.

Mathematics in developing countries

Chairman: Professor H. M. Cundy, Chancellor College, University of Malawi, P.O. Box 52000, Limbe, Malawi. *Secretary:* Mr B. J. Wilson, CEDO, Tavistock Square, London, W.C. 2.

The use of television and film in the teaching of mathematics

Chairman: Professor Seymour Schuster, Department of Mathematics, Carlton College, Northfield, Minn. 55057, USA. *Secretary:* Mr J. Mayhew, Room 75a, The County Hall, London, S.E. 11.

WORKING GROUPS

The place of computers in mathematical education

Chairman: Mr F. Lovis, Mathematics Faculty, The Open University, Walton Hall, Walton, Bletchley, Buckinghamshire. *Secretary:* Mr R. E. J. Lewis, Centre for Science Education, Bridges Place, London, SW6 4HR.

Initial training of elementary teachers

Chairman: Professor W. F. Fitzgerald, Department of Mathematics and Elementary Education, Michigan State University, East Lansing, Michigan 48823, USA. *Secretary:* Mr A. Morley, Nottingham College of Education, Clifton, Nottingham NG11 6NS.

Initial training of secondary teachers

Chairman: Professor H. G. Steiner, Pädagogische Hochschule Bayreuth der Universität Erlangen–Nürnberg, Bayreuth, Germany. *Secretary:* Mr K. Gardner, Brighton College of Education, Brighton BN1 9PH.

In-service education of teachers

Chairman: Professor J. Trivett, Simon Fraser University, Canada. *Secretary:* Mr D. S. Fielker, Abbey Wood Mathematics Centre, Eynsham Bridge, Eynsham Drive, London, S.E. 2.

The mathematics workshop – the use of apparatus, games and structural materials

Chairman: Professor William Schaaf, Florida Atlantic University, Boca Raton, Fla, USA. *Secretary:* Mr J. A. Dodridge, Hereford College, Hereford.

Editing a mathematics journal

Chairman: Dr Shmuel Avital, Ontario Institute for Studies in Education, 252 Bloor Street West, Toronto, Canada. *Secretary:* Dr E. A. Maxwell, Queens' College, Cambridge.

Mathematical competitions

Chairman: Dr E. Hódi, Budapest XVII Rakoshegy, Melczer u. 31, Hungary. *Secretary:* Mr L. Beeson, Bishop Otter College, Chichester, Sussex.

Programmable calculators in schools

Chairman: M. Marcel Dumont, Institut National de Recherche et de Documentation Pédagogique, 29 rue d'Ulm, Paris 5e. *Secretary:* Mr D. Blakely, Marling School, Stroud, Glos.

Middle-school mathematics – ages 9–13

Chairman: Mr D. T. E. Marjoram, H.M.I., D.E.S., Elizabeth House, York Road, London, S.E. 1. *Secretary:* Mr E. McDonald, H.M.I., 1 Meadow Way, Baldwins Gate, Newcastle, Staffs, ST5 5DG.

APPENDIX 2

Assessment in mathematics

Chairman: Dr T. Cavanagh, University of North Colorado, USA. *Secretary:* Mr A. Penfold, London Institute of Education, Malet Street, London, W.C.1.

Vocational mathematics for technicians and business personnel

Chairman: Mr F. W. Kellaway, Principal, Letchworth Technical College, Letchworth, Herts. *Secretary:* Mr M. Bridger, City of Leicester Polytechnic, Mathematics Department, P.O. Box 143, Leicester, LE1 9BH.

Tessellations, space filling, point lattice geometry and their applications

Chairman: Dr J. Hammer, Department of Mathematics, University of Sydney, Sydney, NSW, Australia, 2006. *Secretary:* Mr P. Boorman, Lacon House, Millham Road, Bishops Cleave, Cheltenham, Glos.

Papy–Cemrel international workshop at primary level

Chairman: Professor Frédérique Papy, Centre Belge de Pédagogie de la Mathématique, 1180, Bruxelles, Avenue Albert 224, Belgium. *Secretary:* Mr Frank Gorner, Didsbury College of Education, Wilmslow Road, Manchester M20 8RR.

Mathematics and the socially disadvantaged child

Chairman: Professor W. F. Johntz, Director, Project S.E.E.D., 1011 Keith Avenue, Berkeley, California 94708, USA. *Secretary:* Mrs C. Hoyles, 19 Globe Road, Stratford, London E15 1RF.

Appendix 3 ICMI and Congress recommendations

1 Symposia

Suggestions for symposia were considered at the General Assembly of ICMI and at a meeting of the Executive Committee. It was agreed that ICMI sponsorship should be given to the following:

(*a*) *Luxembourg*, at Echternach, 4–9 June 1973, on *New Topics in applicable mathematics in Secondary Schools*;

(*b*) *Hungary*, at Eger, 18–22 June 1973, on *Theoretical Problems of Teaching Mathematics in the Primary Schools*;

(*c*) *Poland*, at Warsaw, one week in 1974, on *Teaching children of age 5–11*;

(*d*) *Denmark* (?), in 1974 or 1975, on *Aspects of Geometry Teaching at School Level*;

(*e*) *Kenya* (?), a regional symposium on *Mathematics and Language*;

(*f*) *Japan*, 1974, a regional symposium;

(*g*) *India*, a regional symposium possibly on *Integrated curriculum development, including applications of mathematics relevant to the problems of developing countries.*

In addition it was agreed that steps should be taken for a joint ICMI–IFIP (International Federation of Information Processing Societies) symposium on *Computers in secondary education.*

It was agreed that no immediate proposal for a regional conference in Latin America should be made, particularly in the light of the forthcoming third congress of the Inter-American Committee on Mathematical Education.

2 Place of the 1976 Congress

Invitations had been received from Spain, the Federal Republic of Germany, the United States of America and the Netherlands. A decision would be made in 1973.

3 Resolutions

The Executive Committee considered carefully all resolutions proposed by working groups. In addition to those which influenced decisions on future symposia, it decided to endorse formally the following resolutions:

APPENDIX 3

Resolution from the working group on 'Mathematics in Developing Countries'

That all possible encouragement and assistance should be given to developing countries to make changes in their mathematics syllabuses and curricula; such changes to be framed by qualified citizens of those countries to ensure that the cultural background of the pupils and the needs of national development are taken fully into account.

Resolution from the working group on 'Links with other Subjects at Secondary Level'

In view of the interest expressed at all levels in interdisciplinary and integrated studies, linking mathematics with other subjects, this Congress recommends that action be taken to facilitate and encourage work in this field. In particular this could include:

(*a*) providing support (financial and other) to enable teachers of mathematics and other subjects in secondary schools to work together on suitable areas (e.g. by team-teaching);

(*b*) publicising what is already being done in this direction in order to encourage others to attempt cooperative work (a travel grant would be one way of achieving this);

(*c*) providing support and encouragement for individuals and institutions to develop new teaching materials which cross disciplinary boundaries;

(*d*) providing support for the production of source materials suitable for use in secondary schools from the wide variety of existing sources on topics linking mathematics with other subjects.

Agreed

That steps be taken by ICMI to establish a centre for the interchange and dissemination of information on all matters of interest in Mathematical Education, with special reference to symposia, journals and competitions; and also that steps be taken to encourage cooperation between journals in different languages, with special reference to interchange and to re-printing of selected articles.

Appendix 4 Films and videotapes on mathematics and its teaching

During the congress films were shown at some of the working groups and at some of the national presentations. In addition, continuous programmes of films were projected in the Newman Theatre. The films shown are listed below by country of origin, together with a certain amount of information concerning their availability. Information is also given on some of the videotapes which were presented. Some films which it was intended to show at the congress did not arrive because of postal difficulties. These have been included for completeness. All the films are 16 mm.

Australia

Discovery – the Formal Way 1 inch Bell and Howell videotape, 45 minutes. G. L. Hubbard, Hubbard Academy, Brisbane, Australia.

A record of a lesson to grade 10 students from Brisbane State High School. The students had been introduced earlier to symbolic and formal procedures and to relations as subsets of Cartesian products, and the lesson is concerned with the correct logical notation for a function.

France

Calcul des Probabilité – Enfants de 10 à 11 ans. Lunettes – Etude d'une structure de groupe (2 parts). Three 16 mm films, each lasting 20–30 minutes, were shown of teaching at the primary school at Francheville, near Lyons. The lessons concerned probability and structures on a grid. Details may be obtained from Service du Film de la Recherche Scientifique, 86 Boulevard Raspail, 75006, Paris.

Great Britain

The British Broadcasting Corporation produces regular programmes on mathematics. Two representative examples of their work were shown.

Maths Workshop Stage 1 and 2 is a fortnightly series for children aged 9–11. *Round-up* 3 from this series is a magazine programme featuring children's work. 20 minutes.

Countdown is a series first shown in Autumn 1972, designed for lower ability 14–16-year-old children. *Lucky Jim* is the first of the series and is on probability – a club raffle leads to a discussion of some beliefs about the workings of chance. British Broadcasting Corporation, Villiers House, Haven Green, Ealing, W5.

APPENDIX 4

Why Mathematics? Central Office of Information film made for the Department of Education and Science. 32 minutes, colour, sound. Made by Verity Films. Devised and produced by Seafield Head. Written and directed by Nic Ralph, graphics by Trevor Bond.

Available for United Kingdom non-theatrical distribution, on free loan, and sale, from Central Film Library, Government Building, Bromyard Avenue, London W3 7JB, and through its associate libraries in Scotland and Wales.

The film is intended for younger secondary children, and it shows them that mathematics is a subject with interesting and important practical applications.

Further information about DES films can be obtained from the Films Officer, Information Division, Department of Education and Science, Elizabeth House, York Road, London SE1 7PH

Topology Colour, 9 minutes.

Distributed by Educational Film Centre Ltd, 5 Richmond Mews, Dean Street, London W1.

Uses two and three dimensional animation to show examples of topological changes. This film also considers such phenomena as networks, Moebius strips and Klein bottles.

The following two films show some of the work of the Nuffield Mathematics Project.

Maths with Everything (Infants) Colour, 21 minutes.

Can be bought from: Graphic Films Ltd, 1 Soho Square, London W1. Black and White £28.50, colour £90. Can be hired from: Concord Films Council, Nacton, Ipswich, Suffolk.

Observes teachers at a workshop enjoying themselves as they learn to integrate mathematical concepts into the entire curriculum as well as to make the learning process enjoyable for the children. Then shows a teacher applying these methods in the classroom, working closely with individual students aged 5 to 7.

Into Secondary School (First Year Secondary) Black and White, 20 minutes.

Can be bought from Sound Services Ltd, Wilton Crescent, Merton Park, London SW19, price £16.50. Can be hired from Petroleum Film Bureau, 4 Brook Street, London W1.

Illustrates how Nuffield Maths may be successfully continued at least two years into the secondary level. Questions the need for the complete change in teaching methods that normally takes place when British children change from primary to secondary school at the age of 11. Describes how two British secondary schools have tackled the problems of this new approach.

The above two films are distributed in the USA by University of California, Extension Media Center, Berkeley, CA 94720.

Teacher Based Curriculum Development 20 minutes, colour. Directed by Harry Davenport. Distributed by Schools Council, 160 Great Portland Street, London W1.

This film was produced for the Mathematics for the Majority Continuation Project. The project is concerned with less academic, secondary pupils, aged 13–16. The film shows the development of new ideas and materials on a national scale using teachers organised into writing groups. All aspects of the project are covered – teachers writing groups, processing and designing, evaluation, and children using the materials in the classroom.

Number Patterns Black and white, sound, 11 minutes. Made by Beryl Fletcher and Hugh Larcombe, Darlington College of Education.

A college-produced film, showing animations of four different number patterns, for use with children aged 9–13.

A selection of 1 inch Ampex videotapes showed representative work of teaching programmes produced by the Inner London Education Authority, Educational Television Service. These included material from the series *The Nature and Application of Mathematics*, for older school children; a programme for primary children from the series *Pattern in Mathematics*, introduced by two puppets; and a discussion programme at a teachers' centre.

These programmes are available for hire. Enquiries to Educational Television Centre, Tennyson Street, London SW8 3TB.

Israel

Isometries

Square Root by Iteration

Congruent Triangles

These three 1 inch Ampex television tapes, produced by the television service in Israel for 15–16-year-old pupils, were introduced by A. Markus.

Japan

One to One Correspondence Black and white, about 20 minutes. Dubbed in English. Produced by Makoto Yamazaki. Directed by Hisanori Nishiuchi.

A film for secondary school children. Examples of one-to-one correspondence with baggage tags and seat number labels in an aircraft, and other material situations, lead on to the correspondence between even and odd integers. The excellent studio production of this television film gained it a Japan Prize.

Regular Polyhedra A television film which is one of a series intended for the first grade of the lower secondary school. The film is concerned with making regular solids.

The above two films are distributed by Japanese Television; Hisanori Nishiuchi, NHK, 2 Jinnan-Machi, 2-chome, Shinjuku-ku, Tokyo.

Russia

Three black and white films, each of some 7–8 minutes, were made for television, and introduce the fundamental concepts of calculus using a combination of live action and diagram work.

Details from E. Schukin, University of Kaliningrad.

USA

Minnesota College Geometry Project Films Colour, sound.

These films were produced by the University of Minnesota College Geometry Project in cooperation with the National Science Foundation, Washington DC.

World distribution by International Film Bureau Inc. Distributed in Europe by Europa Diffusion, 25 rue Beranger, 75 Paris 3e.

Orthogonal Projection 8 minutes, sale $135, rental $12.50.

The principal use of the film is in connection with a written unit entitled 'Geometric Transformations'. It introduces students to an elementary geometric transformation, which serves as a springboard for treating more complicated kinds of transformation.

Mathematician: D. Pedoe.

Central Similarities 7 minutes, sale $135, rental $12.50.

This film is supplementary to the section on Similarity Transformations in the unit on 'Geometric Transformations'.

Mathematician: D. Pedoe.

Dihedral Kaleidoscopes 8 minutes, sale $135, rental $12.50.

This film is primarily motivational, intending to get students excited about the ideas of symmetry. The first major idea is that of physically exhibiting the dihedral groups by means of reflections in two intersecting mirrors (dihedral kaleidoscopes). The second major idea is a reiteration of the fact that every isometry is a product of reflections. The third and final notion is that by using three mirrors standing vertically on a table so that each pair forms a dihedral kaleidoscope, one obtains regular and semi-regular tessellations of plane.

Mathematician: H. S. M. Coxeter.

Geometric Vectors – Additions 12 minutes, sale $185, rental $15.

Using the study of motion as motivation, the notion of vectors is introduced – and finally defined as an equivalence class of arrows.

Mathematicians: W. O. J. Moser and S. Schuster.

Inversion 9 minutes, sale $160, rental $12.50.

Inversion is the last of the transformations treated in the unit, 'Geometric Transformations'. Inversion is introduced in the film and several of the properties of the transformation are discussed before it is applied to solving Steiner's problem.

Mathematician: D. Pedoe.

Curves of Constant Width 11 minutes, sale $185, rental $15.

The written unit 'Convexity and Combinatorial Geometry' contains a section on 'Curves of Constant Width'. The film ties in directly with that section and is, in some sense, stronger in mathematical content.

Mathematician: J. D. E. Konhauser.

Central Perspectivities 9 minutes, sale $160, rental $12.50.

The film proceeds towards the fundamental theorem of projective geometry, providing motivation by discussing the questions: How many points determine a perspectivity uniquely? Can a perspectivity map one given triple into another? After it becomes clear that a *projectivity* (a product of perspectivities) is necessary to map one given triple into another, the narrator poses the question: How much information uniquely determines a projectivity? The answer to this question, namely the Fundamental Theorem, is not given in the film. It is hoped that the students will gain more of an appreciation of the Fundamental Theorem if they are left to ponder the question that is left open.

Mathematician: S. Schuster.

Equidecomposable Polygons 17½ minutes, sale $285, rental $17.50.

This film treats a problem in the theory of dissection of polygonal regions that was solved by Hadwiger and Glur in 1948. The two polygonal regions can be dissected so that there is one-to-one correspondence between the parts of one and the parts of the other, satisfying the condition that corresponding parts must be congruent, then the two regions are said to be *equidecomposable.*

Mathematician: J. D. E. Konhauser.

Symmetries of the Cube 9 minutes, sale $160, rental $12.50.

The film reviews the manner in which reflections are used to show the symmetries of a square. Mirrors are then used to study symmetries of the cube; that is, the reflectional symmetries are shown to generate all the symmetries, producing the extended octahedral group. The reciprocal of the cube, namely the regular octahedron, is seen to possess the same group of symmetries as the cube.

Mathematicians: H. S. M. Coxeter and W. O. J. Moser.

Isometries 26 minutes, sale $405, rental $20.

Translations, rotations, reflections and glide-reflections are introduced as examples of isometries, namely distance-preserving transformations of the plane.

Mathematicians: W. O. J. Moser and S. Schuster.

Projective Generation of Conics 16 minutes, sale $285, rental $17.50.

Conic sections may be developed in various ways. The methods of construction developed by Pascal, Maclaurin, Braikenridge, Poncelet, and Steiner are all exhibited dynamically by means of film animation.

Mathematician: S. Schuster.

Caroms 9 minutes, sale $160, rental $12.50.

An animated film exhibiting the relationship between a carom – a ball rebounding from a wall – and a reflection.

Mathematician: C. Davis.

Symmetry Colour, 10½ minutes, sale $125, rental $12.50.

Film design and direction – Philip Stapp. Physicists – Judith Bregman, Polytechnic Institute of Brooklyn, Richard Davisson, University of Washington, Alan Holden, Bell Telephone Laboratories. Music – Gene Forrell. Production – Sturgis–Grant Productions, Inc.

'Symmetry' is both a scientific exposition and a work of art. It is not *about* science, it *embodies* science. The film is an abstract mathematical ballet based on two-dimensional symmetry groups of the plane.

Distributed by International Division, McGraw-Hill Book Company, 330 West 42nd Street, New York, NY 10036. Distributed in Great Britain by Contemporary Films Ltd, 55 Greek Street, London W1V 6DB.

The Kakeya Problem 60 minutes. Colour. Sponsored by the Mathematical Association of America. A filmed lecture by A. S. Besicovitch on a celebrated problem. It is shown that a line segment can be rotated in a plane in such a way as to 'smudge' an arbitrarily small area.

John Von Neumann 63 minutes. Black and White. Sponsored by the Mathematical Association of America 1966. A documentary on the life and work of a distinguished contemporary mathematician.

Shapes of the Future I and II – Unsolved Problems in Geometry Directed by Klee.

The above films, four of a series, are distributed in the USA by Amram Nowak Associates. The first two are available on loan in Britain to subscriber members of the Sussex Library of Mathematics Films, University of Sussex, Falmer, Brighton. (Non-subscribers may enquire if copies are available.)

Between Rational Numbers (*Knights*) 11 minutes.
Equivalence Classes in Addition (*Fraction Singers*) 8 minutes.
The Remainder in Division (*Termites*) 8 minutes.
Solving Pairs of Equation (*Pirates*) 10 minutes.

The above four films on rational numbers are from a series of thirty made for the National Council of Teachers of Mathematics.

The Weird Number Sound, colour, about 10 minutes.

A cartoon film introducing some ideas of rational numbers in the style of a popular thriller.

Information on the above five films from Lauren G. Woodby, Michigan State University, East Lansing, Michigan.

West Germany

Number Systems, Place Value
Counting, Adding and Subtracting
Sets, Subsets, Union, Intersection
Compositions, Addition and Subtraction

These four short colour films are part of a series of activity packages consisting of games, books, films and overhead projector material intended for 5–10-year-old pupils.

The films are work films, intended for cassette viewing, developing mathematical ideas from play activities with number apparatus. The system is almost self-teaching. Distributed by Hermann-Schroedel Verlag K6, 3 Hannover, Zeiss-strasse 10, West Germany.

Index

Note: no attempt has been made to list the many mathematical topics, concepts and applications mentioned in this book

INDEX

INDEX